ON PRISON EDUCATION

Available in Canada through

Authorized Bookstore Agents
and other bookstores

or by mail from

Canadian Government Publishing Centre
Supply and Services Canada
Ottawa, Canada, K1A 0S9

Catalogue No. JS82-14/1982E   Canada: $12.95
ISBN 0-660-11051-2   Other Countries: $15.55

Price subject to change without notice

ON PRISON EDUCATION

Edited by

Lucien Morin

This book was published with the cooperation of the Correctional Service of Canada. The views expressed are those of the authors and do not necessarily reflect the views of the Solicitor General.

Dépôt légal : 4e trimestre 1981
Bibliothèque nationale du Québec
Bibliothèque nationale du Canada
Exemplaires déposés :
British Library, U.K.
Library of Congress, U.S.A.

Typesetting, design and cover : Les Éditions Microméga Inc.,
Québec

TABLE OF CONTENTS

PREFACE

I am pleased that the Correctional Service of Canada has been able to co-operate in the publication of this collection of papers. Our Service, like other correctional administrations, has recognized the very important role prison education has to play in the lives of many penitentiary inmates. In Canada we are also fortunate to have been able to provide some leadership in this relatively new field.

It is a central aim of most correctional systems to help prepare inmates to assume their responsibilities as citizens. The question must therefore be asked what this means in a free society.

Freedom is not easy. It means that people have to make choices all the time in their daily lives. Freedom is a burden as well as a joy. There are some who, reacting against the complexity of our times, would be prepared to submit to some kinds of authority — intellectual, political, moral, and so on — in order to escape the burden of freedom. This represents a reaction against the humanism, the rationalism and science which are the distinguishing characteristics of our modern world. The point is that to be free, to be able to exercise freedom, to be a good citizen, it is necessary for a person to be able to make choices. This is the principal concern of education. The first task of education is to enhance the ability to handle freedom, with all the responsibility that freedom involves.

I would like to thank Professor Lucien Morin for his very careful work in preparing this volume. In fact, the idea of the book was his. I hope it will be of interest and value to scholars, critics and others interested in the field of criminal justice. I hope also that ultimately it will benefit the inmates themselves.

Donald R. YEOMANS
Commissioner
The Correctional Service of Canada

FOREWORD

To most contemporary criminologists and penal administrators,
education is a relatively unimportant and rather marginal function of a prison. This is mainly because of assumptions that are
made concerning the nature of crime, the nature of justice, and the
nature of education. Professor Lucien Morin has assembled nine-
teen essays and papers which challenge many of those assumptions, present other points of view, and collectively affirm that
education, conceived of in its dictinctively human dimensions, is
at the heart of the prison's function and is virtually its only hope of
ever being something more than a secure and efficient warehouse
for society's legal outcasts.

In the present century, prison programs have usually been based
on theories of crime causation. There have been organic theories,
sociologic theories and psychologic theories, with corresponding
and derivative methods of treatment — an approach often referred
to as the medical model. That approach has fallen into disrepute.

Almost a decade ago, Robert Martinson sought to answer the
question "What works?" and ended up by reporting that he could
not find sufficient evidence to support the conclusion that anything
works, that any of the ways that have been tried are effective in
"reducing recidivism through rehabilitation." That finding was
quickly accepted by the criminal justice systems of several countries,
including Canada. As a result, the very idea of reformation or
rehabilitation was largely abandoned in favour of a passive type of
"opportunities" model and a rethinking of the role of the prison in
terms of the protection of society. Even Martinson did not go so far
as to reject unqualifiedly the notion of rehabilitation. He admitted
the possibility that the programs offered in prisons may not yet be
good enough. That hypothesis has never been fully examined.

The educational model is different from the medical model. The
medical model was based on the assumption that criminality is
usually caused by a personality disorder arising from deficiencies of
a psychologic or sociologic nature. According to the medical model,

the criminal is in a real sense the victim of circumstances and not primarily the agent. The educational model, on the other hand, assumes lacks in learning and in intellectual and moral development and recognizes a degree of freedom and responsibility — characteristics which distinguish it from the medical model with its more mechanistic presuppositions.

In March, 1980, a post-release study was completed of an educational program which had been conducted in two Canadian prisons since 1972. The astonishing result, that the risk of recidivism for persons who participated in that program for at least a year was only one-quarter the risk for those who participated in other programs, is an inescapable challenge to those who have lost confidence in the very idea of rehabilitation. What conclusion can be drawn from that post-release study? Is it possible that some kinds of education are somehow more effective influences towards reformation than the techniques of the behavioral scientists or industrial-type programs based mainly on the tenets of the nineteenth century work ethic? The educational program which proved so successful was a program of studies in the humanities at the university level, with special emphasis on history and literature.

Education in twentieth century prisons has been conceived of mainly as a preparation for employment, rather reminiscent of the artificial division of the world of learning into human studies and technical studies in the seventeenth century by John Locke, who advocated one system of learning for the wealthy and another for the poor. When he planned for the children of the wealthy, his objectives were the welfare and prosperity of the students. But when he planned for the training of the children of the poor, his objectives lay with the crafts and industries of England of which the poor were to be made dependable, industrious and obedient servants. This idea did not die with John Locke.

Jumping to 19th Century North America, the idea of using schools to teach the discipline, the skills and the so-called dignity of labour became very popular in the heyday of the new industry based on mechanization. There was a veritable campaign for vocational education inspired by the vision of a system of schooling meshed neatly into the economy — guiding the young into jobs matched to the needs of their communities, training them to take their places as competent employees. According to the vision, this was the way to the good life.

This 19th Century perception was of course formed in part by the influence of the 19th Century work ethic, central to which was the faith that diligent and productive work is at the core of the moral life. This legacy of the Benedictine Monks, John Calvin and the Protestant Reformation was still alive in the first quarter of the present century, and, although in the last fifty years the idea has lost much of its force, it remains to this day, in practice, one of the more influential principles of penal administration. Prison industries, for example, occupy a position of great importance and high priority in most modern penitentiaries. Even in the nineteenth century, the work ethic did not dominate North American life completely. The first American dream after all was leisure; and in the longer reach of history the oldest dream of all is Eden.

This book reflects Professor Morin's conviction that education is the best thing that can be given to prisoners and that it must be based on a philosophy of education, a philosophy of God, man, nature and society, and on a vision of what man can become and of what human life can be at its best.

This collection also signals a new and growing interest in the field of penology on the part of scholars and critics in the field of education.

J.W. COSMAN

INTRODUCTION: ON PRISON EDUCATION

Lucien Morin

At first glance, the enterprise seems dubious: associating the most celebrated of liberating endeavors, education, with the most radical of arrestments, prison. Is the project a useless, perhaps impossible theoretical legerdemain? Historically speaking, hasn't incarceration, as the dominant occidental incarnation of the punitive function, always preempted the educational argument? Witness the following statement taken from Charles Lucas' 1838 essay, "De la réforme des prisons": "Education alone can serve as a penitentiary device. The question of penitentiary imprisonment is a question of education". But perhaps from our point of view the problem is concerned more properly with style and approach: with "modern" attitudes concerning new theories in criminal justice, or the psychology of learning, or updated justifications and redefined ideological assumptions for the right to punish. Must refinement in criminal activity itself — say, for example, a shifting away from violent, physical offences to softer, "aesthetic" crimes — necessarily precede legislative amendments and, subsequently, custommade reforms of punishment of which education is obstrusively part and parcel, cause and effect? In the final analysis, is not education itself the postulate to our modern-day concept of the penal system, at least in so far as very few people seem to contest the fact that all punishments are at least "negatively" educational in that they must refer to some correctional or habilitative connotation?

Assuredly, answers to many of these questions are in all our minds which could probably preclude any further questioning. But, to be honest, I do suspect that for most of us the problem does appear somewhat more complicated. Why should we and why do we encourage educational programs in prisons? Isn't the expression "in prisons" a tremendous challenge to common sense? As if education could be abstracted from time and space; as if the prison structure — attitude, environment — could be isolated from its conditioning nature that is, alienated from itself; as if one didn't know that most penitentiary education programs are promoted primarily as effective and happy contrivances for "running the place" or, better said, as tools for controlling individuals; as if penitentiary education couldn't serve a more positive, person-centered end different from the pragmatic, functionalist, system-oriented correction of criminal behavior; as if the concept of penitentiary education were reducible to correcting evil and had nothing to do with creating good.

Of course the spectrum of opinions concerning the place and the role of education in prisons is much wider. There are some for whom solitary confinement automatically leads to profound self-examination and objective scrutiny of one's evil acts, which in turn lead to the disgust and self-condemnation of criminal conduct. Remorse and guilt immediately follow suit as concrete signs of the possibility of correction or, better said, of education — of which must be postulated that it serves not only as cause but as effective support. There are those whose total preoccupation is with causality and instrumental gadgetry, understanding education primarily as a tool to achieve or verify taxonomies of relevant, practical, measurable objectives. Intellectual knowledge for example "causes" correction as, analogically, the watchmaker causes a time-piece to come into being. Because Results are what one expects, truth becomes a problem of workable definitions and operational adjustment: a very subjective affair, in other words. Since the aim is to augment the artifacts of correction, anything that works is sealed with the stamp of acceptability and, more important still, desirability. Thus, penitentiary education is viewed as just as good or just as bad or just as "indifferent" as any other idea or activity in a penal context.

Concerning the symbolic function of education in prisons, much would have to be said on penitentiary education as a justification of punishment, as a determining factor in social reproduction or even as a rationalization of crime. Revealing in a productive sense is a modern and healthy thesis wherein penitentiary education is interpreted as "soul-conditioning". Let me explain.

No one likes to remember the barbaric way in which Robert

François Damiens was executed in March of 1757. There are admittedly few examples in preserved world literature of such horrifying, indescribable physical torture and dismemberment. So when physical chastisement was condemned by De Mably in his 1789 essay, "De la législation", a revolution was born. The object of punishment had suddenly been substituted. By directing itself upon the soul that is, the mind, the heart, the will, the inner spiritual alchemy of the offender instead of the body, punishment had decidedly become something else, something more than punishment: soul-conversion. Today, with the help of our numerous etiological approaches, one could easily substitute the expression "soul-conditioning". One doesn't punish the prisoner any longer, one educates the soul. One doesn't physically harm the prisoner any longer, one "correctionally educates".

Questions. How does one justify soul-education as a judicial imperative? The law provides for the punishment of crime. Where is it written that soul manipulation is to be authorized? Under what pretext? Is soul-conversion a political prerogative? or obligation? How does soul-education of an individual satisfy the collective need for order unless punishment is metamorphosized into education that is, correction that is, prevention? Who can pretend that soul-touching, in a penal context, is not a more refined way of inflicting more acute suffering — distant, non corporeal suffering? Isn't soul-education a kind of compensatory education in reverse? A pretext to qualify an individual instead of condemning an action? A subtle subterfuge by which to legitimize a new trend of questioning and interpreting the penal function, moving away from *what* has this man done to *why* has this man done what he did? An occasion to judge a man ceaselessly instead of judging a criminal act once and for all? A more or less unconscious method of legitimizing one man's curiosity and "interest" in another man's private soul problems or in affirming and justifying one's superior soul difference by trying to redirect another's lost soul? And who furnishes the model for soul re-setting? Would soul-conditioning as punishment have anything to do with God-playing, by any chance? All in all, isn't soul-education as punishment a camouflage to overcome shame, a kind of cathartic, almost aesthetic ceremony by which modern society cleverly avoids having to face incarceration as a doubtful method by which to justify and operationalize the punitive function?

There is more. Without doubt, the visibility function, or the "panopticon" function, is the most important, single function of our occidental philosophies of incarceration. And penitentiary education fits this category like a glove. Very quickly, visibility comes from *videre* of course, which means "to see", "to observe", "to examine", "to know". *Visus*, sight, in traditional western theories of learning has always been associated with knowledge, more specifically with intellectual knowledge — with the power of knowledge, with knowledge as power. To know is to see, to see is to know. Know and see. Know and see where you stand, where things are, where things should be. Learn how to know thyself, proclaims the Socratic *gnoti seoton* that is, know how to dominate, know how to control. The visibility function of penitentiary education belongs to this tradition. First, because it refers to the development of knowledge *by* the inmate — vocational training, academic performance, development of attitudes for life skills etc... — in order to facilitate the amelioration of his general self as a person and as a citizen. But more significantly, the visibility function, more often than not refers almost solely to the development of knowledge *about* the inmate as criminal. Even the educators, it seems, are no exception and offer little resistance to the popular theory; hardly any project can purport to be truly educational in a contemporary penitentiary context unless it is preceded by an unending litany of information *about* the inmate. So much so that many educational programs become obsessively preoccupied with itemizing the characteristics of inmates — concentrating remarkably on the column of deficits — and thus developing into uninspiring, short-winded compensatory matchmakings.

Questions. Does education contradict itself if, to exist, it must be subservient to the visibility function. For isn't the development of knowledge *about* the criminal a kind of biography of crime before the fact? Where is it written in our codes of justice that the penal function shall recommend the punishment of the act by punishment of its history? Why must education depend so extensively on "why" truths or "how come" truths, or "what for" truths, supposedly discoverable within the personality traits of the inmate? Isn't the development of knowledge *about* the inmate more like a tremendous power-technique of control whereby spying on an individual's innermost thoughts and feelings becomes an unprecedented instrument of domination over the concerned individual? This appears particularly frightening in cases where etiology, the genealogy of causes, leads not only to a taxonomy of specific characteristics — which almost automatically consists of a characterization of "have nots" rather than "haves" — but may also lead to the inhibiting of the inmate's capacity and very personalized and unique desire for change. At least, two manifestations of this particular paralysis can be noted:

a) *moral paralysis*, in the sense that the inmate is unrelentingly made to see himself as functionally criminal rather than as functionally human. Not only is he forced to be cognizant of his crime, but forced to realize, judge and condemn his "criminal nature": in short forced to judge and condemn himself;

b) *intellectual paralysis*, in the sense that so much gets to be known about the inmate that there is nothing left for him to know about himself. The inmate inevitably discovers himself not as himself but as the idea someone else has of him and says he is; and, by controlling his willing, and wanting, and feeling, and thinking, says he ought to be. So that the visibility function of education exercises overwhelming control not only over one's past, but also over one's destiny. So that the possibility of autonomous change, the possibility of creating, literally, one's life, the possibility of choosing one's inner being and becoming ends up completely paralysed. So that, in a way, and contrary to its original intentions, education soon becomes a deterministic executioner victimizing more the victim it wants to aid. May I add how this observation seems corroborated from a spatial point of view. For is not the prison architecture of the 1980's still closely attached to the Panopticon prescriptions? What better way to organize human beings than to organize their living quarters? The spatial definition of one's limitrophic belonging, geographical lieu, predetermines to a great degree his moral and intellectual belonging. In this respect, if our penitentiaries have placement, transfer, and replacement policies, who will say that they have a philosophy of space for human residence. Not only does the inmate belong to someone else's idea about himself, he belongs in someone else's geographical notion of his hardly belonging anywhere.

Also quite disturbing are the scientific indispositions. Much of the accumulated knowledge *about* inmates rests upon some peculiar, scientific assumptions. Some although certainly not all of these assumptions, are as follows: that science of the criminal will somehow and some day lead to a science of good and evil, which in turn will lead to automatic education and spontaneous good action; that men, all men, must develop through predictable, linear, stages clearly identifiable through scientific analysis, stages whose interrupted processes — as is the case with criminals — must be corrected or compensated for if normal progress is to resume; that science as "power-knowledge" about the other and over the other will eventually finish up in power belonging to and existing for the other; that knowledge of individual traits will help to better differentiate and respect each individuality — as if heterogeneous discoveries about inmates did not invariably lead to quite homo-geneous categories; in short, that science about criminals is scientific. Unfortunately, nothing has proven less scientific and more contradictory in the past one hundred years than criminal science.

This book of collected papers does not wish to "correct" the situation. It is less interested in correcting criminal mentalities and behaviors than in educating human beings. Naturally, penitentiary education is not indifferent to the postulates of order and conver-gence, causal transformation and unity, structural determinism and explainable continuities, predictable tendancies and so on. But this book wishes to explore and emphasize fresh ideas, new "possibles". It appeals to creative imagination and intellectual adventure, to cultural and spiritual auscultation. As a creative stethoscope for constructive optimism, the idea of this book is to exploit the world of the unknown and, in so doing, to explore all avenues of thought and hope — be they contradiction and plurality, discontinuity and divergence, analogy and heterogeneity.

More important perhaps, this book is about persons helping persons. "Every man", Alain says, "was wrapped first in human flesh, and immediately afterwards in human arms; there is no expe-rience which precedes this experience of the human; this is his first world, not a world of things, but a human world, a world of signs, on which his frail existence depends" (*Les passions et la sagesse*). In other words, human dependency arises out of human resemblance, for to be born into the sign of the other is to be born to the other, by the other, through the other. It is his initial relationship with his fellow-man which makes man; through this relationship he *becomes* and thus becomes himself. Consequently, education in prison obliges us to determine once again the original meaning of educa-tional activity, to rediscover the "other" and to re-learn to distinguish the essential from the urgent. The urgent is the solution of facility, that which "gives immediate results", that which correc-tional education has too often endorsed and followed in the past. The essential, in contrast, lies beyond what is profitable, beyond the universe of provision and nervous security, beyond what is fixed and sterile. The essential is based on giving. For we create what we do. One who punishes, creates punishment. One who corrects, creates correction. One who gives, creates education, which, in its original etymological sense, properly means to nourish. Education in prison has no other justification than that of sharing.

This book is about giving.

Québec
August, 1981.

1. INMATE RIGHT TO EDUCATION

Lucien Morin

> "I will not commit the serious mistake of losing faith in man"
>
> Tagore

Introduction

We * could bypass justification altogether by simply referring to existing legislation or to a certain tradition, and show, with facts, where inmate educational rights are recognized, no matter how thinly so. Still more in our right, we could avoid the question entirely by appealing to a literal interpretation of our mandate and see how the problem is "officially" not ours to discuss. But in both cases, we would be betraying our deepest thoughts and feelings. Intervening here is not a wish but a duty.

First, in itself, the question of human rights is one of those problems which is never completely solved and stored away once and for all. A science does not exist which can claim an exclusive and exhaustive grip on all its facets, nor has any body of knowledge yet been able to establish a satisfactory analysis. On this important question concerning the practical lives of men, a common theoretical justification seems to escape human understanding. It belongs to each generation to explain its allegiance and renew its motivations

This paper was originally published in the "Report to the Solicitor General of Canada Concerning the Educational Program of the Canadian Corrections System", by the Ontario Institute for Studies in Education, February 1979.

for adherence. For it is one thing to recognize a particular human right and quite another to discover and articulate the moral principle upon which it rests.

Second, in the minds of ordinary citizens, the admission of a prisoner's right to education does not follow with blunt evidence. On the contrary, resistance runs deep. On the one hand, because of an unconscious belief that it is necessary to appraise all that pertains to prisoners through the screen of moral lenses, men seem to find it more natural to take away from inmates than to grant them any-thing.· On the other hand, engrained social and cultural prejudices exist and render the task more difficult still.

Third, it appears to the members of this committee that to place the emphasis upon legal right puts the attention in the wrong place and tends to fix it in the wrong direction. As we hope to show in the following paragraphs, we would be deceived and deceiving if only practical, immediately applicable, recommendations were expected of this report. We wish to communicate the philosophy which underlies our conclusions and which we believe can serve as an inspiration that will outlast their immediate usefulness. In this respect, we feel it is our duty to show how, for us, the question of inmate right to education is intertwined with moral convictions and metaphysical beliefs. Our study takes its elan and finds its ultimate meaning in our consideration of this question.

It is not our intention, however, to discuss here all the different meanings that one can give the notion of a prisoner's right to educa-tion, nor do we pretend to be able to recommend a particular resolution that would bring unanimity. More modestly, the commit-tee wishes to articulate its position simply and clearly by the exam-ination of the three following propositions:

1. the idea of right must be subservient to that of fraternal obliga-tion; 2. the inviolability of an inmate's right to education is rooted in the concept of human dignity; 3. education means human devel-opment.

1. Legal right and fraternal obligation

From a certain point of view, the prisoner is an enemy of society and, sometimes, depending on the nature of the crime committed, an enemy of humanity—for example, assassination, deportation, genocide, persecution for political, racial or religious beliefs. Now we must not deceive ourselves, the natural human reasons for loving one's enemy are practically nil. We could probably go even further and observe how in his rough and unrefined nature, man manifests a more instinctive tendancy to apply the laws of vengeance, the ancient law of Talion, "an eye for an eye".

In the light of such a context, it becomes increasingly difficult, even impossible, to understand, let alone promote, the idea of a prisoner's right to education. But this is the *crux* of the problem, isn't it, and the committee did not come to grips with it at the start of its investigation. The earliest obstacles to the recognition of inmate rights to education were much less subtle and refined. Here are some of the major ones encountered.

To certain people, the prisoner is a polished and cunning hypocrite. It would thus seem quite inadvisable to provide him, through education, with the means to refine his vices. For others, it is the opposite which is true. The average inmate is so completely devoid of the ability to learn (except criminal behavior, of course) that it would be perfectly ridiculous to even pretend he has a right to education, especially if education is in any way related to formal academic schooling. There are still others, few to be sure, that take refuge behind the extreme moralistic position that the aim of imprisonment is purely punitive. Any and all measures should be taken to make the prisoner aware that as long as he is "inside" he must be continuously punished. Under these circumstances, it is clear that education, because of its evident consequences of relief and deliverance, is entirely inadmissable. For yet another group, the question is left aside in this sense that the prisoner is considered as a fundamentally and chronically deficient individual whose illness stems from social, psychological, physical and neurological sources. And as for the sick, their primary concern is not education. Rather, they need to be nursed and pitied.

Finally, there are those, more practically minded and less subjective, who see the problem not in terms of human rights but in terms of management: how to gather, under one roof (say a school, for instance), so many individuals of such ill - repute without requiring a heavy and costly security system? How to devise an educational method or system that would adequately keep track of the individual needs and abilities of every one? How to be assured that future employers would recognize the institutionalized training received — in the case of vocational or technical training? How to make sure that the prisoner, once freed, will effectively choose employment in the field in which he has trained?

If one is willing to exhaust himself on these questions, however legitimate they are, it is not surprising that faced with the principle of the prisoner's right to education, one develops the habit of capitulating.

The members of the committee saw at least two ways of dealing with these objections. The first was quite simple. It consisted in re-affirming our profound belief that an inmate was above all a human being, a person. "Men are men before they are lawyers, or physicians, or merchants, or manufacturers" writes John Stuart Mill. "Or prisoners" we would add. While it goes without saying that this view will not be readily acceptable to all, the committee felt it of sufficient importance to choose it as one of its basic premises. And to ensure that this would not be interpreted as mere lip service or as a weak academic abstraction it quickly sought the support of existing documents. For example, article 77 of the United Nations' Declaration on the treatment of prisoners: "Dispositions must be taken to develop the instruction of those prisoners who are capable of benefiting from such instruction..."; for example, paragraph 2.10 of a CCS ruling published in 1962: "...the Commissioner must, wherever this is practical, guarantee to each inmate capable of benefiting therefrom, formal academic schooling or vocational training"; for example, the Commissioner's directive 221: "Among the factors to be considered in determining a prisoner's needs, one would concern his academic interests, his professional training background..."; for example, article 26 of the Universal Declaration of Human Rights:

> 1) Everyone has the right to education. Education shall be free, at least in the elementary and fundamental stages. Elementary education shall be compulsory. Technical and professional education shall be made generally available and higher education shall be equally accessible to all on the basis of merit.
>
> 2) Education shall be directed to the full development of the human personality and to the strengthening of respect for human rights and fundamental freedoms.

Of course, this first way of looking at it does not solve the problem. Avowing publicly one's allegiance to a Universal Declaration of Rights, for instance, and interpreting it in favor of the prisoner is not much more than the assertion of one's dependence on a juridical clause, that is to say, on a right defined as expressing liberally established relationships in accordance with a contract or collective good will. Evidently, this is not enough. A prisoner's right to education cannot be limited to some legal definition nor can it hope to result from some theoretical invention. Said differently, if we restrict ourselves to the idea of *right*, the only consensus that can arise will result from a common conviction directing and motivating practical conduct or action.

But there is a second, more fundamental and, assuredly, more dignified way of approaching the question. It consists in looking not only at the prisoner's right but, more profoundly, at the moral obligation upon which this right rests, that is, the human obligation to fraternity, to brotherly love, to charitable action towards fellow man. This is the course that the committee chose to adopt in trying to justify its ultimate commitment to the prisoner's educational rights. For there are situations and moments in a prisoner's life— and education is one of them—where only an appeal to higher principles can clearly establish the boundaries of rights. In this particular case, it is a question of recognizing the concept of fraternal obligation—a concept nourished by the ideas of generosity and brotherhood and whose overflowing richness suffices to surpass and supersede the notion of right. Basically, what is fundamental to this idea of fraternal obligation is that it implies the desire and the will to do good even to those we feel do not deserve it. "If you love only those who love you, what is your real reward?" "If you greet only those who greet you, what extraordinary feat have you accomplished?" In short, if necessity were sufficient for the establishment of right, man would economize on obligation. But the saving would be mortal, for at the same time man would be skimping on his conscience.

Undoubtedly, we are not accustomed to this brand of apologetics concerning inmates or even to the more general question of rights. A certain tradition has habituated us in conceiving the concepts of right and obligation as inseparable correlative terms: a person has no right without there existing, for another person, a corresponding obligation to this right. In short, and to put it awkwardly, right and obligation seem to go together like a horse and carriage. But in fact, such is not always the case. The apparent antinomy between the two terms exists only from a judicial or legal point of view. Initially, both referred to an ethical imperative and fused into a synonymy of indistinguishable meaning. Now the term obligation has kept this moral connotation and, for this reason, is superior to right. Man has a constant obligation to do good, a fraternal obligation towards his fellow man. It is precisely because of his natural obligations toward children, the disabled, the blind, the mentally handicapped, etc.

that these groups of people finally obtain legally recognized rights. Because it rests on the moral injunction to good, the idea of obligation is anterior and superior to that of legal right or juridical recognition. The inmate has a right to education not because the law says so but because the law of moral obligation says so.

Anchoring inmate right to education can be substantiated by other arguments.

On the one hand, the concept of obligation is a gauge of public morality. It betrays in a crystalline fashion a community's real moral fibre and meta-physical lining. It reveals the degree of its cultural sophistication and the spiritual ideal it offers its youth. The fraternal obligation this community shows its minorities, the underprivileged, the poor and the out-casts, the prisoners is the expression of its interest in the future of humanity.

On the other hand, fraternal obligation appeals to an idea of ethical creativity in the strong sense of the word: being attentive and open to a person's wants and needs in order to invent the ways to satisfy them. It is the good of our human brother that, as such, commands our attention which no "letter of the law", no judicial clause can ever even think of exhausting. For the ultimate danger with the notion of human right is withdrawal into the self where real wants and needs can be confused with self-interest, where legitimate claiming can spring up in the absence of a genuine love for others. To clarify, we would paraphrase a well-known quotation from the late John F. Kennedy: "Ask not what a prisoner's rights to education are but rather what your moral and fraternal obligations are in the face of a prisoner's needs for education".

Finally, the concept of fraternal obligation "personalizes" that of human right. It appeals to the most secret of consciences and demands willed and desired responsibility. This implication of conscience forbids one to hide behind the cold and neutral texts of law. For if, with respect to human rights, one can develop more or less conscious habits, one must, when faced with the practice of fraternal obligation, maintain lucid attention and sustained interest.

In short, the idea of inmate right to education can only be justified through that of moral or fraternal obligation. Suppress this notion, and the concept of right becomes the arbitrary code of some legislative decision. Fraternal obligation has so much ascendency over right that in the advent of a betrayal of right, the only hope that justice will be done comes from our commitment to fraternal obligation. In fact, do not the blunders of morality themselves verify and prove the superiority of fraternal obligation? Those who have been tricked, those who have unjustly lost the just causes they tried to defend, all those whose basic rights have been stepped upon expect from the future, that is, from their blind confidence in the principle of moral obligation, that these rights will be dutifully restituted.

It is clear, for the members of this committee, that inmate right to education can only find its true meaning in the principle of fraternal obligation.

2. Human dignity

The inviolability of a prisoner's right to education is founded in yet another noble concept and principle—that of human dignity.

Andre Gide says somewhere that "a human person is the most irreplaceable of all beings". In a more committed and precise manner Paul Claudel writes: "Even with the coldest of misers, the most foul-tempered drunkard or in the heart of the vilest prostitute, lies an immortal soul, saintly preoccupied with breathing and living" (Cantique de Palmyre).

The members of the committee wish to apologize for adopting these bookish quotations but they do serve to express our deepest convictions. In spite of and contrary to the opinions of those who would accuse us of using loaded words and idle phrases, we want to state forcefully our belief that all human beings however repugnant or depraved, regardless of sex, race, religious belief or social status, have their dignity as persons. And what exactly do we mean by human dignity?

Let us begin by admitting that no one can claim to monopolize truth when it comes to human dignity. Every man, precisely because he is man, can have something and something important to say. So that much has been said and written, though no known theory of knowledge exists to regroup all pertinent affirmations. One such affirmation, and an important one at that, consists in identifying human dignity with the intrinsic worth of man per se. "So act as to treat humanity, enjoins Immanuel Kant, whether in thine own person or that of another, in every case as an end withal, never as a means only" (Metaphysics of Morals). By treating the person as an end it is assumed that a person has intrinsic value or worth qua person. Others have said it differently by stating that the supreme essence of man is man himself. Consequently, and in accordance with the etymological origin of the word (that which is its own end because self-sufficient in goodness and fulfillment) human dignity would be interpreted as the person acting as an end to itself.

Of course, we are not unaware that this important position would need to be greatly commented upon. It is probably not even necessary to adopt such an extreme point of view. As a matter of fact, members of this committee would not hesitate to further qualify this statement by adding that the person itself has a destiny which transcends our understanding. For the ultimate dignity of a person is not only in what a person is, but in its origin and its ultimate becoming. To recall Andre Gide's words, what is most important in the world is man. And what is most important in man is his spirit. But the spirit of man surpasses even man himself. At this level of being, everything is above and beyond the knowledge that we may have about human dignity. If, in the final analysis, to respect human dignity is to accept the fact that human beings are more than just human, who, therefore, has no dignity?

3. Education as human development

From what we have just seen, it must now seem obvious that by "inmate right to education" what is understood is human development. In the light of what we observed during our visits to a considerable number of institutions, this conclusion needs explaining.

The official aim of imprisonment being detention and rehabilitation has unquestionable effects on the interpretation, given by the Correctional system, of inmate rights to education. In other words, since education—understood as human development—is not the first nor the major objective of incarceration, a number of "secondary" views militate, more or less unconsciously, against this idea. For one, education is seen as a means of "killing time". This is seen as doubly advantageous: first, it is a comparatively cheap method when one compares it to the high costs needed to maintain the workshops; second, it is very effective from the point of view of security, since a large group of prisoners can be controlled simultaneously. This last point is particularly anti-educational. A dominating passion for security entertains the unconscious desire to prolong the agony of trial—having been judged guilty of a criminal offense, the prisoner should never be allowed to forget and must pay dearly. Useless to say, this unusual marriage contract between education and security leaves no insight into the prisoner as a human being needing human development.

Again, education is seen as the prisoner's preparation for employment. Since it is assumed that no one can survive in today's society without a high school education, much time and energy are spent on the principle of made-to-measure schooling and vocational training. Unfortunatley, this popular "learn how to do" philosophy all but sneers at the "learn how to be" conception of human development.

It is difficult for such a quickly drawn resume to do justice to each of the arguments presented here. Nevertheless, from our point of view, each of them is short-sighted in its version of inmate rights to education. And the results speak for themselves: indescribable inflexibility in the preparation of school schedules and time tables; meaningless activity; incredible exertion of energy in dealing with minute details; endless and useless reorganizations and restructurings; an agonizing feeling of stupid sterility and demoralizing scepticism. Most of all, it is the prisoner himself who ends up with the worst part of the deal. Faced with an immense need to be helped, he is abandoned to himself, left with his very human difficulties in a very inhuman solitude.

Evidently, the members of this committee cannot adhere to a philosophy of education leading to such consequences. A radical change is imperative and to bring about such a change a new and deeper understanding of the inmate right to education must be promoted. For this committee, there is only one real option: human development. Education, be it in a penal environment or otherwise, is meaningless if it isn't first and foremost envisaged as human development. There are at least two main aspects to this proposition: education as human development implies the acceptance of the inmate as a total being-becoming person; education as human development implies that values education be a major concern of any educational project. Here, we will concentrate on the first.

Educating the inmate as a total being-becoming person resists the idea of an education restricted solely or almost exclusively to training the powers of the mind. Let us briefly see why.

A recent American theory on criminality, which is quickly gaining popularity in Canadian circles, seems to rationalize criminal behavior by using the expedient notion of cognitive deficiency. More simply said, criminal conduct is seen as a matter of free, if not always intelligent, choice. The implication is that education must tackle the problem by developing the intellectual capabilities of the prisoner.

This is a theory to remember. It reaches far deeper than others which tend to justify criminal behavior and explain criminality in terms which totally absolve the criminal of any responsibilities. Nevertheless, it represents a special danger when seen in relation to ethics (a danger which is overlooked by authors of the theory). For it can lead one to believe that intellectual powers alone relieve one of moral obligation. And this, of course, is going too far. From time immemorial, man has wanted to abolish the contradictions between is and ought by using radical means. Socrates devoted his life to the problem. The aim seems to be to build a "good" world by intellectual knowledge alone and to demonstrate that "good behavior" can only be achieved through the science of the good. In other words, if a person were able to fully develop his mind, his knowledge of the good would "automatically" entail good behavior. Now we do not agree that man can behave solely through reason or logic. "The science of logic", writes William James, "never made a man reason rightly, and the science of ethics (if there be such a thing) never made a man behave rightly" (*Talks to Teachers*). In other words, when dealing with human development, logic is not sufficient. Within the realm of being and becoming, the total person has to be involved, involved with the passions, the emotions, the feelings as well as with the mind.

Educating the inmate as a being-becoming person also resists the idea of an education restricted to training in practical know-how. Here again we must qualify our resistance.

There is a prevalent educational theory in the prison world pretending that it is concrete know-how, know-how to do, know-how to make, know-how to produce that alone fosters the betterment of an inmate. In other words, an exclusive development in technical or manual skills would automatically raise human consciousness and produce good men. Awkwardly put, because Jean-Pierre is a good welder and Jean-Paul a good mechanic, they will fundamentally be good, honourable human beings.

The idea supporting this view is also very seductive and should be remembered. It suggests that the obligation to systematic, organized conduct, for instance, to assiduous attendance at work, to consistency in one's effort, to regularity at work, etc. will automatically breed the habit of goodness. This habit will in turn breed the spontaneous habit of good actions, perhaps even the deliberate will to do good. So much so that the repetition of good actions or activities—in the workshops or vocational classes for example— would suffice to instill good being and becoming. In short, by repeating the acts and activities of men on the "outside" inmates would instinctively become good persons.

Once again we would like to caution the reader against such an extremist attitude. We stress the fact that superficial imitation of "good actions" and professional competence alone are not sufficient in the promotion of human development. Being and becoming a person presupposes mature internalization and the deepest commitments.

To summarize, education as human development means growth in the plurality and totality of one's human dimensions. We would volunteer the concepts of learning to become and learning to know oneself. This, of course, is true of all education. For the inmate, this vision is full of hope and promise. It introduces him to the search for life's meaning, it allows him to grope with the fundamental whys and wherefores, with the what for and what questions. Like all members of the human race, the inmate inasmuch as he is a being-becoming person needs answers, significant answers to these questions. For the idea which he has of himself will justify his existence, give meaning to his life and determine, in large measure, his conduct and behaviors. "We should learn to know ourselves", said Pascal in the footsteps of Montaigne. "Even if the enterprise does not produce the discovery of truth it at least serves to regulate one's existence". All in all, saying that human development will bring out the total person is recognizing that education is senseless if it doesn't seek the inner man.

NOTE

* The "we" refers to the Review Group responsible for the "Report to the Solicitor General of Canada Concerning the Educational Program of the Canadian Corrections System", (February 1979). Although the author was asked to write in the name of the Group, the views expressed in this paper are those of the author and do not necessarily reflect those of all the members of the Review Group.

2. PENITENTIARY EDUCATION IN CANADA

J.W. Cosman

Introduction

The nature of penitentiary education in Canada is mainly the result of certain presuppositions concerning the nature of man, the nature of society, and the nature of education. These presuppositions, always implied but not always stated, go unexamined. As in other fields, so in the field of education, if basic presuppositions are not discussed it is only because they are assumed to be true. At least four such presuppositions largely determine the nature of education in Canadian penitentiaries: that criminality can be explained by a mechanistic approach to human behaviour; that human development can be realiably guided by a psychology which assumes that the self is atomic in nature, somehow real by itself, and discoverable in terms of its private mental states; that society is primarily economic in nature; and that the aims of education are essentially to occupy time and to provide skill-training for the employment market.

It is remarkable but not surprising that in contemporary penological literature a mathematical concept is used to describe the process whereby a person incarcerated in a prison rejoins his community. The process is called "integration." This reflects both a generally accepted mechanistic interpretation of criminal behaviour and also a

This paper appeared in Education Canada, *Spring/Printemps 1980, and in* Learning, *Summer, 1979.*

special psychological approach to education.

The extension of the mechanistic conception of the physical world to the non-physical world in the seventeenth century resulted in due course in the flowering of the behavioural sciences which have tended to reduce man, as a whole, in all his activities to the level of a conditioned and behaving animal, subject to the laws of large numbers and long periods, which eliminate as immaterial whatever does not conform or is not automatic. Explanations of criminal behaviour have followed this pattern. Some investigators have asserted that the causes of crime are organic; others have affirmed that adverse environmental conditions give rise to crime; still others have found psychologic factors at work and have adopted psycho-analytic concepts to explain what is called criminality. Such is the pervasiveness of the modern faith in the mechanistic concept and in the applicability of the scientific method to all phenomena!

In the case of criminal behaviour, it is ironic that two scientists have discovered the futility of the mechanistic approach. In their work, *The Criminal Personality* (1977), the late Dr. Samuel Yochelson, a psychiatrist, and Dr. Stanton Samenow, a clinical psychologist, report on sixteen years of intensive research and follow-up studies which they conducted in the field of criminology under the auspices of the U.S. National Institute of Mental Health. On the basis of the evidence, they abandoned, one by one, the accepted causes of crime. Their report literally shatters the stereotype of the criminal as the subject of early emotional socio-economic deprivation. Counter to their own training and preconceptions, Yochelson and Samenow were forced to the conclusion that crime has little or nothing to do with poverty, social injustice, mental illness, emotional disorder, drug addiction or any of the other conditions that have been postulated in modern criminology as causes of crime. It is illuminating and a matter of some interest in the history of thought that one of the findings of scientific study in the field of criminology in the last half of the twentieth century is that the mechanistic approach is inadequate and raises the same questions concerning freedom and morality that were raised by the same conception four centuries ago.

Galileo and the Renaissance scientists, having proposed to mechanize the universe, automatically re-opened the old problem of reconciling the world of nature with the work of the spirit, which had been solved in medieval times by Thomas Aquinas. It was this problem of reconciling the mechanistic conception of the world with the conception of God as omnipotent and of the human spirit as free that confronted René Descartes in the seventeenth century.

Although the thinking self of Descartes seemed a splendid self in that it was rational, in the last analysis it was an empty and atomic self, lacking in imagination and emotion, and stranded without resources in the immediate universe. Descartes projected into modern thought the idea that man could be known and could function as himself alone. He did that not just through his dualism, but through his description of man, which was in terms of mental functions and states. The thinking self of Descartes is not only a self separate from other selves, but it is an isolated, particularized self, independent of reality in general.

It was on the basis of the Cartesian metaphysics that John Locke wrote his influential essays and treatises including his views on education. With Locke and the English empiricists, Descartes' thinking self became the basis for a rampant individualism which showed itself in many spheres of life. The era saw the rise of Russia, Prussia, England and the American colonies. France and Austria, representing military despotism, non-commerce and conservatism were arrayed against England and Prussia, standing for the new spirit of individual freedom. This was no ordinary freedom. It was a freedom which knew no bounds, for man had become raised, as a rational being, into a position of supremacy over everything. The world was now seen in the light of one's personal interests. Knowledge, morality, religion and the state became subordinated to man in his particularity, and John Locke began his philosophy from the standpoint of private experience.

Locke accepted Descartes' dualism and his thinking self, and knowledge therefore had to become a matter of private experience. Material and spiritual reality had to become assumptions. Thus Locke left the individual more isolated and stranded than ever. All he had left were his private states of consciousness, a mythical world without, and a mythical self within.

In turn, George Berkeley denied the reality behind the world, and David Hume rejected the reality behind the self, arriving finally at the position that all knowledge derives from sensations and feelings and consists in perceptions or mental states. External bodies are only conjunctions of sensations; within, there is only a multitude of ever-varying sensations, ideas and feelings. Beyond impressions and the copies of impressions man can make no assertions.

Thus Descartes isolated the self; Locke made knowledge a matter of private experience; Berkeley rejected material substance as unknown and unnecessary; and Hume denied the very self. The individual had disappeared. There was nothing left but an assortment of conscious states. The individual is completely psychologized and is lacking in unity. This method of treating the self, that is, in terms of private states of consciousness, not only showed itself in moral theory for the next hundred years but was also the forerunner of modern behaviourism.

By the nineteenth century Locke had become very influential. His "mental states" became the basis for much of modern psychology. While there have been other treatments of the self, most modern psychologists, in wrestling with a detailed account of the self, have almost invariably fallen back on John Locke's idea of experience as a series of effects from causes, although they often introduce some general, determining condition, such as integration, co-ordination, fusion or contiguity, which, while having the potency, have also the ambiguity of the work of the mind in Locke. Reason is very difficult to explain, without accepting the unity of life as actual. Modern behaviourists, in their attempts at precision, have employed a method of reduction which has left only one possibility — to enumerate the detail of life in terms of bodily responses.

According to this type of psychological approach, the discovery of the self is not considered a rational development. It is not known in terms of a content which is a series of ordered functions and relations arising from a governing and objective totality. It is not discovered as sharing the world but as an atomic state. According to this approach, the individual exists by himself alone or in terms of some distinctive characteristic, not as a self that is achieved progressively through its interaction with the world, deriving its meaning from its community with an objective order which goes beyond its immediate and specialized states.

The psychological presupposition that the self is atomic or real by itself and known as a simple empirical fact irrespective of what the world generally involves has had an important impact on education, including education in penitentiaries, where behavioural scientists have been extremely influential. On that presupposition it is not surprising that educators in recent times have concentrated their attention more on the social and motivational aspects of education than on the intellectual aspect, that the school has come to be seen mainly as an instrument for teaching social and emotional skills.

It is not at all surprising that penitentiary education has not been very much concerned with the content or with the development of creative power but with process. For it has been bound by a psychology according to which man is atomic in nature and definable in terms of his private mental states. On that basis education as the pursuit of knowledge loses some of its authenticity, and it becomes difficult for an educator to discriminate between the study of ballroom dancing and the Oresteian trilogy.

(On this same psychological presupposition, in another field, as Christopher Lasch observes in his recent book *The Culture of Narcissism*, mental health becomes a matter of extreme egocentricity approaching pathological narcissism.)

The third presupposition which has affected the nature of penitentiary education is that society is primarily economic in nature. Thus, penitentiary education has been thought of mainly as a preparation for employment, although there is no evidence that employability in the manpower sense leads to reduced recidivism. In prisons, inmates tend to be thought of as means, even sometimes as a means of running the prison. In a rather desperate utilitarian dialectic, even within the context of helping the inmate to prepare himself for "integration" into society, the nature of the society involved is not questioned. It turns out that the society into which the inmate is to be integrated is assumed to be a society of labourers or job-holders (*animal laborans*), a purely economic society. The inmate, therefore, is really thought of as economic man, deriving his reality and meaning from some economic function he is to perform, from serving as a means to an economic end, from simply making a living.

This is an outrage not only to human nature but also to history. It is only recently, in the modern age, that there has developed a glorification of labour and a transformation of the whole of society into a labouring society. There have been other kinds of society at other times. A genuinely human approach to education can have only one style, which is to treat the student as an end in himself and not as a means to serve institutional or social objectives.

What a contrast there is between the idea of learning as secondary, as subservient, for example, to the training of a man to become a good cook or a good computer programmer, and the view of Comenius that "learning, virtue and piety" are inseparable, "bound together as if by an adamantine chain," the three providing the basis for the imitation of the ideal life!

At most penitentiaries education is conducted under the supervision of an education officer who functions as the principal of the penitentiary school. Two of the senior teachers are usually designated supervisors, one of whom assists with the supervision of the academic department and the other with the supervision of the vocational department.

At the regional office there is a regional education officer who acts as a regional school superintendent. At the national office, in Ottawa, there is a director of education, a chief of academic education, and a chief of vocational education. There are between 9,000 and 10,000 inmates in federal prisons. Most of them are undereducated, although the I.Q. distribution among the inmate population is not significantly different from that of the general population. Approximately 90 per cent of all inmates are under 45 years of age. A complete description of the education program in Canadian penitentiaries is contained in the OISE *Review of Penitentiary Education and Training, Phase I: Report to Reviewers, August, 1978.*

In the mid-nineteenth century in Canada, penitentiary education was thought of in association with spiritual development and was the responsibility of the chaplains. The first major recommendations advocating substantial education in penitentiaries were made in the report of the 1936 Royal Commission to Investigate the Penal System of Canada — *The Archambault Report.* In short, the Royal Commission was appalled by the perfunctory manner in which the limited elementary academic programs were being conducted in federal institutions and by the small number of inmates exposed to any opportunities for educational advancement, and it called for a complete reorganization of the educational system.

The Royal Commission recommended that the revision and remodelling be of sufficient depth to ensure the provision of a well-rounded program of adult education structured to meet the needs, interests and abilities on an individual basis of the potential student body, the majority of whom they found to be academically under educated, vocationally unskilled and culturally deprived.

In 1947, General R.B. Gibson was appointed Commissioner to consider the recommendations contained in the *Archambault Report* and to ascertain the extent to which those recommendations had been implemented. General Gibson was not impressed.

Nine years later, in 1956, the Fauteux Committee also expressed dissatisfaction with the state of affairs.

Finally, in 1977, the Parliamentary Sub-Committee on the Penitentiary System in Canada also was critical of the educational services of federal penitentiaries. The Sub-Committee's report drew attention to deficiencies in terms of quality, course content, curriculum, qualifications of teachers, and the meeting of external accreditation requirements. The Parliamentary Sub-Committee's criticisms were justified. Penitentiary education in Canada has been characterized by a general lack of interest in genuine educational achievement, by inadequate standards of teacher selection and training, by a lack of discrimination in matters of curriculum between the trivial and the important, a lack of discipline and structure, and by a complete lack of educational research.

Although there are a few bright spots, for example, in British Columbia, where a unique university degree program has been developed, penitentiary education has been mainly thought of either as a time-filling activity whose main purpose is to relieve boredom and soothe the conscious state, or as a means of providing skill-training for the employment market, although no relationship has yet been discovered between criminality and employability.

Even academic education in penitentiaries is largely a matter of skill-training, of the development of reading skills and vocabulary and basic mathematics up to the grade 10 level, and of correspondence courses, aimed at the passing of high school equivalency tests, which are, of course, not tests of true equivalency at all in terms of subject content but only indicators of probable success in more advanced programs of study.

Penitentiary education has simply not been conceived of in terms of the development of the powers of the intellect, in terms of enlightenment and the strengthening of reason, in terms of the development of man an historical person, as a member of a society and a civilization. Education in Canadian penitentiaries has been thought of mainly in terms of behavioural psychology, with human intelligence functioning merely as an instrument of human adaptation. How different from the traditional concept according to which education is analogous to the cultivation of a plant, with the action of education being like that of the sun!

The future outlook for penitentiary education, however, is hopeful, although there is a serious risk that it will not receive the attention it needs. In the last few years, there has been a growing sense of disappointment in criminal justice circles following the high expectation of the past 20 years for the effectiveness of correctional programs based on the medical model of treatment. There is a danger that this pervasive air of disillusion will be indiscriminate and will result in the de-emphasizing of effective programs along with the ineffective, and in the hindering of the development of programs based on more appropriate models of intervention.

The educational model is different from the medical model. The medical model was based on the asumption that criminality is caused by personality disorder usually arising from deficiencies of a psychologic or sociologic nature. The medical model thus aimed at the modification of certain personality characteristics. The educational model, on the other hand, assumes lacks in learning — deficits in cognitive development comparable to the pre-adolescent deficiencies in intellectual as well as in moral development.

Paul Wagner, in his paper "Punishment and Reason in Rehabilitating the Offender" (*The Prison Journal*, Spring / Summer, 1978), asserts that in any comprehensive program of rehabilitation that is based upon the concept of man as a deliberative and reflective agent, the first requirement "must be a sustained and concentrated effort to develop inmates' skills of ratiocination. Simply having inmates process through basic education programs and acquire high school equivalency certificates does little to develop the intellectual skills necessary for a person to become (and to care to become) a reflective, deliberative, and responsible being."

As a result of the findings of the Parliamentary Sub-Committee on the Penitentiary System in Canada, arrangements were made early in 1978 for a group of prominent educators from across Canada to carry out a critical review of the educational programs throughout the Canadian Corrections Service. The purposes of this review, which was conducted under the auspices of the Ontario Institute for Studies in Education, were as follows:
1. to establish the groundwork for the development of a five-year plan for an educational and training program of high quality designed to meet the needs of inmates of federal penetentiaries; 2. to identify and define specific penitentiary problems requiring professional educational research; 3. to lead to the creation of an Educational Advisory Committee to the Commissioner of Corrections; 4. to encourage university faculties of education to develop courses in teaching methods for penitentiary teachers; 5. to plan an international scholarly conference on penitentiary education and training; 6. to stimulate interest in the subject of penitentiary education and training on the part of academics and other professionals in the field of education.

The reviewers completed their report in March.

Unfortunately, although in recent years criminality has been a subject of much interest to psychologists and sociologists, it has not attracted the attention of many original or critical minds in the field of education. Yet there is an important need to develop a body of research and specialized knowledge specifically in the area of penitentiary education. Some research is already being initiated, even before the recommendations of the OISE reviewers become available. It is hoped that the report of the OISE review will stimulate substantial educational research by clarifying some of the needs. In the long run, this may prove to be one of the greatest benefits of the study.

3. REHABILITATION THROUGH EDUCATION: A CANADIAN MODEL

Stephen Duguid

In an essay in the September issue of *Corrections Today*, Arthur Berliner posed what must remain the crucial question for all of us involved in the criminal justice system: is rehabilitation a myth or a reality? We are far too sensitive and indeed too moral a society to be content with the simple utilitarianism of incapacitation or punishment as the sole end of our vocation. Berliner took a positive view, arguing that under certain specific conditions rehabilitation does in fact occur. I would like to second his argument and at the same time report on an education program in a Canadian federal prison which incorporates much of the spirit and substance of Berliner's model.

Education in prisons is generally recognized to be a "good", "humane" and "personally beneficial" activity. In recent years, post-secondary education has been advanced as a rehabilitative device, particularly post-secondary education which is directed at value and/or attitude change. Unfortunately, the record of such attempts at rehabilitation through education has not been marked with great success if such success is measured by the subsequent behaviour of the prisoner-students after release. Evaluations of the extensive Newgate programs, a program for young adults at Camp Hill, Pa., and a program at Pittsburgh all reveal varying degrees and types of change in the students but also reveal no significant differences in rates of recidivism compared to matched and control groups (Seashore et al., 1974; Lewis et al., 1973; Blumstein and Cohen, 1974)

The program discussed here, the University of Victoria program,

A first version of this paper was presented to the Correctional Education Association, Salem, Oregon, September 1980.

has achieved quite different results. In a recently completed follow-up study covering 65 men over a three year period, the rate of recidivism for the students was 14% compared to 52% for the matched group of non-student prisoners. As well, all of the value, cognitive and social changes represented in the other studies were found to be operative. There could be many factors involved in generating this success, but we argue that the theoretical and structural foundations of the program are in fact the key factors and therefore that the results and the program may be replicated elsewhere (Ayers et al., 1980)

The program is based on an amalgamation of several psychological theories about human behaviour, starting with a concern for the role of perception in causing certain behaviours. Perception is seen as the crucial cognitive step between reality and the individual's conception of reality (Claster, 1975: 101). Thus school, family, or society in general may or may not be corrupt or oppressive, but certainly most criminals perceive them to be so. Crime may or may not be worth the risk, but obviously most criminals perceive that it is. Arrest and imprisonment may or may not be deterrents, but obviously a great many individuals perceive them not to be. Most of us have reached a consensual perception on these issues which is at odds with the perceptions of most criminals. This perceptual dissonance, obvious to anyone in contact with prisoners, makes it essential to focus initially on the nature of the potential students in prison education. More specifically, who are our students and can we say anything about them as a group which will help us in deciding what kind of education we should be offering?

By emphasizing perception instead of mechanistic drives emanating from social class position, poverty, deprived childhoods, or inherited genetic strains, we arrive at the central rationale for prison education: not job training or the imparting of social graces, but the changing of perceptions of reality. There are three aspects to this process:

1. Cognitive Development
2. Moral Development
3. Socio-potilical Development

I will discuss each of these in turn and describe the manner in which the University of Victoria program has tried to deal with them.

We know enough about criminals to make some important

generalizations. We know that socio-economic factors have a significant relationship to varying rates of crime, but do not explain the individual delinquent in relation to his non-delinquent peers. We also know that the impulse to commit delinquent acts is simply not that unusual in juveniles, studies in England and North America indicating that such acts may instead be the norm. David Matza has shown that criminals are not amoral or without a conscience — in fact quite the opposite though they have evolved techniques to neutralize that conscience (Rowan, 1978: 119; Wright, 1973: 3; Matza, 1957)

We also know that for the men we deal with in federal prisons, usually mature adult criminals, the criminal life is largely a chosen life, a vocation. They have by this time accumulated a history of offences, have strong ties with criminal social groups, have abandoned all but a tactical link with legitimate modes of making a living and have adjusted to prison sufficiently to negate deterrence as a major inhibiting factor. Further, research has shown that delinquents and adult offenders maintain a firm belief that despite an admittedly efficient police force and despite increasing risks, they will not be apprehended for future offences — what one of my students refers to as a sense of omnipotence.

In an attitudinal sense, we know that these men share a long-standing contempt for the average "straight" citizen and his moral/legal code. They are highly egocentric and manipulative. Their membership in delinquent gangs, adult criminal groups and time spent in prison has led to the adoption of a social code and set of values which acts as a powerful stimulant to future criminal associations and behaviour. All of this when coupled with the socio-economic and cultural sanctions imposed on an ex-offender, makes any kind of change highly problematic.

It is our argument that there are no socio-economic or genetic inevitabilities here. It is also our argument that at the base of this persona is more than just an attitude. We turn instead to the issue of perception and cognition — in particular to the notion of cognitive style. The problem lies with the way in which the world and the self's relation to the world is perceived and the cognitive structures which assimilate that perception. We are, of course, making a case for rationalism, for a direct connection between perception, cognition, and behaviour.

Piaget proposed a universal and invariant four stage process of cognitive development, culminating in what he termed formal operations or the ability to engage in abstract thinking. We are primarily concerned with the last two stages; concrete operations and formal operations. We argue that most criminals have remained at the concrete operational stage, a "way of thinking" most characteristic of adolescence. Here are some attributes of concrete operational thinking:

— reliance on authority
— intolerance of ambiguity
— rigidity under low levels of stress
— collapse under high stress
— inability to see alternative solutions to problems
— poor ability to role play and think in hypothetical terms
— poorly defined self-concept
— tendency toward extreme and polarized judgments (Goldstein and Blackman: 139)

A retarded level of cognitive development does not, however, make criminals at all unique as adults. Estimates vary, but it is generally accepted that a majority of North American adults fail to make a complete transition from concrete to formal operations (Dulit, 1972: 299) Also, it is argued that one may develop abilities in formal operations for only certain aspects of one's life, engaging in abstract thought at work, for instance, and concrete operations or even lower in one's personal life. Moreover, for many tasks facing adults in this society, concrete operations are perfectly functional and thus sufficient. Thus our students are in no way special in the structural level of their thinking.

The issue then, is neither level of development nor intelligence, but rather cognitive style. Cognition is not just perception, rather, it involves a "… systematic interpretation and reorganization of the information that is received as a result of interaction with the environment" (Cropley, 1977: 84). Even within stages of cognitive development it is possible to discern differences in the ways in which different people carry out this organizing process. I would argue, moreover, that it is possible to discern how certain groups of individuals share certain cognitive styles, in particular criminals. There have been a few attempts to identify a criminal cognitive style, but they do not appear to me to be very successful. It may be more practical to include criminals within another, better substantiated group usually referred to as authoritarian.

The theory of the authoritarian personality or, as I would refer to it, the authoritarian cognitive style, has a sound empirical base

(Kreml, 1977). Keeping in mind the earlier description of our prisoner-students and of the characteristics of concrete operational thinking, here are some attributes of an authoritarian cognitive style:

— need to perceive the world in a highly structured fashion
— intolerance of ambiguity
— excessive use of stereotypes — ignoring of nuance
— adherence to whatever values are conventional in one's setting
— preoccupation with virility — exaggerated assertion of strength
— pessimistic assumptions about human nature
— inability to be introspective, to acknowledge one's feelings (Greenstein, 1965: 86-87).

The two dominant features of the authoritarian are rigidity and intolerance of ambiguity. Cognitions are compartmentalized and walled off from each other so that opposite or conflicting perceptions can be maintained and contradictions denied. There are strong correlations between the emergence of this type of cognitive style and certain forms of child-rearing practices as well as with class origin (Goldstein and Blackman: 39). The absence of varied role taking opportunities within lower class communities, isolated communities or highly dogmatic environments tends to foster this rigidity and intolerance. It is suggested that individuals with limited role experience cannot take the roles of others outside their reference group, that they cannot understand or sympathize with such outsiders and therefore feel hostile toward and reject members of such groups. In an odd turnabout, we and all that we represent are the outside group. Merely pointing out contradictions in his thinking, or offering "facts" to contradict his perceptions, will get us nowhere with the authoritarian / criminal, because his cognitive structure or style has developed ways of absorbing contradictions without change.

What we are concerned with, then, is not the content inherent in the criminal's thinking, or lack thereof, but the actual structure of his thinking. It is for this reason that critics of prison education can accuse many prison education programs of producing mere educated criminals or job-holding criminals, because they have not addressed themselves to the crucial issue of the structure of thought.

Education in and of itself is not sufficient to confront this problem, rather it must be education with a particular goal, a particular content, and a particular style. It is clear, however, that if cognition is in fact a key element in the behaviour of criminals, then education can be a critical factor in changing such behaviour. The education program becomes what Feuerstein calls a "mediated learning experience", the lack of such mediation being perhaps the causative factor in the decisions which led to criminality (Feuerstein s.d.).

The kind of program needed in prison education is not one oriented to facts or information but rather one emphasizing problem-solving strategies, fundamental concepts and the basic structures of the academic disciplines, because these are the basic tools of thought used in making sense out of experience, organizing plans of action and making decisions (Rest, 1974: 242). Above all there is a necessity for what Piaget called cognitive conflict. Movement in cognitive stage is not automatic but rather proceeds in a very dialectical manner — the result of conflict and the resolution of conflict. This conflict is achieved by introducing students to a style of thought that involves greater subtlety and complexity than they are used to. It is the on-going debate over issues that acts to re-order cognitive structures and alter basic perceptions of reality, beginning the process of addressing behaviour. The goals, then, of this kind of education are centered on:

— awareness of the variety of possible problems that beset human interactions and a sensitivity to the potential for such problems whenever people get together
— capacity to generate alternative solutions to problems
— articulating the step-by-step means that may be necessary in order to carry out the solution to a problem
— considering the consequences of one's acts in terms of their impact on other people and oneself (Spivak, 1976: 12).

This set of goals leads us to the next major issue — the content of a prison education program. It is at this point that my argument becomes most controversial because I am going to make a case for moral education. There are many approaches to moral education and moral development and the one I have followed most closely is associated with the work of Lawrence Kohlberg. He posits a series of six moral reasoning stages which parallel Piaget's stages of cognitive development (Kohlberg et al., 1974). If cognitive development is meant to improve the quality and clarity of the individual's perceptions through increasing sophistication of mental structures, then moral development is meant to affect how those perceptions are interpreted and acted upon. Thus how a person selects, arranges, and sequences perceptions of reality is more than a cognitive operation — it is also a process intimately connected to the beliefs and values that guide one's life. These beliefs and values are subject to a developmental process which can be directly affected by education.

To affect a series of developments which might later be labeled rehabilitative, this educational process must be more directive in nature than that employed by traditional theories of adult education. To quote Parlett, "There is, in the scope of the teaching day, a hidden agenda which is, in the final analysis, directed toward the development of moral stages through which the majority of criminals have not passed because of the vicissitudes of their lives" (Parlett, 1980: 36). In the prison context the agenda cannot remain too well hidden but neither can it be seen as preaching. Assuming that within the typical prison classroom there are students representing the whole range of Kohlberg's moral reasoning scale, the overwhelming influence of the inmate code, the presence of an authoritarian prison environment, and the numerical predominance of students at Kohlberg's Stage 2 (egoistic, pre-adolescent moral reasoning) will inhibit a natural process of discussion. The instructor must at times become an advocate and not merely in a Socratic sense in order to promote examples of higher stage thinking (Duguid, 1979).

The contentious issue of content should not distract us from the far more important issue of principle and structure. To address these principles we have chosen not to rely on the classic "moral dilemma discussion" approach, but rather to use the standard liberal arts curriculum. Just as we argue that cognitive development is best served by education, we see moral development as emerging from that same educational process. We do not specialize in courses on ethics nor do we modify courses in other disciplines to emphasize moral or ethical issues. In practice, while instructors may be familiar with the theories discussed here, we do not train or even solicit these instructors to alter their course content or teaching style to purposively bring about such development. Such actions, besides resulting in objections from many faculty, would be seen through very quickly by the students and the education program would become just another therapy/treatment program. To this extent the agenda is in fact "hidden".

The actual curriculum is probably less important than might be supposed. The curriculum provides a vehicle, a rationale for the student to be in the educational setting and it sets a certain tone or level of discourse within that setting. As well, it requires hard work, time organized by academic term, and provides the necessary reward system. We have chosen English Literature and History as the core of the curriculum because these disciplines seem most likely to couple cognitive growth with the development of moral reasoning. Both have the advantage of being broad-based disciplines concerned with argumentation, philosophy, ethics, analysis of data and both require the development of a strong sense of empathy.

Other disciplines offer different contributions to cognitive-moral development. Anthropology attacks the ethnocentrism of the student and that in turn may relate to his egocentrism. Mathematics and physics challenge imbedded cognitive processes, forcing the student to consider other paradigms, other ways of receiving and organizing information. Philosophy acquaints the student with the complexity of what may have appeared to be simple truths. We avoid specialized courses on crime or deviance, individualized "explorations in personal awareness", or any other curricular innovation tied to the prison situation. In a program with a multiplicity of courses the student will take several courses over several terms, interacting with different instructors and with different groups of students. Characters in novels, historical situations, psychological theories, and philosophical arguments all act in combination to produce the desired effect. Thus no one course or instructor is the key to the developmental process. Instead, the education program as a whole is responsible and the primary cause or change agent may vary with each student.

The developmental theories described earlier were derived from an analysis of the problem, i.e., crime and the criminal. Education has been proposed as a mechanism through which the theory may be applied. It only remains to outline the structure within which that education should take place in order to maximize the theory's potential and thereby address the problem. As Berliner so clearly outlined in his proposed social work/counselling approach, the structure with its attendant network of social and personal relations is more than just another factor, it is the key factor. In the education program described here, it is the structure which allows for the process of socio-political development of the individual, the movement of the development process from the private realm of the individual to the realm of his relations with society.

We must in the end be concerned with behaviour and the connection between cognitive-moral development and behaviour is not all that well established. For Piaget and Kohlberg, not only that connection but the very process itself is tied to what we can call praxis, the active participation of the individual with his social environment. For Kohlberg, for moral development to occur, that praxis must take place in what he calls a just environment, one employing democratic norms with principles of justice as guides to interaction. This, of course, raises all kinds of problems when such a development process must occur within a prison. Berliner proposes to rehabilitate the prison in order that it may serve as a source of rehabilitation for the prisoner. If possible, that is obviously the best solution. If not possible or practical, however, it is possible to create an alternative community within the traditional prison.

The students must attain a new perspective on the law, a new understanding of the nature of a democratic society, and must develop some kind of social conscience. All of these are "social" developments in the sense that they occur in conjunction with others, not in isolation. Moreover, unlike the Freudian tradition, this approach sees the evolution of a sense of justice as being autonomous, not something passed on from parent to child. While the parent or teacher can play an important mediating or modeling role, justice is only internalized through interaction with peers in the context of mutual respect and solidarity.

The prison as an institution and a community is clearly authoritarian by nature and encourages the formation of social relations among individuals for the purpose of self-protection (Kohlberg Stage 2) or outright deferral to unquestioned authority or force (Kohlberg Stage 1). The prison and the prison staff are perceived by the prisoner as being unjust and authoritarian and are thus negated as a factor in cognitive-moral development. In response to this, the University of Victoria in effect created an island within the prison, an area where all Kohlbergian stages above Stage 2 were operational or possible. The cognitive development associated with taking courses provided the base from which to build these new possibilities for social relations. Just as important, the staff of the university, not being part of the prison hierarchy, felt no pressure to conform to the Stage 2 environment and were thus able to model and encourage thought and practice at higher levels. To avoid the opposite problem, staff identification with the prisoners, the program emphasized sessionial, part-time, and term staff appointments rather than permanent positions in the prison program.

Comprising about 20% of the prisoner population at each of two British Colombia penitentiaries, the University of Victoria program has enjoyed consistent support from corrections staff at all levels. In large part because of this support the program was able to envolve internal procedures and practices that were highly democratic in both a formal and informal sense. Relations between university staff and the prisoner/students were emphatically non-authoritarian, while at the same time the student-teacher relationship was maintained. There were few points of contact with prison staff during the working day, administrative relations with the institution being handled through the superintendant of education and disciplinary matters taken care of by the students themselves or in consultation with staff. In eight years of operation there have been no incidents of violence or occasions to request intervention or assistance from prison staff on any but administrative matters.

The more formal democratic structures evolved as the community matured, as the students demanded practices more in line with their more advanced perceptions and reasoning. Participation in decision-making was not "given" to the students, but rather was acceded to when they argued for it in a rational manner. The situations confronted by the community were neither artificial nor abstract. Rather, they were as real as the men would confront outside the prison, involving rights, privileges, conflicts of claims, material interests and group welfare. The conflict, stress, and passion implicit in these situations serves to confront each student with a series of decisions which require emotional, reasoned, and moral responses, thus giving ample opportunity for the exercise of both new and old problem solving skills.

There are, of course, a myriad number of problems associated with starting and administering such a community and these problems would no doubt be unique in each situation. What remains common, however, is the principle and the theory behind the principle. To resist the temptation to opt for easy authoritarian solutions in times of crisis, controversy requires that the staff and student leaders know that there is a very real reason for choosing the more difficult democratic option. To go beyond simple compliance or identification, the student must internalize the cognitive structures and moral principles offered by the education program and in my view he does that only by testing those structures and principles in the practice of his social and political life, by seeing their superiority in actual practice.

REFERENCES

AYERS, J.D., et al.
1980: Effects of University of Victoria Program: A Post-Release Study, Ottawa, Ministry of the Solicitor General.

BLUMSTEIN, Alfred, and Jacqueline COHEN
1974: An Evaluation of a college level program in a maximum security prison, Carnegie-Mellon University.

CLASTER, D.
1975: Perceptions of Certainty: Delinquent and Non-Delinquent. In R. Henshel and R. Silverman, Eds., *Perception in Criminology*, New York, Columbia University Press.

CROPLEY, A.J.
1977: *Lifelong Education: A psychological Analysis*, New York, Pergamon Press.

DUGUID, Stephen
1979: History and Moral Development in Correctional Education, *Canadian Journal of Education*, 4 (4).

DULIT, Everett
1972: Adolescent thinking à la Piaget, *Journal of Youth and Adolescence*, 1 (4).

GOLDSTEIN, Kenneth, and Sheldon BLACKMAN
Cognitive Style: Five Approaches and Relevant Research, New York, John Wiley.

GREENSTEIN, Fred
1965: Personality and Political Socialization, *Annals of the American Academy of Political and Social Science*, 361.

KOHLBERG, Lawrence, et al.
1974: *The Just Community Approach to Corrections*, Harvard, Moral Education Research Foundation.

KREML, William
1977: *The Anti-Authoritarian Personality*, New York, Pergamon Press.

LEWIS, Morgan, et al.
1973: *Prison Education and Rehabilitation: Illusion or Reality?*, University Park, Pa., Institute for Research on Human Resources.

MATZA, David
1957: Techniques of Neutralization, *American Sociological Review*, 22.

PARLETT, T.A.A.
1980: Education-A necessary if not sufficient modality in the correction of penitentiary inmates, *Learning*, 3 (2).

REST, James
1974: Developmental Psychology as a Guide to Value Education, *Review of Educational Research*, 44 (2).

ROWAN, John
1978: *The Structured Crowd*, London, Davis-Poynter.

SEASHORE, Marjorie J., et al.
1976: *Prisoner Education: Project Newgate and Other College Programs*, New York, Praeger.

SPIVAK, Geirge, et al.
1976: *The Problem-Solving Approach to Adjustment*, San Francisco, Jossey-Bass.

WRIGHT, Erik
1973: *The Politics of Punishment*, New York, Harper and Row.

4. TOWARDS A PRISON CURRICULUM

William Forster

Introduction

Whilst it is the purpose of this paper to consider the development of an educational curriculum within prison, and not to discuss penalogical and sociological theory, a few points must be made to solve as a context for the body of the text.

1. The unique nature of each UK prison makes it impossible to generalize accurately about the "system". This variety is partly a result of national policy which has produced a wide range of functions for different prisons — there are, for example, high security prisons (both old and modern), open prisons, local prisons and a range of other establishments for the young and female, as well as "training" prisons which place great emphasis on education and training — and partly the result of different "styles" of regime and historical accident. Not only does the British system of allowing a great deal of autonomy to a governor give him the opportunity to stamp his own personality upon "his" prison, but each prison has developed an historical "image" which it is very difficult for either management or inmates to dispel.

2. Even the most "closed" of prisons is to a large extent influenced by the outside world. And this can occur in three ways:

Paper presented to the World Congress in Education: Values and the School; Symposium on Prison Education, Université du Québec à Trois-Rivières, July, 1981.

a) Ultimate governmental responsibility for the penal system means that the Home Office can do no more in the prison service than public opinion "allows". One well-publicised error of judgement, or a particularly heinous crime can provoke a general outcry for a hardening of the system; one example of brutality can swing public opinion in the other direction. Such events do not provoke sudden shifts in policy, but the Home Office must be aware of them.

b) Fashions in penology and criminology similarly have an ultimate effect upon the way prisons are run; as indeed do ideas about education in the outside world.

c) Resources within the Prison Service come ultimately from the same source as other resources, and prison life is not immune to the waves of expansionism or recession which affect the outside world. The present cuts in public expenditure in the UK are affecting the prison education service as much as the national education service. Moreover, this is linked with (a) above; generally it is regarded as a "good thing" that prisoners should be usefully employed in manufacturing, but this attitude changes rapidly as soon as Trades Unionists, for example, see their own jobs affected by a recession.

3. A highly complex topic is the constant shift of power within the structure of the UK prison service. Ignoring the political aspect of control, there are four broad categories involved in the management of prisoners; the civil servants, the governor grades, the uniformed staff and the specialists — educationalists, psychologists, doctors, welfare officers and so on. In the past, there has often been tension between the first two categories, in recent years the third category — the uniformed officer — has entered the lists. The specialists are not real contenders for power, but their ability to operate depends in general terms upon the attitude of the currently dominant group and, at a local level, upon a great deal of political skill.

4. Three particular problems affect the prison education service:

a) The rising prison population underlines the urgency of the "treatment and training" role of the education service.

b) Both the abolition of capital punishment and the tendency of the judiciary have increased the number of "long-term" prisoners with their own special problems.

c) The establishment, after the Mountbatten Report, of a number of "high security" prisons throughout the country, presents very special problems of control and care.

Factors affecting curriculum development

Ideological

First it must be said that the person responsible for planning a prison curriculum is subject to the same constraints, and must take into account the same factors, as anybody responsible for a similar exercise elsewhere. This communality between the prison education service and the public adult education service is a factor which runs through this paper and which is a main objective of Home Office policy and practice. It is expressed structurally in the links between the Home Office and the Local Education Authorities in such matters as professional oversight, staff employment, career structure and training; the intention is that the prison education officer should approach his students and situation primarily as an adult educator, and that movements and ideas in the adult education world outside should be reflected in prison provision.

Indeed, any institutional consideration of objectives must immediately come to terms with this, for one of the major thrusts behind the development of curriculum in prison has been the idea that education should be provided in prison, "as of right". One of three attitudes must provide the foundation upon which the curriculum is built — first, that crime demands a reduction of attention, secondly that, like food and physical exercise, education is a human right which should be available at a minimum level to all, and thirdly, that the deviant require special and extra provision. Certain factional views in the UK would adhere to the first view, but increasingly the prison education service is able to work with the second view in mind, occasionally venturing towares the third. Within this framework, there are two specifically penal objectives in view. The first, which if it can be demonstrated, inevitably attracts public support, is what one might call the "anti-recidivist" — the intention is to prevent offenders from returning to prison. The second, and a far more difficult one to "sell" to public opinion, is to see the educational curriculum as supporting the official Home Office policy of "humane confinement". In a period of long sentences and high security, the vital role played by education in helping prisoners to serve their time and to remain sane cannot be overemphasised; moreover, it is a role which assists not only the individual prisoner but the community which ultimately receives him back.

The institutional factors, as I have called them, are of course subject — quite properly — to constant debate. Whether the recidivism rate is low or high, there are so many other factors involved as well as education — social background, age and so on — that it is difficult to demonstrate any relationship between it and education. And education which is provided mainly to help prisoners survive a long sentence has frequently come under attack — often from the "liberal" side — as being an extension of the "control" system rather than a part of the "treatment" system. But the central debate, affecting them all, is whether the prison education system is "special", or a simple extension of the world outside.

Practical

One could sub-title the "ideological" section as, "What One Can Get Away With"; and this is important. But those of us actively engaged in developing educational programmes know that there are practical considerations of, "What One Can and Can't Do", which loom just as large. It is I think, worth listing some of the practical constraints which inevitably operate upon the development of a prison curriculum no matter how idealistic the intentions informing the system.

a) *Security and Routine*. These vary widely from one prison to another, but are ever-present. The constraints of the penal system can affect the time of day when educational programmes can be run, the prisoner's ability to attend any course of study consistently, the provision of materials (it is only recently in British prisons that VHF Radio has been allowed), the free access to the prison of part-time teachers and, indeed, the continual presence in the providing prison of any one student prisoner. These factors are obvious, but are potentially so frustrating and, indeed, crippling, that they must be noted.

b) *Location*. Although some of the older prisons in the UK are situated centrally in cities, many, for reasons both of security and public opinion, are situated "nowhere" — islands, moors, rural fastnesses. This can create tremendous problems in the provision of part-time teachers — a vital factor in the construction of a wide curriculum.

c) *Length of Sentence.* While the long — and the medium — term prisoner is an important factor in the UK's prison population, numerically the short-term prisoner swamps the system. The minor nature of the bulk of crime, the slowness of the courts (which means that many a prisoner serves the bulk of his sentence on remand), the reception system and the parole system, all combine to create a situation where the education officer hardly has time to interview the prisoner, and certainly no time to make any appreciable impact upon him.

d) *Accommodation.* Many new prisons have got adequate and pleasant purpose-built Education Wings. But many more are struggling with quite inadequate converted cell accommodation; this is often far too small, noisy and under constant pressure from the demands of an over crowded prison. It is interesting to note though that this inadequate accommodation often gains from its central position in the prison; there is less complication with security and less conscious decision making attached to a visit to a centrally placed education room.

e) *Cost.* It is worth emphasising that, both at national and local level, the cost of resources is an important part of curriculum planning. Expansion and retraction outside is usually mirrored in the prison education service.

f) *The Hierarchy.* I mentioned in my introduction the need for the education department in a prison to achieve a place within the constantly changing power structure of a prison. Basically, the daily routine of a prison is made possible only by the co-operation of the uniformed staff. The recent national dispute, for example, completely closed many educational programmes for weeks on end; similar temporary closures have sometimes occurred on a local basis.

But it is worth mentioning that the response of uniformed staff to the education programme is often highly complex and, even when the system is under stress, a programme of remedial education can be given high priority. On the other hand, the more advanced any academic work is, the more vulnerable it can be. And officer reactions can also vary depending upon who the student is. This introduces another range of practical constraints upon curriculum development within an individual prison.

The present curriculum

There is no intention here to describe the present curriculum in British prisons in any detail, but these few notes indicate the general heads under which the curriculum is described and which, incidentally, profoundly affect peoples' perception of educational provision.

a) *Remedial Education*. A survey of 18% of the prison population in the early '70s showed that 30% of the sample had a reading age of under 12 years of age. Neither the urgency nor the size of the problem needs emphasising and in many ways the prison education service has risen to the challenge — so much so, that when the National Literacy Campaign was organised, a great deal of expertise from the prison service proved invaluable. Basic Literacy and Numeracy are given a high degree of priority, and there is an increasing awareness of what "functional" literacy is all about. The concepts of "life-skills" and "coping-skills" are gaining ground, and there have been several interesting projects concerned with, at one level, assisting prisoners to deal with an increasingly bureaucratized life and, at another, to cope with the field of human relation ships often through group work.

Almost without exception, the Literacy and Numeracy programme receives public and institutional support, although this sort of provision suffers badly from the brevity of contact with many prisoners. Real efforts are being made, via the Probation Service and the National Association for the Care and Resettlement of Offenders, to link released prisoners with basic education programmes outside.

An interesting area of research would be the relationship between remedial education provision in prison and the development of the academic programme. Whilst many factors affect the scope of the present academic programme, there can be little doubt that one early pressure came from the need to provide successful remedial students with some way of applying their new skills of Literacy and Numeracy. There are degree students in British prisons who learnt their alphabet within the prison system.

b) *Recreational Arts and Crafts*. The provision for crafts and hobbies is the direct responsibility, financial and organisational, of the prison education service. An extremely popular range of activities is provided within the prison walls, ranging from painting and drawing to woodwork, soft toy making, pottery and constructional activities. Time for this sort of activity is allowed within the prison routine, and most activities are jointly funded, with the main costs being met by the Service and a contribution towards materials coming from prisoners.

An instructional element is embodied in most activities, but in some cases they become "cell hobbies" with prisoners allowed the discretion to work in their own accommodation. Although these activities are almost completely un-researched, it is impossible to over-emphasise the part they have come to play within the prison culture. Traditional activities, and traditional — almost "folk" — designs within those activities have spread throughout the prison system. The benefits are legion, ranging from the most obvious immediate therapeutic values to a maintenance of the family relationship, via gifts for children, to a real sense of personal achievement and enhancement of self-image.

Difficulties do and can arise, of course, from the "closed" environment within which the activities are pursued; it is difficult to establish a true sense of relative values, especially in those fields where values, as opposed to manual dexterity, are concerned. A "successful" prisoner artist, for example, often finds that his "success" lasts no longer than his sentence. This difficulty is often enhanced by the tag "Recreation"; the emphasis often tends to be upon simply letting the activity go on, and (especially as so many prisoners are attracted) a valuable opportunity to inject some tough, critical teaching is neglected.

c) *The Academic.* The major discussion part of this paper is devoted to the "academic". At this stage I would simply present a table from the informal and "new" statistics of 1978-79 to give some idea of the spread of academic provision in prisons in England and Wales.

Two points need to be made here about definition. The first is that this table is based solely upon examination results. A truer picture would include not only all those students who attend the non-examinable academic courses of bodies such as university extramural departments and discussion groups of an informal nature which are run within many prisons (and which you and I would call

		STUDENTS				
		Prisons	Remand Centres	Borstals	Detention Centres	Total
GCE	'O' Level	797	—	122	15	934
	'A' Level	94	—	6	2	102
RSA	Stage 1	515	45	668	—	1228
	Stage 2	148	—	175	—	323
	Stage 3	52	—	20	—	72
C&G	Part 1	273	1	476	4	754
	Part 2	77	—	40	4	121
CSE		30	—	4	5	39
Open University		95	—	—	—	95
First Aid		230	4	220	45	499
Royal School of Music		75	—	—	—	75
OTHERS ⋆		544	289	534	472	2039
TOTAL		2930	339	2265	547	6081

⋆ Including a wide range of activities at various levels; HNC, post graduate work, specialist professional examinations, etc.

"academic"), but also all those students who attend courses with no intention of sitting for an examination.

The second point really illustrates why I wish to take this area as the central part of my paper; it is that, in official definition terms, "academic" does not exist. This, I suspect, is because most of the more formal academic programme can best be seen as it relates to other more easily defined activities. Written examinations up to "O" level can be seen as extensions of the remedial programme; and this can be extended up to degree level. Many examinations with a mathematical element, or those concerned with the world of commerce, relate to the vocational thrust of the programme. Other activities can be seen as recreational — music, literature, history and so on. It is this amorphous quality of the academic programme which seems to me to make it of paramount interest in the field of penal curriculum development.

Curriculum development in prison; some considerations

Anybody concerned with curriculum development must be concerned with at least four factors; first, the wants and needs of his student population; secondly the constraints — practical and ideological — within which he operates; thirdly (and this is important in the context of prison) that the proposed curriculum properly reflects the universe of ideas and practice it represents; fourthly, that the curriculum presents a maximum opportunity of choice and progress to the student. The broadening of choice and the consequent development of a "ladder" of progress is not only a matter of constant review but is an accepted historical achievement. The same may be said of the relationships between the prison curriculum and the wider currents of educational developments outside — this has been touched upon. And constraints are ever present.

For this passage, I would like to concentrate upon the expressed wants and the implicit needs of prisoner students. This is an extremely large and very complex topic, and I would not pretend to deal with it adequately here. I have searched back through my own notes, both on my research and my experience as a teacher in prison, and have freely adapted the work of others. As a rough and ready guide to discussions on how the needs of individual prisoners relate to curriculum development, I have constructed a series of side-headings and added a brie gloss to each one. I have largely ignored their inter-relatedness, and I trust that they will be read within the framework I have already detailed. They are the self-expressed needs and wants of prisoner students, a vital factor in the curriculum planner's strategy.

Choice. To engage in the curriculum at all is a voluntary activity and represents a choice, and indeed it is a continuous choice as to whether to stop or continue. The selection of a subject area represents a further choice and, moreover, the whole educational process contains an element of selection, judgement and seeing the consequences of those choices. This is in sharp contrast to the ethos of the rest of the prison system and has profound implications within any treatment scheme.

There is a strong case for the prison education service to enhance as far as possible this element of choice and, in particular, to engage the student whenever possible in studies which involve value judgements.

Assessment. There has been a rapid increase in recent years in courses which are assessed by external bodies. All mature students, prisoners or not, approach the external examination in a different frame of mind from the younger, full-time student. But this process has a peculiar potency in prison, especially for the prisoner with a background of educational deprivation. Most prisoners have a low self-image — they are "failures", even as criminals; the education department in a prison is often the only area in which a prisoner can clearly see the relationship between his own endeavour and the process of assessment. And, of course, the process of self-assessment plays a strong part in this.

Time and Achievement. Any achievement comes as a "reward"; not only for the quality of effort put in, but also for the quantity of effort over a period of time. Not only does this use of time — as an investment for the future rather than as a dreary "serving" — again contrast sharply with the rest of the prison, but many prisoners commented upon their awareness of the discipline involved in waiting for the "reward" as contrasted with the sought immediacy of the criminal "reward".

Relationships. In a largely uniformed and "gubernerial" institution, participation in the education programme engages the prisoner in a whole new range of relationships. One interesting area of research would be the prisoner's perception of the full-time education officer (in the British system, "of but not really" the system); he is certainly seen as the person who both offers choice and, at times, has to deny it. But the prisoner is brought into contact with a wide range of part-time teachers, both male and female, and time and time again, student prisoners emphasised the importance of this contact to them. Not only do such visitors present a window to the world but their different perspectives of prisons are a vital part of the educational progress.

A Sense of Membership. Really an extension of (iv) above is the oft-expressed value of an externally assessed course resting on the sense it gives of engaging in an activity which is the same as that of "normal" people outside. This feeling is at its strongest when there is the idea of "membership" of a clearly defined outside body such as the Open University.

The Importance of the Subject. Even though it be in humiliation, the prisoner is at the centre of the prison world; nothing — to him or to the system — is more important than he is. But the education programme again presents an alternative, and many prisoners confessed to the difficulty of adapting to the situation where the subject under discussion is, albeit temporarily, more important than either of the discusants. This runs closely alongside another confessed difficulty; that of adapting to a process of discussion in which the "authority" figure invites contradiction, which can be conducted without aggression and which is aimed at some concept of "truth" rather than praise or blame.

A "Useful" Occupation of Time. "Freedom" is a difficult concept to define, but perhaps the greatest sense of loss on the part of a medium — or long — term prisoner, is of the loss of time which otherwise could have been usefully employed. The prison system is such that, within the limited range of occupations available, education is the one activity which can be seen as a "useful" occupation.

"Milestones". The passage of the days, weeks, years in prison is a painful business; it is not for nothing that prisoners do not like clocks. Of enormous value to the prisoner is the simple "milestone" function of a course involving regular teaching contact, essay presentation and examinations. Here, a sense of progress and a sense of usefulness is closely linked to the process of coping with a long prison sentence.

Widening Horizons. All educational programmes should widen awareness and, therefore, choice. But this truism gains added potency in prison where, not only is the system designed for deprivation, but by definition a high proportion of students come from tragically deprived backgrounds. This not only invests the simplest educational process with a power beyond the imagination of many people of average education, it presents enormous problems in attracting students who, in many cases, do not know what "education" is and have not the basic awareness to distinguish between subject areas and categories of activities.

The "ladder". A sense of progress as well as of choice is vital to the sane survival of many prisoners. And — as in the world outside — development at any stage in the educational ladder implies the need to provide a further rung. The UK system now runs from basic literacy to post-graduate work. This "ladder" concept is important not only to progress those who start at the bottom, but to cater for those prisoners with a wide variety of educational experience outside. Whilst, numerically, the "disadvantaged" provide a high proportion of the prison population, the higher general level of education outside is mirrored inside prison and an urgent need in recent years has been to make provision for prisoners with an already high level of educational achievement.

Self-respect. Many prisoners expressed close links between their educational activity and their sense of self-respect. This varied in expression; many of the previously deprived spoke movingly about a new process of self-discovery, others looked back upon previous educational achievements and saw their current educational activity as the only means available to them of maintaining that part of them — the "cultural" — which they could dissociate from both crime and punishment.

These notes, albeit inadequately, summarize a whole series of conversations in which a wide range of convicted prisoners were answering the basic question: "Why is education important to you?". It must, first of all, be made clear that not all prisoners gave equal weight to all answers. There was a wide range of prisoners — those from the deprived background — who laid great emphasis upon the "new horizons" aspect; others, usually "lifers", who saw the notions of "milestones" and "progress" as the centre of their experience. And there is a wide range of other categories to be taken into account; the offender from a professional occupation (banker, teacher) whose offence debarred him from going back to that profession and who hoped to use a qualification to "sidestep" into some other occupation; the relative youngster who had been in the educational system and who had "opted out" (drugs, "political" offences) and who saw academic work as a way of regaining his previous position; the lost soul, sometimes highly educated and cultured, groping for some way to protect himself from the worst effects of prison life. As well as developing the curriculum to allow all these possibilities, there is the difficult and sensative task, on the ground, of matching needs to provision.

A second point of great importance is to note that no curriculum development of real significance is entirely "safe". I will fail in my intention if the list above gives the impression that educational development in prison is obviously a "good thing" and that, in the face of all these immediate benefits to our penal system, massive and immediate investment in infinitely widening the curriculum would solve all problems. If education anywhere means anything, it affects and changes people, and this inevitably involves risk and danger.

It can be seen, for example, that most of the coins I have proffered for view have an opposite side. To face a man with the completely new experience of choice can, and does, produce bewilderment as well as delight; this can lead to rejection and even deeper institution-alisation. Even more seriously, it is impossible to present a man with the opportunity to be assessed and to progress without, at the same time, providing a further opportunity for failure. And this failure can be utterly disastrous. Any examination system introduces a high degree of anxiety into an already intense life — especially as there is self-judgement and the judgement of one's peers involved. And there are occasions when aggression or breakdown results.

Perhaps most dangerously, certainly in the higher reaches of academic education, an alienating obsession can take over. Is it right that we imprison a man, and then provide him with so rich a diet of educational experience that he can, more or less, emotionally and intellectually reject his surroundings? And prisoners can become alienated from their peers in the system, their family and the system which contains them. There is a range of subjects (mainly in the arts) which, pursued obsessively, can take a man away from prison; another range is from time to time frowned upon by the establish-ment because, obsessively pursued, it can cause a morbid over-concern with the immediate situation. Psychology can very quickly become a study of deviance; Sociology the Sociology of Institutions. And the maintenance of "self respect" can be a way of denying that a crime was ever committed.

All of this can be said about Adult Education outside prison; what we have to take account of is the sharpening and heightening of these feelings in the unique hot-house of the closed prison. But there are two important factors which operate inside prison and not outside, which curriculum planners have to take into account.

1. It is not possible within a closed prison to provide a "wide" or "broad" education as we mean it in the world outside. Under-graduate, part-time adult student, school-child — our educational experience is always "leavened" by a wide range of other activities; family occupations, conversations at work, social life and so on, ad infinitum. This provides us both with a "check" to our evaluation of the direct educational experience, and with the opportunity to "apply" our education and to widen its meaning by using it. This opportunity does not exist in prison, nor does the opportunity to

learn and form judgements by the process of "serendipity". This last I don't think has ever been measured, but my guess is that well over 50% of my education emanated from what can only be described as the broad human equivalent of "browsing". This worries me a great deal, particularly where the study of humanities is concerned — the proliferation of different subject areas does not in itself provide a wide education. And I can see no answer in the closed institution.

2. The prisoner student's attitude to education is qualified by his awareness that, to a much greater extent than is true in the outside world, his education is subject to the control of others. And "others" can range from the prison officer in the corridor to the Home Secretary himself; in between these two extremes are the "flu viruses" which might affect his teacher, the library supply, a change in prison routine, a transfer to another prison. He feels vulnerable and, as well as increasing the anxiety element implicit in the process, it has two effects. First it makes it doubly difficult for him to invest himself thoroughly in such an unreliable process; secondly, it encourages him to perceive the educational programme as another counter in the constant "authority" game of prison life. And so our concept of choice within the prison curriculum is constantly modified by the fact that the choice operates within an authoritarian regime.

The way forward

1. Perhaps the most significant achievements in curriculum development in UK prisons over the past two decades have arrived almost indirectly as the result of the Home Office policy to forge links with "non-prison" bodies. The most obvious example of this is the way in which, although the Home Office pays for prison education, the provision within a prison is the responsibility of the Local Education Authority. But there are many other examples of how "outside" bodies have fed their ideas into the prison system; and one could argue that it is just as important that the educational programme and "feel" of a prison should mirror its outside equivalent, as that it should be good. This is a continuous process, and the debate about the "special" nature of prison education must not be allowed to inhibit the importation of new educational thinking into prison.

And so one would hope that those responsible for curriculum development within the prison would maintian a careful watch upon trends and, indeed, "fashions" outside. It is not only that education is one of the few real contacts with the outside world for the prisoner; if the intention is that the educational experience should be continued post-sentence, then the released prisoner should be able to move into a world which is recognisable in terms of the one he has left.

2. Within the constraints intimated in 1 there is plainly a good case for developing the prison curriculum so that the principle of choice is maintained. To be educated (or not) is the first level of choice; the second level of choice occurs when the student prisoner views the "shopping list" (and at this stage discrete professional guidance is most important). But beyond this stage there is a strong case for making available a type of work which involves the student in choice — aesthetic or value judgements and rational selection.

3. In the real world the curriculum developer is of course faced with choices of priority. The problem of desperate urgency in UK prisons is that of literacy and numeracy and it is recognised that a strong case can be made for concentrating resources upon that problem, especially if adequate provision could be made for the short-term prisoner.

4. We have a situation where the curriculum must reflect the outside world, and must recognise the need to husband resources and establish priorities within the system. And it should be recognised that the UK prison system already offers a wide range of subject matter at different levels. But, this said, two practical developments could be of enormous value within the system:

— A greater standardisation of provision in different prisons could be of benefit in a system where prisoners are constantly liable to be transferred. Obviously, the process of continuity would be of direct benefit to the student but there would be what I believe to be an even profounder benefit. The added security conferred upon the student could lead to a greater willingness to self-commitment, and if the "right" to continue study were more easily perceived then the tendency to regard education as a control tool should diminish.

— It is debatable whether the attempts to mirror outside provision should stretch to the common (in the UK) practice of providing the bulk of education in periods of a three-term year, thus leaving gaps of several weeks in the programme. This is the inevitable result of using teachers with full-time jobs in the academic world, and linking full-time education officers' terms of service to their LEA colleagues'. And it can be justified on the grounds of providing no more within prison than without.

But against this, it must be recognised that the prisoner does not have the range of choice of experience in these gaps that his free counterpart does. Moreover, the very status of the education service in prison would be enhanced were it seen to accord with the 52 week year of the prison; not only would it be perceived as being more "serious", but, especially where prisoners are released from other activities for educational purposes, then it would flow more easily with the system.

5. The next major thrust in the field of penal curriculum development should be, I think, not so much in the broadening of the curriculum, but in a reassessment of the relationships between its present constituent parts — defined as the "recreational", "remedial", "vocational" and "academic". There are institutional advantages in these semantic divisions, but already in reality there are considerable overlaps in function. Learning basic skills of literacy is plainly "vocational" and it can lead to the "academic". Again, any mathematical component of the "vocational" is plainly "academic".

Additional consideration, with little or no further call on resources, could be given to the relationships between these areas. An element of critical discernment could be introduced into the recreational, crafts programme, and the manuel dexterity of this programme could move closer to the assessed skills of the vocational training programme. And the vocational training programme could benefit from an injection of a "liberal" programme. The precise nature of these contrived "overlaps" — the "Critical Workshop" in the Art Class, "Sociology of the Work place" as part of the Vocational Training programme — must obviously be left to the discretion of the local operative, but a wider debate could do a great deal to stimulate a re-examination of the boundaries of these domains.

5. EDUCATION IN PRISONS: A DEVELOPMENTAL AND CULTURAL PERSPECTIVE

J.D. Ayers

"Perspective", the dictionary tells us, has as one of its meanings the capacity to view things in their true relationship or relative importance, and it is in this sense that the term is used in this paper. Achievement of a perspective on education in prisons that might lay claim to being final or definitive is surely an overly ambitious goal for this or perhaps any occasion, but it is hoped that even a modest essay in that direction may not be without benefits.

Perspective is achieved in various ways — by standing back, by viewing elements from several vantage points, by considering those elements with a certain detached attitude rather than as through the eyes of one intimately involved as participant or actor in the matter under review. For obvious reasons, it is not possible to achieve complete detachment. The author, in his role as coordinator of the Programs at the British Columbia Penitentiary and Matsqui Institution, is not a passive bystander but maintains constant supervision of the programs while remaining apart from the day to day operations. Moreover, a great deal of the author's perspective is based on the study of exemplary educational programs in British, American, and Canadian prisons (Ayers, 1974; 1975).

Appropriate and Inappropriate Intervention Models

Some four years ago when preparing the report for the Canadian Corrections Service on educational programs operating in selected

This paper appeared in the Canadian Journal of Education, *6: 2, 1981.*

United States prisons, the terms "corrections", "clients", "inmates", and "residents", were purposely avoided, although they were widely used at the time. These terms were considered inappropriate because they connote aberrant or deviant behavior that requires correction. They assume a medical model of criminality that has come under increasing attack, particularly since Martinson (1974), Bailey (1966), Michael (1968), Adams (1973), Younger (1974), and Clarke and Sinclair (1974) have emphasized the ineffectiveness of "rehabilitation" programs based on this model. The resulting change in attitude is reflected in the following statement by John R. Manson, Commissioner of Connecticut's Department of Corrections (Cockerham, 1977: 42):

> "...I was going to ask the legislature this year to change the name of the department to the Department of Prisons... but it would cost too damn much money... I've no intention of abandoning educational and vocational programs in the institutions, but I'm also not putting much hope in terms of rehabilitation."

At the International Conference held in Canterbury in June, 1977 in recognition of the bicentenary of John Howard's publication, "The State of the Prisons", it was apparent that there was a pervading air of letdown in criminal justice circles following the high expectations of the last ten or twenty years concerning the effectiveness of rehabilitation programs (Freeman, 1978). There is a real danger that this disappointment with research to date, together with society's clamour to be more punitive, will swing the pendulum too far, resulting in the elimination of effective as well as ineffective programs and thereby curtailing further experimentation with programs based on more appropriate models.

Over the past twenty years, most policies and practices in penal institutions have been based on the medical model which lead to an erroneous analogy with the physician's practice of diagnosing an individual's disease, prescribing a treatment, and effecting a cure. In a similar manner, the prisoner would be cured of his illness, that is, his criminality. While the medical model has been able to label certain types of criminals, such as psychopaths, dangerous or asocial offenders, etc., there is little evidence to indicate the effectiveness of this model. Moreover, such practices as indeterminate sentences, living units, and group therapy, are open to serious questioning on ethical grounds (Irwin, 1970; Johnson, 1971; Thomas, 1973; and Balch, 1975).

The most fundamental limitation of medical treatment models for personality change is that they are based on the unfounded assumption that personality is consistent across situations. While historically and intuitively individuals appear to display pervasive behaviour, virtually all research is discrepant with such a position (Mischel, 1968; and Bem and Allen, 1974). The model also neglects to consider the prisoner independent of the institutional setting. As a consequence, programs have been prescribed for all offenders, such as the living unit concept with compulsory group counseling. One might characterize, then, the rehabilitative thrust of the last twenty years as "coercive reformation".

Much of contemporary criminological thought appears to be accepting sociological theories of causation (Reasons, 1975). In these theories it is recognized that an individual is legally culpable for certain actions, but it is believed that many societal factors, such as economic and family conditions as well as peer group pressures affect everyone's behavior, including those who commit criminal acts and are officially labelled "criminal". The assumption is that the criminal is a victim of social conditions and is conditioned to criminal activities. Thus, the treatment must involve reconditioning by manipulating the social conditions in the family, the peer group, and particularly the community. Community based corrections are emerging in response to this new penology. While community work-release programs have a common sense appeal, they have not been found effective (Waldo and Chiricos, 1977).

The switch to the environmental reconditioning model is also increasingly making inroads into the prison, for example, in the re-introduction of no work, no pay in federal prisons. Work programs have seldom been effective in the past and there is no reason to expect they will be effective now (Glazer, 1964).

One might characterize past rehabilitation efforts as going from one fad to another in reaction to political pressures or currently popular theories. Limited consideration is given to a review of past research or to the development of a rational and coherent theory in support of an innovative program. Seldom, too, is the type of prison, the prisoner, or the after care taken into consideration. Rather, each new program is applied to a part of the criminal justice system in the hope that it will offer a universal solution.

In summary, then, there have been two main theories of reformation, both derived from the social sciences. The medical models assume that most prisoners have personality defects in the form of serious maladaptive behaviours that violate the societal norms and need to be replaced by other more desirable behaviours. Treatment could be considered as coercive reformation. The reconditioning model assumes that the causes of criminality are mainly in society itself and that the criminal's inappropriate behavior has been conditioned by economic, family, and peer group pressures. The treatment involves a reconditioning through manipulation of the environment.

An alternative and more tenable model to the medical therapeutic and environmental reconditioning models is an educational growth model. It assumes that most prisoners are deficient in certain analytic problem solving skills and in certain interpersonal and social skills that are required in order to function in straight society. Most criminals may be likened to the pre-adolescent who is deficient in intellectual, social, and moral development. Support for this position is found in a number of recent studies that are summarized below and in the work of the author, which is also reported below, under "Student Evaluation of Educational Programs".

Yochelson and Samenow (1976), in a comprehensive and extended study of the so-called criminally insane, showed that the criminal had immature and inappropriate thought patterns that required training to develop more effective thought patterns. Feuerstein in Israel (Narrol and Narrol, 1977) has shown that delinquency can be reduced by training problem teen-agers in the analytic thinking skills that are required in non-verbal and verbal intelligence tests. Parlett, Ayers, and Sullivan (1975), and Ayers (1977) have shown that cognitive and interpersonal skills are developed through humanities and social science courses that emphasize the discussion of political, social, and ethical issues. Kohlberg, Kauffman, Scharf, and Hickey (1975) have proposed that the level of moral development can be improved in a "just community" where discussions centre on the solution of moral dilemmas and of day to day problems in operating the just community. Spivak, Platt, and Shure (1976) contend that the simplest explanation for much of delinquent behaviour is that there are lacks in certain kinds of thought processes that get delinquents into difficulty. They concluded that problems are not ones of conflict or aberrant motivation but that delinquents suffer from a form of cognitive deficit that repeatedly leads them into social difficulties. As a consequence they have developed a series of cognitive exercises in their problem solving approach to adjustment.

The appropriateness of the cognitive learning model has now been extended to the area of psychotherapy. Ellis and Harper in the introduction to a very widely used book on assertiveness training entitled, *A New Guide to Rational Living*, have stated (1978: IX):

"We also believe, as part of rational-emotive theory and practice, in the *educative* aspects of psychotherapy. RET doesn't exactly follow the usual medical model of disturbance, which essentially holds that emotional problems consist of diseases or aberrations, curable by an outside person's (a therapists's) authoritarianly telling people what they have to do to improve. Nor does it follow the somewhat similar conditioning model (held in common by both psychoanalysts and classical behaviorists), which claims that humans get *made* disturbed by early influences, and that they therefore have to get restructured or reconditioned by an outside, parentlike therapist who somehow forces them into new patterns of behaving. It follows, instead, the humanistic, educative model which asserts that people, even in their early lives, have a great many more *choices* than they tend to recognize; that most of their "conditioning" actually consists of *self*-conditioning; and that a therapist, a teacher, or even a book can help them see much more clearly their range of alternatives and thereby to *choose* to reeducate and retrain themselves so that they surrender most of their serious self-*created* emotional difficulties."

While the Ellis and Harper approach emphasizes cognitive thinking skills and is critical of the medical and environmental approaches, it differs from the Yochelson and Samenow; Feuerstein; Parlett, Ayers and Sullivan; and the Spivak, Platt and Shure approaches in one important respect. It assumes an educational retraining model whereas all of the other educational theories reviewed assume that the delinquent or criminal is arrested in his development, that he has deficiencies which he can grow out of with appropriate training. There is no replacement or retraining required.

The Ellis and Harper (1978) quotation contains an explicit assumption that is not made clear in most other models, that is that a person has a choice to re-educate or retrain himself. He is not a victim of his emotional difficulties. He is self-created. Both the medical-therapeutic model and the environmental-reconditioning model make the implicit assumption that the delinquent or criminal is a victim of his upbringing, while the educational models referred to above make either an implicit or explicit assumption that the delinquent or criminal is more a decision maker than a victim. For example, Yochelson and Samenow admitted that they initially started their work with deterministic premises, but concluded that professional prisoners are in part created by their specific environment but have also had a strong element of choice in deciding to become criminals.

Based on the studies reviewed, an adequate educational model would comprise three basic assumptions: (1) that delinquents and criminals have deficits in cognitive, social, and moral development, (2) that development of cognitive skills is a necessary condition for the development of interpersonal skills and for moral development, and (3) that the delinquent or criminal is more a decision maker than a victim or pawn.

Purposes of Incarceration and
Organizational Structures for Habilitation

It is assumed that the function of incarceration is to protect society for a period of time and to return the prisoner to society as a better person. It does not accept the position as many do, that the two primary tasks of the penitentiaries are security and rehabilitation. Rather, the tasks are *habilitation* and *security* in that order. What is required is habilitation through *education*, making the prisoner capable to re-enter society.

It is also assumed that the tasks of habilitation and security cannot be performed effectively at the same time. For prisoner/students to achieve any degree of growth or development it is necessary that security be minimized, or at least that its pervasiveness be minimized. To achieve habilitation is difficult in an organization that at present only pays lip service to returning the prisoner to the street a better person. In practice, penitentiary industries, penitentiary schools, and penitentiary socialization, and so on, have been considered mainly ways of occupying inmates' time, of keeping them busy, of keeping the place "cool". In other words, these activities have been perceived mainly as means of managing the "joint". Such are common observations of prison administrators and of the instructors in the University of Victoria Program.

The traditional prison, thus, appears to have no aim, purpose, or ideal beyond pragmatic custody and control. The old tools of punishment, authority, and petty rules are retained and override any real consideration of the value of work, or vocational and educational programs, such that neither staff nor inmates believe in these rules and sanctions or consider them fair. In practice, arbitrary rules are sometimes harshly enforced, sometimes ignored (Sykes, 1958; Goldfarb, 1976). Traditional prison settings, then, lack any of the elements of experience required for intellectual, social, and moral growth. From the author's perspective, what is required are strategies that will maximize the separation of programs aimed at habilitation so that they are not identified with day-to-day operation of the prison.

To achieve some degree of habilitation, organizational structures must be developed to make programs as independent as possible of security. Contracting out all professional services, not only in education, but in other areas as well, such as parole, is one way of achieving this end, and probably in the long run, the ideal way. At the present time, however, in federal prisons the only programs that provide for some contracting out to individuals and community agencies are in education. A less desirable practice would be to combine contracting out with a country-wide unit, centralized in Ottawa, that would be responsible for educatinal programs in all prisons, similar to several American statewide school districts, such as in New Jersey or Texas, which provide educational services to all of the prisons and sometimes other institutions within a state's jurisdiction. Such a structure would allow some coordination in the development of programs and the implementation of those that are found effective. It could also lead to more effective selection and training of teachers. But its primary thrust would be to make programs more independent of the local prison administration except for day-to-day operations. This would help in establishing an identity for the school separate from that of the prison such that the prisoners would perceive the teachers as being from "outside", somewhat in the way that the instructors in the University of Victoria Program at the British Columbia Penitentiary and Matsqui institution are viewed. This requirement is a prerequisite for the establishment of conditions that facilitate learning in a prison setting which will be elaborated further below.

Student Evaluation of Educational Programs

When the author visited a number of prisons in Canada, the United States, and Great Britain in 1974-75, a major purpose was to obtain the views of prisoner / students on the effectiveness of various educational programs. The institutions were selected to represent a variety of educational programs with an emphasis on post-secondary. The choice of the programs surveyed at each institution was determined by availability of students for interview and the length of time a program had been in operation; in general, the longer being chosen. The six tables included in this section list the programs surveyed in each institution, together with a very brief description of their operation, and the length of time the students had been in attendance.

The three questions used were the same in all three surveys and were open ended in order to avoid leading the prisoner to respond in terms of the purposes of the program and to allow for the reporting of unanticipated side-effects.

Classification of Responses

Responses to Question 1, "What effects, if any, has the program had on you?", have been classified under eight headings and several sub-headings, which have been combined into three major categories for purposes of discussion: (1) those effects which are primarily *educational*, (2) those which are essentially *cognitive*, and (3) those which are more *affective*. The eight categories selected are essentially the same as those used in previous surveys evaluating the University of Victoria Program in the federal prisons in Canada. Experience indicates that these categories permit a high degree of interrater consistency in the classification of responses (Parlett, Ayers, and Sullivan, 1975). Because the responses were typically immediate reactions to impromptu interviews, it is assumed that they are relatively unaffected by undue reflection or other extraneous influences and thus are valid indications of the effectiveness of the respective programs.

A study of the tables reveals a number of interesting patterns or consistencies across similar programs in various institutions and countries. The first is that most responses, except in university programs, fall in educational categories (V to VII). The first two, "Broadened Outlook-Awareness" and "Communication Improved", (Categories V and VI), are not reported frequently, but most students make comments about courses providing opportunities for jobs or for further education (Category VII(a)), and sometimes make specific statements about individual courses, their enjoyment of them, or their effectiveness (Category VII(b)). It should be noted that "vocational courses" are not perceived to provide any more job potential than "academic courses". This may simply reflect a realistic evaluation of the situation. For example, it is well known that the training in some trades can be out of date, that many employers ask for general educational qualifications rather than specific vocational training, and finally, in penitentiaries many men take vocational programs for their general educational effect or just to do good time. In summary, Categories V to VII(b) represent educational effects that are normally expected from such programs. Category VIII, on the other hand, has to do with "Good Time" and "Parole", which are not really relevant purposes of educational programs.

Another pronounced trend in the data is that post-secondary programs, especially those that emphasize humanities and social science courses at the university level, have both a high proportion of responses in the cognitive and affective categories, I to IV. (See especially Tables 3 and 6). In addition, students in post-secondary programs report both more effects and a greater variety of effects.

In the three surveys an attempt was made to obtain random samples of students in each of the programs surveyed. This was more often accomplished in the Canadian institutions than in either the British or American. There are probably a number of reasons for this. The major one being that schooling is more often a full-time or at least a half-time activity in Canadian institutions and students were thus available for interviews while in most British programs and in many American programs the students are part-time and evening so that students interviewed tended to be the ones that were more readily available. Despite these differences in selection of students for interviewing, the results obtained appear to be quite similar for equivalent programs with one minor exception. In the Canadian survey a few students in adult basic education upgrading programs indicated that they were doing "easy time", whereas in both the British and American surveys only one made such a response, and the remainder reported that schooling was "good time" in the sense that they looked forward to it, it kept their minds busy, that they might as well make use of the opportunity presented; in general, schooling was constructive use of time.

In the American survey information was collected on prior schooling which was used in the initial classification of responses. Except in the case of Leavenworth (Table 2), the number of new students was not large enough to report as a separate category. There was, however, a tendency for the cognitive categories, I and II, to be reported more frequently by those who had taken few courses rather than many courses. New students may be more aware of these effects due to recency in change of perceptions. The somewhat higher proportion of responses in the cognitive categories for the University Programs in Canadian prisons (Table 6) compared to the same programs in American and British prisons (Tables 1, 2, and 3) is probably due in part to two factors: (a) a greater proportion of humanities courses in the Canadian programs, and (b) generally full-time attendance in Canadian programs versus half-time or evening attendance being the norm in American and British prisons.

Education prior to incarceration does not appear to affect the results. However, the level at which a course is pitched and expectations in terms of commitment and assignments, do seem to be critical. Prisoner/Students respect the assertive teacher with high standards but not the authoritarian or lax teacher.

The effects classified in the first two categories probably reveal that students have made certain cognitive changes in their way of thinking. In addition, many of the statements include or imply an expression of change in values. Under "Style of Perceiving Problems", are included all statements which indicate an awareness that problems and issues have more than one interpretation or solution, or that an open mind is necessary to appreciate alternative points of view. Specific examples include responses such as "can take an outside perspective", and "can see both sides of an issue". Other comments indicate that the students are more analytic in their thinking and consider the consequences of situations — "judgments are now based on understanding". All of the responses are indicative of a more mature, rational approach to the solution of problems.

In the second category, "More Accepting of Society", were included those responses which imply either directly or indirectly that the students are acquiring a greater awareness of the purposes and functions of society and its institutions, as well as the roles which they as members are expected to play. Included in this category were such statements as, "police have a job to do; there are roles to be performed", as well as the less obvious, "becoming more conservative in thinking".

Responses in Categories I and II are made mainly by students in university programs and to a lesser extent in community college programs in the United States. What is not revealed by these tables but obtained during the interviews was that most of these effects seem to be attributable to humanities and social science courses with instructors who challenge students by confronting them with their assumptions and by providing opportunities to discuss ethical, social and political issues. In fact, when these practices are emphasized, it is not unusual to have more than 50 per cent of the students make responses classifiable in these two categories as revealed in Table 6 and reported by Parlett, Ayers, and Sullivan (1975).

The next two categories appear to have a large affective component. A response was classified as, "Better Understanding of Self and Others", when the respondent referred to insight into human thought and action, particularly with respect to a better understanding of himself and his interpersonal relationships. Many of the prisoners indicated that they "now understood what conditions our behavior in interacting with others", or that their "outlook had changed toward other people", and that they were now able "to see how they affected other people".

The fourth category, divided into two sub-sections, "Committed-Goal" and "More Confidence" included expressions of incentive and satisfaction provided by a program. It was not unusual for students to report that they "first used the program to get out of work" or that they "started it to do easy time", but soon became totally involved. Sometimes a student would say that this is the "first commitment" that he had ever made. Expressions of confidence are often outcomes of effective remedial programs, particularly those at the basic literacy level, as for example, at Ranby Prison (Table 1), or early in other programs as a consequence of initial success; whereas commitment is more frequently associated with very challenging courses with a high level of expectation in terms of work and assignments. "Better Understanding of Self and Others", is usually an outcome of courses, either formal or informal, which emphasize interpersonal relations. The large proportion of students in the community college programs at Fort Worth (Table 2), and at Corona (Table 3), who reported that they had a better understanding of themselves and others and had more confidence in themselves, is specifically related to special "psychology" courses in human relations that had recently been completed. Life Skills programs can have similar effects. It is interesting to observe that the Life Skills program at Vanier (Table 4), which was primarily informational, had no effects classified in the affective area, whereas the Life Skills programs at Springhill and Dorchester which used the Saskatchewan Newstart materials had a significant proportion of responses in this area, particularly at Dorchester where the instructor had special skills and training. Understanding of interpersonal relations was also reported as an effect in some formal psychology courses and in the study of literature, particularly drama.

In Great Britain the Younger Report on Young Adult Offenders (1974) proposed that social and ethical issues be discussed in an educational setting because such issues cannot be left in the hands of chaplains, and that counseling and group therapy are inappropriate because they look at personal relationships from an inward rather than an outward looking view. This position was fully supported by most of the interviewed students who had been involved in "compulsory" group counseling or living units.

Student evaluation of programs, particularly with courses in the humanities and social sciences that emphasize the discussion of social, political and ethical issues, or of programs that develop problem-solving skills and interpersonal relations, indicate that there has been significant intellectual, social, and moral growth. These evaluations lend support to the major thrust of this paper, that appropriate educational interventions can habilitate prisoners and delinquents.

Preliminary data from a follow-up study based on 60 to 85 subjects who were contacted two to three years after their release from a five-month university level program primarily in the humanities show that the beneficial effects are real and for many long-term. For others, however, particularly the known addict, the effects are very fragile and appear to require additional support, as for example, via specialized half-way houses for students continuing their education on the outside.

Kohlberg et al. (1975) also observed that the results of this first experiment were positive but weak because discussion meetings three times a week hardly matched the meaning of being in a reformatory twenty-four hours a day. This is why he established a separate unit for women at Niantic with provision for release through a halfway house.

Acculteration by Education

Our public schools at present are not aimed specifically at providing the types of cognitive and interpersonal skills discussed in this paper, nor do they actively promote moral development. However, most children, especially those from structured home environments, gradually develop survival skills through guidance and interaction with parent models. An educational program, particularly one provided by mature instructors from outside the prison, operating in an open humane school community within the larger prison, can effect significant growth in skills which have been previously undeveloped in the delinquent and criminal.

One could view most of the educational programs reviewed above as *acculteration* of the delinquent or criminal. For excample, the analytic cognitive skills and the affective interpersonal skills developed in the University of Victoria Program, and some other programs, could be viewed simply as providing the prisoner/ student with skills that would help him survive in straight society. This is habilitation or fitting out. One would also surmise that similar programs in the high schools would develop better citizens for our society and perhaps reduce criminal activities.

REFERENCES

ADAMS, S.N.
1973: Correctional education: status and prospects. A survey and analysis prepared for the Justice Study Group. Syracuse University Research Corporation, 1973 (4).

ADKINS, W.R.
1974: Life coping skills: a fifth curriculum, *Teachers College Record*, 75 (5): 507-526.

AYERS, J.D.
1974: Evaluation of academic education programs in Canadian correctional institutions. Report to Canadian Corrections Service, Nov. 74.
1975a: Observations on education in penal institutions in Great Britain. Report to Canadian Corrections Service, June 75.
1975b: Observations on education in penal institutions in the United States. Report to the Canadian Corrections Service, Aug. 75.

BAILEY, W.C.
1966: Correctional outcome: an evaluation of one hundred reports, *The Journal of Criminal Law, Criminology and Police Science*, 57 (2): 153.

BALCH, Robert W.
1975: The medical model of delinquency: theoretical, practical and ethical implications, *Crime and Delinquency*, 21 (4): 116-130.

BEM, D.J., and A. ALLEN
1974: On predicting some of the people some of the time: the search for cross-situational consistencies in behavior, *Psychological Review*, 81: 506-520.

CLARKE, R.V.G., and I.A.C. SINCLAIR
1974: Towards more effective treatment evaluation. In Methods of evaluation and planning in the field of crime, Council of Europe.

COCKERHAM, W.E.
1977: Profile: John R. Manson, *Corrections Magazine*, 3 (6): 42-47.

DUGUID, Stephen
Forthcoming: Latent effects of prison education programs on criminal choice, *Canadian Journal of Criminology and Corrections*.

ELLIS, A., and R. HARPER
1978: *A new guide to rational living*, North Hollywood, Wilshire Book.

FEUERSTEIN, R.
1977: *Instrumental enrichment: studies in cognitive modifiability*, Jerusalem, Hassadah-WIZO-Canada Research Institute, Report No. 3.

FREEMAN, John, Ed.
1978: *Prison past and future*, London, Heinemanns Educational Books.

GOLDFARB, Ronald
1976: *Jails*, New York, Anchor Books.

GOODRICK, D.D.
1976: Operations research and correctional treatment: a social skills training perspective. Paper presented at American Psychological Association Convention, Washington, D.C., 1976 (9).

GLAZER, Daniel
1964: *The effectiveness of a prison and parole system*, Indianapolis, Bobbs-Merrill.

IRWIN, John
1970: *The felon*, Englewood Cliffs, N.J., Prentice-Hall.

JOHNSON, Elmer H.
1971: A basic error: dealing with inmates as though they were abnormal, *Federal Probation*, 35 (3): 39-44.

KOHLBERG, L., KAUFFMAN, K., SCHARF, P., and J. HICKEY
1975: The Just community approach to corrections: a theory, *Journal of Moral Education*, 4 (3): 243-260.

LETKEMANN, Peter
1973: *Crime as work*, Toronto, Prentice-Hall.

MARTINSON, R.
1974: What works? Questions and answers about prison reform, *The Public Interest*, 35 (Spring): 22-54.

MICHAEL, C.B.
1968: Changing inmates through education, *Education and training in correctional institutions: proceedings of a conference*, University of Wisconsin, Center for Studies in Vocational and Technical Education: 95-105.

MISCHEL, Walter
1968: *Personality and assessment*, New York, Wiley.

NARROL, H., and P. NARROL
1977: An introduction to Feuerstein's methods of assessing and actualizing cognitive potential. In S. Miezitis and M.Orme, Eds., *Innovation in School Psychology*, Toronto, OISE: 104-117.

PARLETT, T.A.A., AYERS, J.D., and D.M. SULLIVAN
1975: Development of morality in prisoners. The teaching of values in Canadian education, Edmonton, *Yearbook of the Canadian Society for the Study of Education*, June 75.

REASONS, Charles E.
1975: Social structure and social thought: competing paradigms in criminology, *Criminology*, 13 (11): 360-372.
1978: Two models of race relations and prison racism: A cross-cultural analysis. In B. Rich and C. REASONS, Eds., *The sociology of law: an international perspective*, Scarborough, Butterworth.

SPIVAK, G., PLATT, J., and M.B. SHURE
1976: *The problem-solving approach to adjustment*, San Francisco, Jossey-Bass.

SYKES, Gresham M.
1958: *The society of captives*, Princeton, University Press.

THOMAS, Charles W.
1973: The correctional institution as an enemy of corrections, *Federal Probation*, 37 (3): 8-13.

WALDO, G.P., and T.G. CHIRICOS
1977: Work release and recidivism: an empirical evaluation of social policy, *Evaluation Quaterly*, 1 (2): 87-108.

TABLE 1
Percent of Student / Prisoner Responses by Type of Effect, Institution and Program in Great Britain

ENGLAND AND WHALES

Effect of Program	Erlestoke Detention Centre		Gaynes Hall Open Borstal		Dover Closed Borstal	
	Evening Compulsory Soc. St. & 3 Options	Remedial English (Reading)	Business Studies Ord. Nat. Cert.	Cert. of Off. St.	ROSLA	General Cert. "O" Level
Length of Attendance	5 Wks	2 Mos.	4 Wks.	4 Wks.	2Wks.	7 Wks.
COGNITIVE						
I Style of Perceiving Problems						20
II More Accepting of Society						
AFFECTIVE						
III Better Understanding of Self and Others				25		20
IV (a) Committed — Goal			33	25		20
(b) More Confidence		20				
EDUCATIONAL EFFECTS						
V Broadened Outlook — Awareness						
VI Communication Improved						20
VII (a) Job Potential Improved			33	50	75	
(b) Specific Course Cited	87	80	66	100	75	80
VIII (a) Good or Easy Time	25		33			
(b) Parole or Family			33			
Number of Inmates Interviewed	8	4	3	4	4	5
Number of Inmates in Program	24	12	6	7	30	12
Average Number of Responses	1.1	1.0	2.0	2.0	1.5	1.6

TABLE 1 (Cont.)

SCOTLAND

Ashwell Open Prison		Ranby Closed Prison		Wakefield Closed Prison	Edinburgh Young Offenders	Castle Huntley Borstal	Greenock Young & Adults	Greenock Adults
Evening Optional	Construction Including Training for Trades	Remedial English (Reading) (2 Groups)	Evening Optional GCE	Open University	"O" Level	Mechanical Engineering	SCE "O" Level	Family and Home Skills
Up to 8 Mos.	6 to 16 Wks.	Up to 5 Mos.	4 Wks.	4 Mos. to 4 Yrs.	2nd Session	6 Mos.	5 Mos. or more	3 Wks of 4
					17			
				14				
	12		20	28	17			
	25			14	17	20		
33		43		14	17		33	
33	12		40				33	
	25	28		14	50	100	100	67
33	62	100	60	43	33			67
100	38	14	40	71	33	20		
					33			
3	8	7	5	7	6	5	3	3
7	36	16	10	30	12	30	12	6
2.0	1.75	1.9	1.6	2.0	2.2	1.4	1.6	1.3

TABLE 2

Percent of Student/Prisoners Responses by Type of Effect, Institution and Program in United States Federal prisons

Effect of Program	Sandstone GED	Sandstone GED	Leavenworth Many Courses	Leavenworth Few Courses	Leavenworth Total	Forth Worth GED	Forth Worth Com. College	Terminal Island GED	Terminal Island Evening Bus. Admin.
(Schedule)	Half Days Continuous Entry	Half Days Continuous Entry	(Evening University)			Half Days Continuous Entry	Half Days	1-1/2 hrs/day Continuous Entry	1 or 2 Course 2-1/2 hrs/Week
Length of Attendance	2 to 4 Mos.	3 to 7 Mos.	End of Semester	End of Semester		1-1/2 to 5 Mos.	End of Semester	1-1/2 to 2 Mos.	End of Semester
COGNITIVE									
I Style of Perceiving Problems			17	14	8				
II More Accepting of Society				71	46				
AFFECTIVE									
III Better Understanding of Self and Others			33	14	23		63	20	14
IV (a) Committed — Goal		17		14	8		25		
(b) More confidence		17		29		33	38		
EDUCATIONAL AND OTHER EFFECTS									
V Broadened Outlook — Awareness			17	14	8		13	20	28
VI Communication Improved	17		17		8	33	25	20	14
VII (a) Job Potential Improved	67	100	67	43	8	100	13	60	43
(b) General					54		50		
VIII (a) Good or Easy Time	67	17	33		23		13	20	43
(b) Parole or Family			33	14	23				
Number of Inmates Interviewed	6	6	6	7	13	3	8	5	7
Number of Inmates in Program	20	50			200	20	33	14	16
Average Number of Responses	1.5	1.5			2.2	1.7	2.4	1.4	1.4

TABLE 3

Percent of Student / Prisoner Responses by Type of Effect, Institution and Program in State Prisons in the United States

Effect of Program	Illinois Menard GED	Illinois Menard University	South Carolina Manning & Central GED	South Carolina University	Texas Wynne College	Arizona Fort Grant GED	Arizona Fort Grant Trade School	California Corona High School	California Corona College
(program description)	1 hr/day	Full-time 3 or for Courses 2-3/4 hrs per Week	Half Days	Full-time Typical 4 Courses	Liberal Arts and Business Evening Average 2-1/4 Courses	Continuous Entry 20 hrs per Week	Full-time	Continuous Entry Half Days	Half or Full-time
Length of Attendance	4 Mos. to 1-1/2 Yrs.	End of Quarter	Few Wks.	End of Semester	End of Semester	3 Mos. to 1 Yr.	End of Semester	Recent	End of Quarter
COGNITIVE									
I Style of Perceiving Problems	14	22		14	20				14
II More Accepting of Society		22		14	10				14
AFFECTIVE									
III Better Understanding of Self and Others	14	33		28	30		31	25	57
IV (a) Committed — Goal	14	11		28	10		6		14
(b) More confidence		22		28	30	25			28
EDUCATIONAL AND OTHER EFFECTS									
V Broadened Outlook — Awareness	14	22		14	10	25	6		14
VI Communication Improved		11		57	30	25	38		28
VII (a) Job Potential Improved	29	33	20	14	50	75	56	25	14
(b) General	71	22	60		10	25	25	75	14
VIII (a) Good or Easy Time		44							28
(b) Parole or Family	—	—	—	—	—	—	—	—	—
Number of Inmates Interviewed	7	9	5	7	10	4	16	4	7
Number of Inmates in Program	160	107	33	24	240	15	45	80	50
Average Number of Responses	1.6	2.4	0.8	2.0	2.0	1.75	1.6	1.25	2.3

TABLE 4

Percent of Student / Prisoner Responses by Type of Effect, Institution and Program in Three Provincial Prisons and in Federal Prisons in the Atlantic Provinces

Effect of Program	Vanier (Ont.)	Regina	Haney (B.C.)	Haney (B.C.)	Springhill	Springhill	Dorchester	Dorchester	Dorchester
	Life Skills	Upgrading Grs. 5-10	BTSD-2 Gr. 8	BTSD-3 Gr. 10	Upgrading Grs. 6-10	Life Skills	Upgrading Grs. 6-10	Grs. 11-12	Life skills
	2 half days per wk. for 5 wks.	Full-time 2 to 3 mos.	Half days 6 wk. cycle	Full-time 4 mos.	Full days Cont. entry	Half days 3 mos.	Full days Cont. entry	Corres. + half days per wk.	Half days plus ind. counseling
Length of Attendance									3 mos.
COGNITIVE									
I Style of Perceiving Problems									—
II More Accepting of Society									25
AFFECTIVE									
III Better Understanding of Self and Others		33				40	25		100
IV (a) Committed — Goal									—
(b) More confidence									25
EDUCATIONAL AND OTHER EFFECTS									
V Broadened Outlook — Awareness	25					60			50
VI Communication Improved		33	50	50				50	
VII (a) Job Potential Improved	100	67	—	50	40	—	75	50	—
(b) General		33	—	25	100	100	50	—	25
VIII (a) Good or Easy Time					—	—	50	50	—
(b) Parole or Family									
Number of Inmates Interviewed	4	3	4	4	5	5	4	2	4
Number of Inmates in Program	12	16	20	8	48	24	25	9	12
Average Number of Responses	1.25	1.6	0.5	1.2	1.4	2.0	2.0	1.5	2.2

TABLE 5
Percent of Student/Prisoner Responses by Type of Effect, Institution and Upgrading Program in Canadian Federal Prisons in Ontario and the West

Effect of Program	Collins Bay	Stony Mountain	Saskatchewan		Drumheller		B.C.P.	Matsqui	
	Grade 12	9-10 Upg.	Basic Literacy	5-10 Upg.	5-9 Upg.	High School	GED	GED	6-9 Upg.
	Full-time 12 wk. cycle	Half-days Cont. entry	Full-time Cont. Intake	Full-time Cont. Intake	Full-time	Full-time	Full-time 3 Mos. cycle	Full-time 3 Mos. cycle	Full-time 3 Mos. cycle
Length of Attendance	12 Wk.	3-4 Mos.	1-2 Mos.	3-4 Mos.	3 Mos.	3 Mos.	2 Mos.	2 Mos.	2 Mos.
COGNITIVE									
I Style of Perceiving Problems									
II More Accepting of Society						17			
AFFECTIVE									
III Better Understanding of Self and Others	20					33		25	
IV (a) Committed — Goal		33		50	11	33	11		
(b) More confidence					33	33	11		
EDUCATIONAL AND OTHER EFFECTS									
V Broadened Outlook — Awareness				50	11	33	22	25	
VI Communication Improved						17			
VII (a) Job Potential Improved	40	50	50		25	33	44	50	67
(b) General	80	33	50		75	33	44	50	33
VIII (a) Good or Easy Time						17			
(b) Parole or Family									
Number of Inmates Interviewed	5	6	2	2	9	6	9	4	3
Number of Inmates in Program	12	12	8	6	22	31	40	18	18
Average Number of Responses	1.8	1.2	1.0	1.0	1.7	2.5	1.3	1.5	1.0

TABLE 6
Percent of Student / Prisoner Responses by Type of Effect, Institution and College or University Program in Canadian Federal Prisons

Effect of Program	Collins Bay — St. Lawrence College — Bus. Admin. 8 Month Terms	Collins Bay — St. Lawrence College — Poly-Tech. 8 Month Terms	Stony Mountain — U. of Manitoba — University Program 4 Month Terms	Saskatchewan — U. of Sask. — University Program 4 & 8 Mo. Terms	Drumheller — Mount Royal College — University Program Fall	Drumheller — Mount Royal College — University Program Spring	Drumheller — Mount Royal College — University Program Total	B.C.P. — University of Victoria — University Program 4 & 8 Month Terms	Matsqui — University of Victoria — University Program 4 & 8 Month Terms
Length of Attendance	8 Mos.	8 Mos.	4 - 12 Months	8 Months	3 Mos.	8 Mos.	—	5 Mos.	5 Mos.
COGNITIVE									
I Style of Perceiving Problems	33	—	50	33	30	20	27	56	86
II More Accepting of Society	—	20	16	67	10	—	7	6	36
AFFECTIVE									
III Better Understanding of Self and Others	—	40	50	67	50	—	33	50	57
IV (a) Committed — Goal	33	—	—	50	30	50	33	63	100
(b) More confidence	—	20	33	33	40	30	40	25	21
EDUCATIONAL AND OTHER EFFECTS									
V Broadened Outlook — Awareness	33	40	33	17	70	60	67	63	43
VI Communication Improved	—	20	16	—	20	—	13	13	7
VII (a) Job Potential Improved	—	40	—	—	—	—	—	—	—
(b) General	66	20	16	33	20	40	27	18	7
VIII (a) Good or Easy Time	—	—	—	—	—	—	—	—	—
(b) Parole or Family	—	—	—	—	—	—	—	—	—
Number of Inmates Interviewed	3	5	6	6	10	5	15	16	14
Number of Inmates in Program	7	7	18	14	44	19	63	41	41
Average Number of Responses	2.0	2.0	2.2	3.2	2.7	2.4	2.6	2.9	3.5

6. CAN CORRECTIONS BE CORRECTIONAL?

Douglas K. Griffin

The purpose of the present paper is to justify the reformative purpose of the modern prison, both in terms of cultural and ethical traditions, and in terms of the historical evolution of prison architecture.

I want also to illustrate how some traditional views of prisons, prisoners, and crime, affect our contemporary views of the prison.

The Cultural Heritage

One of the earliest references to prisons occurs in the first book of the Bible. *Genesis* Chapter 39, verse 20 says "and Joseph's master took him, and put him into the prison, a place where the king's prisoners were bound".

You may recall that this was one of the earliest frameups of recorded history. Joseph had been sold into slavery by this time and he had become a very successful overseer in the house of the Captain of Pharaoh's guard. Joseph was also successful in attracting the attention of the Captain's wife, and the story goes that on his refusal to sleep with her, the Captain's wife grabbed Joseph's sport jacket and showed it to her husband as proof that Joseph had tried to seduce her.

So Joseph was thrown into prison, in the midst of a plot which,

Paper presented to the Learned Societies Conference: Canadian Educational Research Association Symposium on Education as a Cultural Alternative for Prisoners and Delinquents, Saskatoon, Saskatchewan, June, 1979.

although 5,000 years old, is as contemporary as tomorrow's soap opera. Joseph was thrown into prison, and from the bare bones of the account, it appears that he was not treated to any psychiatric analysis, any academic or vocational assessment, nor that the judge acted with the benefit of a pre-sentence community report. The King's prisoners were not only thrown into prison they were also bound, according to this account. In spite of the harshness of the conditions of the prison Joseph prospered there as well as you may know, and he became a kind of trusty overseer in the prison as he had been in the Captain's house.

The ability which Joseph demonstrated in prison was not acquired through academic learning, nor was it the result of skilled vocational training. His ability was that of interpreting dreams, and when Pharaoh dreamed his dreams of the seven fat cows and the seven lean ones, Joseph was fetched from the dungeon. Verse 14 of Chapter 41 of the book of Genesis tells us that "they brought him hastely out of the dungeon and he shaved himself and changed his garment and came in unto Pharaoh".

What we learn from this is that even the trusty overseer of the prisoners was apparently denied the facility of even having a shave and that his clothes probably gave off too strong an aroma to allow him to appear before Pharaoh in them. As a result of interpreting Pharaoh's dream Joseph was of course rehabilitated, and instead of simply being an overseer in the Captain of the guard's house, he became the most powerful person in all of Egypt, after the Pharaoh. He was given the priest's daughter for a wife and we are happy to learn he did not recidivate.

This very early story illustrates a theme which is to occur often in the Bible, and which still influences our thinking today, namely that prisoners were usually victims of arbitrary and unjust political power.

The men who originated the Judaic Christian cultural tradition on which European and American culture is based, had a great deal to say about evil and its consequences, but they did not associate imprisonment with wrongdoing, as has been done during the past few hundred years. The prophesy regarding the coming of the Messiah in Chapter 42 of the book of Isaiah says that the Messiah will "bring out the prisoners from the prison, and them that sit in darkness out of the prison house". Later in chapter 53 verse 8 the prophesy is of the Messiah who would be "taken from prison and from judgement"; and... "was cut off out of the land of the living".

For the Christian, Christ is certainly the most famous prisoner in history. The criminal justice system of his day arrested, condemned and executed him according to the law. The implication must be very clear, that if the most perfect man in history could be punished by the ultimate sanction of the criminal justice system, then there was something wrong with the system. The prophet Isaiah says in Chapter 61 verse 1 "the Lord has sent me to proclaim liberty to the captives and the opening of the prison to them that are bound". There was an early tradition according to which not only imprisonment, but also the law itself was seen as unjust in certain instances. The famous story of Daniel in the lions' den is an illustration. You may recall that Daniel was held in high regard by the Emperor Darius, King of the Medes and Persians, because he also was adept in the interpretation of dreams. The King's high regard for Daniel however, was the cause of great jealousy among the other princes of the land. Chapter 6 of the book of Daniel tells us that the Princes and Presidents assembled and decided that they would create a law which would serve their purpose of attacking Daniel. They designed a law, according to which petitions could only be asked of the Emperor Darius himself. When Daniel broke the law by asking a petition of his own God, he was cast into the lions' den for his trouble. Here is an example of how the law itself, the punishment for breaking the law, and imprisonment, are all portrayed in biblical sources as instances of injustice.

I emphasise these and other Biblical references, because I believe that the concepts and notions contained in the Bible continue to influence contemporary thinking even among people who are unaware of the Biblical source of these ideas. Biblical influences are strong in matters related to proper and improper behaviour, to matters of the law, correction, and justice.

In addition to the theme of the injustice of prisons and imprisonment which occurs throughout the Bible and which still influences us today, I wish to illustrate three other themes which are present in a very different way. The first is that there is a clear distinction between people who do evil and people who do good, in the Bible. This is surely one of the strongest themes throughout the 4,000 year period over which the different parts of the Bible were written. A second theme is the correction of mistakes. The correction of tendencies toward evil must be understood as something different from punishment and must be understood as something which leads to the happy condition of the individual, rather than to his sorrow.

The book of Job in chapter 5 and verse 17 says "happy is the man whom God correcteth: therefore despise not thou the chastening of the Almighty": The book of Proverbs, chapter 3 verse 12 says "for whom the Lord loveth he correcteth: even as a Father the son in whom he delighteth". This kind of correction is the loving action of a parent or a God who seeks the happiness of his child. It appears that the individual being corrected in such a case is not a person actively doing evil, but is someone who is simply mistaken. Although his basic orientation is for good the individual in this case has merely gone astray and if left on his mistaken path will eventually come to evil and to harm. Proverbs Chapter 22 verse 15 says "foolishness is bound in the heart of a child but the rod of corrections shall drive it far from him".

The third theme, which I referred to briefly earlier, is a theme which has perhaps regained the popularity which it had lost, at least in the popular media, for a couple of decades. This is the notion that there is a qualitative and not a quantitative difference between good and evil. The enormously popular movies Star Wars and Superman are based on the clear and simple distinction that these technically sophisticated movies make between the forces of good and the forces of evil. Similarly, the works of J.R. Tolkein, written forty years ago, have only recently found a readership enthusiastic about his straightforward portrayals of the struggle between good and evil. In numerous other realms of our current existence such as concerns over the environment, distinction between things that are good and things that are not good is being made more and more frequently. We are not content as we apparently were during the 50's and 60's to simply measure in terms of quantity. "More" is no longer equated with "better".

The Bible, of course, makes vivid qualitative distinction between good and evil. Isaiah Chapter 59, verses 4 to 7 describes evil people in the following terms: "they conceive mischief, and bring forth iniquity — and weave the spider's web — their webs shall not become garments, neither shall they cover themselves with their works; their works are works of iniquity, and the act of violence is in their hands. Their feet run to evil, and they make haste to shed innocent blood — wasting and destruction are in their paths". It does not require any painful wrench of the imagination to apply this description to any flock of evil-doers who perpetrate the crimes in a standard series of contemporary television shows. The unwashed criminal that Kojak slams against the New York telephone pole is one whose "feet run to evil, who makes haste to shed innocent blood". "Wasting and destruction" are certainly in his path.

The proposed remedies for evil must interest us. In the Old Testament evil is generally opposed by another evil. The principle of "an eye for an eye" has continued since the early days, and in non-Christian societies still remains the principle of retribution. The Christian ethic moved beyond this.

In the New Testament, the solution to the problem of evil is revised. In the New Testament, Paul writes (in *Romans* chapter 12 versus 17-2) "recompense to no man evil for evil — avenge not yourselves, but rather give place unto wrath; for it is written, vengeance is mine; I will repay, saith the Lord. Therefore if thine enemy hunger, feed him, if he thirst give him drink, for in doing so thou shalt heap coals of fire on his head. Be not overcome of evil but overcome evil with good".

The New Testament doctrine does not teach the passive submission to evil, as is commonly supposed, but rather the overcoming of evil by good. This, I believe, must be recognised as a very advanced and important idea, and one that is in danger of being thrown out and supplanted by more primitive notions.

Having traced this historical development of the cultural and ethical traditions of our civilization, I would now like to trace briefly the history of prison architecture to illustrate how that evolution influences our present situation in corrections.

The Architectural Heritage

In the 4th Century B.C., Plato suggested in *De Legibus* that a city should have three kinds of prisons. One could be for persons awaiting trial and sentence. A second would be for correction of petty criminals, and the third would be in a distant location, to house and punish dangerous criminals.

Similarly, in the 6th Century B.C., it is known that the City of Jerusalem had three prisons. The first of these was a house of detention. In the second we are told that prisoners were restrained in chains, and in the third prisoners had both their hands and their feet chained.

At the northeast corner of the Forum Romanum near Capitoline Hill in Rome, the Mamertine Prison has been shown in reconstructions to have been an underground cistern which consisted of two sections. The upper one was lit by a hole in the roof and the lower one, a dome-like dungeon of Eutruskan origin, was entirely dark. Prisoners were normally confined to the upper room and those condemned to death were thrown into the lower dungeon to starve.

Roman slaves were usually kept in a House of Detention whereas Roman citizens were chained to soldiers by the wrists and received severe punishment.

During the Middle Ages the usual places of detention were the dungeons of castles. During the fifteenth and sixteenth centuries the number of these castles greatly increased and all of them were notorious for the ghastly conditions in the cells in which thousands of prisoners were tortured and killed or were left to die in misery. Some of the most famous of these were the Seven Towers of Constantinople, the Castle of Spielberg, and the Bastille. In those days there was only maximum security. Men, women, and children who were not thrown into prison would be executed, or whipped, branded, maimed, or tortured and killed in some other hideous fashion. Unless a prisoner had powerful political influence he was helpless. Very wealthy individuals often possessed their own private prisons, in which they would incarcerate their opponents or their competitors.

It appears that the first amelioration of these savage conditions occurred in England during the reign of Henry the IInd. The extension of Royal Justice and the King's Peace coincided with legislation to provide places of detention for those awaiting trial and sentence. In 1166 it was decreed that the Sheriff of each country should build a jail, or that otherwise prisoners were to be kept in the royal castle. This was a bare beginning. During the next 400 years conditions did not noticeably improve.

In 1557, the Royal Palace of Bridewell which had been built by Henry VIII in 1522, was converted to an institution which was to house beggars and vagrants and to provide compulsory employment for them. Other similiar institutions were also called bridewells, taking their name from the palace. These were in theory work houses or houses of correction, rather than prisons. They consisted of large open dormitories and common rooms.

The idea of bridewells spread to Europe and many were built in Germany and Holland in the 17th century. The bridewells or houses of correction which were built in Holland formed the model for prisons in that country and in Germany, Holland, and Scandinavia. They were still going strong when John Howard visited them 200 years later. The most famous European bridewell was the workhouse for men in Amsterdam. There were originally only nine rooms in this building and the rooms served both as bedrooms and workrooms. Each room held four to 12 prisoners. There was no heating in the prison but there was a school, a church, and a dining room. It was the Dutch that first segregated men and women prisoners. The first prison for women was built in 1593 in Amsterdam.

In England, two types of institutions existed at this time: the jails which held debtors and others awaiting trial, and the bridewells or houses of correction. These two types gradually merged, and conditions were terrible. John Howard visited a 200-year-old jail in 1774, and wrote that it had two rooms, was overcrowded, had no glass in the windows, had no chimney, no water, and no employment for the prisoners. The Jails were even worse than the bridewells and there was no segregation of the sexes in either of them.

The first real improvements in prison conditions came as the result of the work of Filippo Franci, who started a work house for vagrant boys in Florence, in 1650. It was the Roman Catholic Church which inspired the construction of this prison, as well as Saint Michael's Prison in Rome, fifty years later. St. Michael's was the first celluar prison in the world. About this time, the Quakers in America, who strongly disapproved of the prisons in existence in the areas of West Jersey and Pennsylvania, which were copies of English bridewells, established a new type of prison. William Penn eliminated the use of corporal punishment under the Great Law of 1682 which established that most crimes would be punished by hard labour. This law was reversed in 1718 when the British compelled the return to the use of fines and corporal punishment. After the American independence in 1776 the Quaker system of imprisonment was revived and was developed into the Pennsylvania and Auburn systems of solitary and partial confinement.

With the exception of the Italian and American reforms, conditions in prisons in other countries during the 17th and 18th centuries were hideous. The conditions in France were among the worst. It is painful to imagine the intense suffering that prisoners underwent during years of solitary confinement in wet, rat-infested cells, or in overcrowded rooms from which men, women, and children were taken for execution or torture.

Saint Michael's Prison in Rome, referred to above, was built by Pope Clement XI and was completed in 1704. It influenced prison architecture for the next 200 years. It provided individual cells for prisoners arranged around a central court yard so that prisoners could see the altar in the centre aisle and so participate in religious services. Saint Michael's Prison had three levels of cells, each level containing 10 cells. The centre hall was large and well lit, and was used as a work room. This basic design still exists in the majority of European prisons today. Now, however, the central hall is used for the supervision of the inmates rather than for the inmates' view of religious services. Other countries were very slow in the adoption of this new design. For example, congregate prisons, (that is prisons without individual cells) were still in use in England. In Russia capital punishment was replaced in 1753 by transportation to Siberia and huge prisons were built to hold prisoners before transportation. Three and four thousand prisoners were sometimes housed in these Russian prisons, which some authors have described as the worst in the world.

The Power of New Ideas

It appears that these terrible conditions in prisons existed largely as the result of neglect and apathy, rather than according to any coherent plan. When men of intelligence and humanitarian orientation addressed their attention to prisons, it is remarkable how powerful their ideas were in producing change. The ideas generated by a very few creative men were successful in completely revolutionizing the character of prisons in Europe and North America. These changes show very effectively the relative power of ideas over physical structures and systems.

The first important thinker was Cesare Beccaria. *His Essays on Crime and Punishment* of 1764 recommended the abolition of torture, and talked for the first time about reformation rather than repression in prison. Beccaria profoundly influenced John Howard, Jeremy Bentham, Benjamin Franklin and other prison reformers. In contrast with these advanced views the famous Newgate prison, built in 1769, incorporated none of them, and reflected an emphasis on cruelty and repression rather than on reformation.

An Architectural Breakthrough

Two important events occurred soon after this. The first was the construction of a cellular prison in Ghent and the second was the appointment of John Howard as Sheriff of Bedford. The prison at Ghent resembled the cellular design of Saint Michael's and originated the radial design, in which cell blocks radiate from a common centre. This design is still basic to most Europen and American prisons. The prison at Ghent was the first planned for the classification of prisoners. Separate sections were planned for criminals, petty offenders, women, and juveniles.

John Howard was perhaps the greatest prison reformer of all time. Having had no interest in prisons previously, he visited the prisons for which he became responsible when he was appointed Sheriff of Bedford. He was horrified by what he saw. He published *The State of the Prisons* in 1777, in which he described prisons he had seen in Russia, Europe and England. He single-handedly changed the conditions of imprisonment in England and introduced the cellular design which had originated in Europe. As a result of his work the Blackstone Act of 1778 established new conditions for prisons, and included among them the statement of a need for moral and religious instruction. The act was not immediately put into effect but English prisons have never been the same since.

The conditions in American prisons improved only after this time. The first prison used in Connecticut was an abandoned copper mine with congregate dormitories 70 feet below the surface. This prison was abandoned in 1827 when it ceased to make a profit. The Quakers in America were successful in influencing prison design. Benjamin Franklin and Benjamin Rush of Pennsylvania used the Quakers' ideas as well as the ideas of Howard, Beccaria and Jeremy Bentham. The first actual construction of a modern type of prison was the Walnut Street Jail in Philadelphia built in 1790. This was the first segregated prison in America.

It was with the innovation of the segregated cellular design in America that the term "penitentiary" came into use. In their segregated but shared living the inmates were supposed to reflect upon their sins and to change their ways. The Walnut Street prison in Philadelphia, along with Saint Michael's prison in Rome and the prison at Ghent, are seen as the three most important prisons in the evolution of prison design.

The American system had two variations. Under the Pennsylvania system inmates were completely segregated day and night, and did individual work in their cells. This was called the solitary system. Under the Auburn system, called the silent system, which developed later, inmates were housed alone in their cells at night but worked in association with other inmates during the day.

Implications of the Architectural Heritage

It should be clear from the preceding description that prisons which were designed for repression and punishment alone, bear little resemblance to modern prisons, although the debate in which punishment is set against reformation continues. The history of architectural design in prisons shows that the physical structure of modern prisons is based on a philosophy of reformation. This fact is often overlooked. If we wanted to design prisons simply for punishment and repression, we have some very effective models to use. Fortunately, these have disappeared in Western Europe and America. The most recent history of intervention in prisons is not really based on a debate between punishment and reformation. It is based on a debate whether reformation can be effectuated through the manipulation of conditions which affect the criminal, or whether reformation involves the criminal's active will and conscious decisions.

Historical Implications for Reformation

In strictly historical terms we must dismiss the notion that imprisonment is strictly for punishment, as being clearly out of date by at least 200 years. The introduction of the term "penitentiary" and of the reformative type of architecture establishes the objective of the prison. It appears that the early idea of reformation in which the offender played the active role temporarily went out of favour in the middle of the twentieth century. During this time there was great optimism that social engineering would solve all human problems.

The medical and sociological models of reformation essentially removed the primary responsibility for change, from the offender. These approaches identified the source of the offender's problem as either deriving from a mental illness for which he was not responsible, or arising out of social conditions to which he passively reacted, and of which he was a victim. In the past ten years we have witnessed an enormous disillusionment generated by the failure of social engineering approaches in corrections. It seems now that the enormous advances in terms of control, manipulation, and predictability in the physical sciences which took us from the Pony Express to Lunar modules could not be duplicated in the social sphere. Having decided that reformation could not be accomplished by the manipulation of the offender as a passive recipient of stimuli, we are faced with the enormous problem of how to produce self-motivated reformation. If we cannot determine, predict, and control behaviour, motives, attitudes, and actions, that we desire, the only alternative is to evoke these from within the individual so that he himself sets out on a different path.

Why Corrections Must be Correctional

I shall now attempt to integrate the various themes I have illustrated above, and draw a plan of action from them. I believe that as a society we have reached a stage of confusion in which we are forced to look back to our cultural origins. We are forced back to an essentially moralistic stance. We are forced to take the position that social facts cannot be controlled and measured using purely quantitative terms. We must use qualitative measures if we are to provide a proper, adequate, and satisfactory classification of social facts. We are forced to recognize that some actions are better than other actions. Some actions are responsible, whereas others are irresponsible. Further, we are forced to the recognition that the reformation process which is to occur in a prison is essentially an educational endeavour and must be an educational endeavour in which the qualitative differences between responsible actions and irresponsible actions must be clarified.

One of the most important contributions that Samuel Yochelson, Stanton Samenow, Frank Schmalleger, and other writers have made to criminological literature is to identify the fact that criminals, regardless of the harm that they have caused other people, uniformly regard themselves as good people. These authors have recognized that the criminal uses thought patterns which justify and rationalize his actions. These authors have demonstrated that criminals think logically and consistently. They plan, using basic premises, but in terms of basic considerations of responsibility and irresponsibility, their actions are immoral. They are immoral, because they result in harm and injury to other people, but they are built on an internal consistency. (Harm and injury are commonsense terms referring to what most people think, most of the time.)

As a correctional educator I am a moralist. This is *not* because I believe that the job of correctional education is to preach morality to inmates. Rather, I accept that there is a moral distinction to be made between classes of actions, I accept that actions which lead to the well-being of other people are good, and acceptable, while actions which lead to harm to other people are irresponsible, unacceptable products of a thinking process. Unlike the computer age which assumes that all givens are of equal value and can be manipulated with equal justification, I maintain that basic premises are not equal. I also believe, with Doug Ayers and his colleagues, that irresponsible thought patterns are essentially immature. The development of responsible patterns of thinking and action requires a maturation process, in educational terms. Social responsibility and social maturity are related, at least conceptually, but certainly not all influential members of society are socially mature or socially responsible people.

I believe that correctional education has the central role to play in the reformation process for which our prisons exist. I believe that the basis of correctional education must be a program which not only encourages offenders to develop the powers of thought and analysis which will enable them to elaborate and implement their basic premises of action, but also must be one which will allow them to make moral distinctions among the kinds of basic premises upon which thought and action are based.

Conclusion

What we have, then, is an architectural heritage which is based on the reformative principle, which left punishment for its own sake, far behind. We have a cultural and ethical heritage which, at its highest stage of development, encourages us to overcome evil with good and maintains that good is more powerful than evil. As for how this correctional reformation process is to be carried out, we know that we must use an educational approach within these architectual and cultural frameworks, since our recent experience has demonstrated that deterministic social-engineering methods are unsuccessful.

Traces of very old and inappropriate traditions still persist, and influence contemporary views of the prison. There continues to be a vague suspicion that all imprisonment may still represent arbitrary or unjust imposition of power by the strong members of society against their enemies. Prisons are still suspected of being places of punishment and retribution. This leftover sediment from other ages cripples efforts to make prisons reformative. A healthy society cannot licence destructive and irresponsible behaviour, nor can it indulge in the luxury of returning evil for evil. While rejecting actions which are harmful to its members, it must itself behave in a manner which is responsible towards wrongdoers, and must replace retribution with reformation.

7. THE BENEFITS OF ADVANCED EDUCATION IN PRISONS

T.A.A. Parlett

Looking at society we can see that there seems to be two styles of life; the physical and the intellectual. Livelihood is gained in one of these two manners: either through physical work or through occupations requiring mental dexterity. (This is not to deny that most physical jobs require the worker to use his brain to some extent.) More important, there is also a social split of the same nature. Socially, there are two ways in which situations may be dealt with — physically or by reasoning. This is particularly noticeable in disputes, and in recreation. The physical worker usually resolves his arguments by administering some level of physical force on his antagonist. Our society, however, like most societies, is ruled by intellectuals and resolving issues by physical force is normally illegal.

This is not to suggest that physical people are unintelligent. Many people who we would call physical types show a remarkable level of native intelligence. The core of being an intellectual seems to be the ability to respond verbally to situations rather than physically. This appears to be a result of education or training rather than any native or inborn ability.

The English psychologist Philip Vernon in discussing intelligence and cultural environment has spoken of this as "the effective all round cognitive abilities to comprehend, to grasp relations and reason, which develop through the interaction between the genetic potential and stimulation provided by the environment". His statement seems to be a nice scientific way of saying that this important

Address delivered to the American Correctional Education Association, Indianapolis, Indiana, July, 1975.

part of intelligence is the ability to reason and to see how things go together, and it all comes from what you are born with and the type of family background you grow up with. Vernon further states, "it seems reasonable to regard the Puritan ethic of the middle class worker as producing the greatest development of intelligence". Again, he is simply saying that children of Protestant middle class workers develop intelligence quickly. Vernon also declares, "the greatest promise of quick advance lies in the field of language teaching — i.e. a sophisticated language suitable for abstract and technological thinking, such as English". We may conclude from what he says that if you don't use a propositional language well you cannot be regarded as intelligent.

There appears to be more than what is generally termed "intelligence" involved in being an intellectual. Intellectuality doesn't call for an ability to quickly resolve problems involving spatial relationship, or progressive matrices which are big in intelligence tests, especially the so called culture fair tests. What seems to be important is being clever with words, and being able to speak about music, literature, politics and so on. We might call this a kind of coping skill or survival skill. Even in the jungle, the word-wise witch doctor is more powerful than the warrior.

The contrast between the physical and the intellectual and the penalties attached to poor facility with language can perhaps best be seen in comparing native Canadian Indians with native born Canadian whites. Looking over prison populations we notice that about forty-six percent of the native Indian inmates have been sentenced for crimes of violence. Only sixteen percent of the whites are in prison for crimes of violence. Inability with language it seems leads to acting out of frustration with physical aggression rather than the more subtle means. It is also notable that the more intellectual (verbally skilled) inmates are in prison for more sophisticated crimes, big and little confidence rackets, embezzlement, forgery and so on. Perhaps the most startling demonstration is given by the sexual offender who is usually very poor in verbal skill.

In North America, education and social position are tightly connected. The old school tie is not just a part of the older cultures but is easily visible in newly-developing and recently-developed societies. There are also levels of respect towards thinking and ways of speaking which a culture shows in its schools and universities and this respect coincides with the level of respect given to various occupations. All of this seems to point up the fact that if we want to change the level of criminals towards non-violence we should be training at the levels of higher occupations. We could assume that training the violent offender in the rough trades will not lessen his violence nor will it change his choice of companion.

When we look at our Western Canadian prisons, we notice that the higher level courses (first and second year university) are the only areas in which the inmate is required to do the same amount of work as his counterpart on the street. A full university load in prison calls for as much work from the prisoner student as does a full university load for Joe College living in residence on campus. On the other hand, it is a well known fact that in most areas of the prison, it takes three inmates to do the work of one civilian worker. As an example, one of our institutions with 350 men needs over 40 inmates in the kitchen, and reports being unable to manage with fewer.

Advanced education provides an opportunity for life problems to be presented in an outer-directed manner. It is much easier to present ethical problems at the higher educational levels than the lower, and relatively easier to discuss the moral issues set forth in the Greek tragedy, and in Shakespeare, than it is to discover if there are any moral issues in the material usually prescribed for lower level courses. It will be noticed here that education as we perceive it deals with social and personal ethical problems as they relate to society. This is far removed from the many so called "therapies" which have been popular in prisons and which appear to do no more than feed the self-concern and self-centredness of the individuals.

In previous researches, I and a team of researchers from the University of Victoria, discovered that inmates have what is called high cognitive needs. We called them "gleaners". We called them this because they seemed to have a desperate need to collect all sorts of odd and sometimes useless information. Many of them had a huge mental storehouse of all kinds of odd and unrelated facts which they had gleaned from reading and listening. Our feeling about this is that it is an attempt by the inmate to raise his verbal and social status. He, we thought, was striving for the same goals that we try to put forward. In his case, the striving lacks organization. He does not know what to glean and how to separate the wheat from the chaff.

This gleaning trait was more noticeable in inmates who had served a lot of time. It seemed that it was an attempt not only to change his own personality, but in some way to diminish his anxiety stemming from his feeling of being alone in the world, the so-called existential anxiety. It seemed to us that this type of inmate fills the statement that the biologist Rene Dubos made in *So Human an Animal*.

> Man... does not react passively to physical and social stimuli. Whenever he functions, by choice or by accident, he selects a particular niche, modifies it, develops ways to avoid what he does not want to perceive, and emphasizes that which he wants to experience.

We also found another interesting aspect of the inmates' functioning which is called "cognitive clarity". This is the ability to understand and make meaningful experiences. They appeared to be low in this factor. The psychologist Albert Cohen, speaking of cognitive need and cognitive clarity suggested that people with high cognitive need are easier to change than others provided there is cognitive clarity. It appeared to us that if we could improve clarity we were well on the way to being able to change the attitude of our prisoners.

We have looked very carefully at both of these aspects and they seem to be part of what psychologists call "cognitive style". This whole style phenomenon is concerned with the way subjects see all kinds of experiences. Some people see experience in a rather cluttered way. They can't get what has happened to them all together. For others experience is structured. They understand and see their experiences as linked and reasonable. The cluttered person is known as a "global" type; others are referred to as "analytic". Most of us are in the middle, sometimes we are a bit cluttered, at other times we are analytic. When we are cluttered, we are confused and uncertain of what has happened to us.

A number of tests have been developed to measure how global or how analytic a person is. The usual test is called the rod and frame test, but it requires rather ingenious instruments and takes time to carry out. An easier test is one which can be done on paper with a pencil, called the Hidden Figures Test. This test which only takes half an hour deals with the ability to pick up a geometrical figure from a maze of straight lines. There are 36 figures in the test and the average score that people get is from 12-20 figures identified.

We have carried out a number of studies on prison inmates and found that they attain low scores — six or seven on the Hidden Figures Test, meaning that they are quite global. We also found that being taken through a university program helped raise their scores.

We carried out two sizable experiments in cognitive style involving inmates from minimum, medium, and maximim security institutions. We divided the inmates into two groups on one occasion. Half of them were in low level education courses, and half in university type courses. The ones in the advanced courses increased their scores from an average of 7 to an average of 20. The lower level increased from an average of 7 to an average of 9. A small change from 7 to 9 really means no change at all. A change from 7 to 20 is a significant change. Statistical treatment showed that there was only one chance in a thousand of us being wrong about the others. On another occasion using an extremely tightly controlled experimental situation we got similar results. In some way or another, university seemed to give the inmates the ability to be more coherent in their cognitive abilities.

We knew when we carried out this experiment that most people need more evidence than paper and pencil tests that a programme works. Most people want to know how many committed more crimes when they left. This criterion is usually called the rate of recidivism, and it is quite awkward to obtain figures. As a general rule we would expect that about 30 percent of people released will return within two years. Only 16% of the subjects in the experimental group have returned to prison. Three of our cases are given below.

1) Charlie "C", a Cree Indian with a long history of violent crimes has been out for two years. For the eight years before that, the longest time he was out of prison was two months. He is employed, married and says that he is successful and happy.

2) Mike "W", a heavy user of heroin, 20 caps a day before he was sentenced is in his 20th month of freedom. He isn't using and it is the longest period of time since age 18 that he has been out of jail. He is 32 and reports that for the first time in his life he is able to relate to people.

3) Ron "H", another Indian has worked continually for the last eighteen months. This is longer than he has ever worked in his 28 year life. He says, "I've got it all together now."

It may be remarked that of the three cases, only Mike has a sedentary occupation. None of them are involved in academic pursuits. Thus, the concept of higher level education producing literate "bums", as is occasionally suggested by those who wish to see inmates back in the stone-breaking gang in order to encourage "good work habits", is not substantiated.

In addition to these three, 7 of the subjects have been in a half way house, continuing on with their education for over a year. Six of them were hard core addicts. One was an alcoholic. The six junkies are clean and are good students. The former alcoholic is the only one who looks as if he could run into trouble. Six out of six junkies over a year is a much better rate than most programmes can show.

We were also interested in the moral development of these men. Recent research suggests that moral development is by stages which go with age and intellectual development. Stages cannot be missed and once a person has reached one stage he doesn't go back to a lower stage. Much of the work in the area of moral development has been carried out by Lawrence Kohlberg, the Harvard psychologist. We theorized that because of trouble with the law at an early age, and interference with intellectual growth, most prisoners would be morally retarded. We tested eighty-two prisoners to find out the level of moral development and found that they were at an early stage 3, a stage which is usually attained by age 13 and 14.

In our studies we took a group of twenty-nine inmates through advanced level courses and compared them to forty soldiers, sailors and airmen, and to 30 teachers in a philosophy course. The educated inmates attained the same moral level as the teachers (which was stage 5, a high level of principled moral development.) As in the test for cognitive style, the statistical chance of our being wrong was 1 chance in a thousand.

There are strong indications that education at an advanced level changes subjects to a more analytic mode of perception, and in addition accelerates moral development. On these two bases alone, disregarding the aspect of recidivism, it may be speculated that the rewards of advanced level education may be in terms of more thoughtful and more moral prisoners. There are also clear indications that criminality may be caused to diminish.

8. THE HUMANITIES IN PRISON: A CASE STUDY

Morgan Lewis

Since this is a paper on the correction of crime, I think it is appropriate that I begin with a confession: I confess that the study that is the topic of this paper was begun with more hope than realism. Those of us who conducted this project thought that exposing a group of young offenders to the humanities would lead to value changes that would be reflected in post-release behavior. I no longer think the humanities in a prison setting are capable of producing those kinds of changes.

The project was based on a belief, or hope, that young men who find themselves in prison would be open to examining the dominant values of their lives. It seemed likely that these values had never before been explicitly considered yet their values had led to actions which resulted in these young people being in prison. The humanities, we thought, offered an ideal vehicle to assist in an examination of their lives. We tried to find material of interest to the participants in our study that would lead them to think about where they were, why they are there, and where they were going.

The realism of this thinking was somewhat wanting, but I do not think this was the main flaw in the project. The psychological testing which we conducted indicated the project caused some changes in our participants. These changes were of the kind the project tried to produce. The critical flaw in our design was a failure to appreciate

Paper presented to the World Congress in Education: Values and the School; Symposium on Prison Education, Université du Québec à Trois-Rivières, July, 1981. It is based on the report, Prison Education and Rehabilitation: Illusion or Reality? *published by the Institute for Research on Human Resources, the Pennsylvania State University.*

the influence the prison environment would have on the project and the influence their post-release environments would have on the behavior of the participants. These environments overwhelmed the effects produced by exposure to the humanities. In this paper I expand upon these points in greater detail. First, I describe the general design of the project and the influence the prison setting had upon the conduct of the experimental phase. I then present the results found during the experimental and follow-up phases. In the third section I speculate on what can reasonably be expected of prison-based educational efforts.

Conducting the Humanities Program

The Participants

The humanities project was conducted as part of the regular educational program at the State Correctional Institution at Camp Hill, Pennsylvania. At the time of the project, Camp Hill incarcerated minor (under twenty-one years of age) males convicted of the types of crimes usually committed by adults. Its typical inmates were eighteen years old, and had committed major crimes, such as rape or murder, or had a long series of less serious offenses. Most were not simple delinquents or incorrigibles. They had been committed to Camp Hill either because of the seriousness of their offense or because they could not adjust to other institutions or community placements.

When the study was conducted, Camp Hill had the most extensive education and training program in the state correctional system. The program extended from basic literacy through college courses. Inmates who were over sixteen but had not completed high school were assigned to a program designed to prepare them for the General Equivalency Diploma (GED) test. Passing this test demonstrates an education level equivalent to an average high school graduate. Inmates in this GED program were used as the source of participants for the humanities program.

The study was conducted as a true experiment which means the participants who received the experimental treatment, the humanities program, were randomly selected. A matching procedure was used to construct groups of subjects of similar age, race, and IQ. Within each group the most similar subjects were paired and one of each pair was randomly assigned to the humanities program and the other to the GED control group. To provide another comparison group, inmates in the Camp Hill vocational training program were classified into the same categories used with the GED students and those with the best match to the experimental and control group inmates were selected to be included in the evaluative phase of the study. A total of fifty-nine participants were originally assigned to each group.

The Program

The humanities classes were conducted as part of the regular school program at Camp Hill during the 1968-1969 academic year. The participants attended class three times a week for a total of five hours. The humanities were broadly defined as materials that had the potential to help the participants develop a sense of personal identity which provided a sense of meaning in life and a set of values consistent with life in society. The original planning led to a thematic structure which began with a consideration of walls — both literal and metaphoric — including both their negative functions (in limiting freedom) and positive ones (giving meaningful shape to different kinds of experiences). The second topic was to be the isolated individual and topics three through six were to deal with the individual as related to the family, the group, the institution, and his total environment. The final topic was to be the self-actualizing individual. Each of these topics was to be approached through films, short stories, and visual arts in a manner intended to evoke discussion of the underlying issues.

This plan and its basic assumption — that the material presented would lead the participants to evaluate their own attitudes and values — proved to be flawed. The first feature film that was shown, *On The Waterfront*, is a good example of the planned format and its weakness. The protagonist of the film, played by Marlon Brando, is a young man who comes to question the values that have influenced the crucial decisions in his life. These values are reflected by the corrupt union which dominates the lives of the men who work on the docks. He eventually rejects these values and at great personal risk leads a revolt against the union.

This film was well received by the participants, but it did not produce the type of discussion anticipated. The attempts of the teachers to stimulate discussion of the film were met with brief one or two word responses. The students could not or would not discuss what the film meant to them, personally, or even what it was about.

This first experience was repeated several times in the first month of the project as the teachers attempted to work within the planned structure. Gradually they came to realize that the original design was not appropriate to these participants and that other ways would have to be tried. These "other ways," however, generated their own problems.

Throughout the planning, orientation, and first month of the project, the teachers had been encouraged to identify and respond to the interests of the students. As some degree of trust began to develop between the teachers and the humanities students, it was soon apparent that the major interest of the black students concerned their race: their place in contemporary society, the contributions blacks have made to society and specifically to America, proposals for an independent black state in the United States and similar topics.

Many of the whites, in turn were protofascists and wanted books dealing with the Ku Klux Klan and Nazi Germany. The teachers attempted to respond to these interests by designing one course on minority history and a second on political forces that could treat these topics within a broad social context.

The proposed syllabi for these courses revealed little of an inflammatory nature. In the climate then prevailing at Camp Hill, however, the prison staff was very reluctant to allow these courses to be presented.

Four months before the humanities program began there had been a full-fledged racial battle on the athletic field, with the blacks and whites attacking each other with baseball bats. A few weeks after the program had started, several blacks had assaulted three guards, nearly killing one. The two courses were proposed to prison officials during the very week that the trial of the inmates charged with attacking the guards was held. The Camp Hill authorities were concerned that the white inmates might view the minorities history course as a concession to the blacks and that this would cause the whites to organize for their own protection. The prison officials believed that the white inmates looked to the custodial staff, which was predominantly white, to control the blacks. If the staff was seen as conceding to the blacks, the officials were afraid they would have an even more polarized situation. The prison officials were also concerned, since the choice of the courses would be voluntary, that only blacks would choose minority history and only whites political forces. Without a racial mixture in the classes, discussion may have only reinforced existing attitudes and prejudices.

In addition to these specific objections, the prison administration had a general rationale for the avoidance of sensitive topics. Their position was that the humanities classes were unlike any other prison activity. In these classes the students were encouraged to be frank about their feelings and opinions, and the teachers specifically tried to bring about discussion and debate among the inmates. The prison staff was concerned, first, whether the humanities teachers were capable of controlling the situation if a really intense argument developed. Even if it were granted that the teachers could do so, the administration's second and more important concern was that after a session in the freedom of the humanities classes, the inmates had to return to the much more restrictive environment of the rest of the prison. If the inmates were not able to manage the transition, a chance remark from a guard or another inmate might cause the constantly present staff-inmate or racial hostilities to burst forth.

Since it was not possible to convince the administration, it was necessary to adopt another approach. The approach chosen was to emphasize process rather than content. An improvisation drama and a film-making course were developed. The basic interest of the inmates found expression in these courses. The drama course, which began with both blacks and whites, gradually became all black and a play concerning life in the ghetto evolved. Likewise in the film class, the students frequently filmed mock fights between blacks and whites.

For students not interested in these courses, a course in the modern novel was offered, and the prison officials approved some books by black authors which had previously been banned.

These courses constituted the most productive period of the program, and the inmates demonstrated their acceptance in a conclusive manner. From September through mid-April, attendance in the humanities classes had been mandatory as part of the regular evening school at Camp Hill. As the end of the spring semester classes approached, the project staff believed they were making real progress and asked the prison officials to allow the program to continue for an additional six weeks on a voluntary basis. There was skepticism among the regular prison staff that any of the humanities students would be willing to attend classes after the end of the regular school year. To do so meant giving up highly valued alternatives such as "yard time" when the inmates were allowed the freedom of the athletic field, television viewing, and card playing. Of the forty-one students who were then enrolled in the program, twenty-five attended the additional six hours a week for the six-week extension.

Evaluating the Program

Experimental Phase

Acceptance of the Program. The number who chose to attend the additional six weeks of classes was the most objective evidence of the acceptance of the humanities program by it students. Other evidence of a questionnaire type was also collected. Brief anonymous questionnaires were administered to the participants twice during the experimental phase, midway through the program and on the last night of compulsory classes. Table 1 presents the results from these questionnaires.

The questionnaire results were verified by the responses obtained from personal interviews conducted after the program ended. Interviewers who had no previous contact with the project were used, and both experimental and control subjects participated. The interview data were used to compare the reactions of the humanities students to the humanities program, the prison educational program and the education program of the high school they attended before entering prison. The students were not asked to make direct comparisons of these programs; instead, the same questions were asked about each program at different times in the interview. When the responses were compared statistically, thirteen of the fourteen comparisons were significant. The students responded most favorably towards the humanities program and most negatively towards the prison school in every case. Table 2 presents the coded responses to four representative questions from the interviews.

Changes in the Subjects. Acceptance of the program and its teachers was necessary if the humanities program were to bring about change in its students. This, of course, is not evidence that the program produced any changes. To assess these changes a number of psychological measures were administered before and after the program. Table 3 presents several of the main scales from these measures.

More significant changes were found among the humanities students than among the comparison groups, but overall there were fewer changes than non-changes. The changes that did occur were not all in a "positive" direction, but the humanities program was not

TABLE 1
RATING OF THE HUMANITIES PROGRAM
(percentage figures)

	December 1968 (N = 44)	April 1969 (N = 39)
	%	%
1. Did you like the program?		
I liked it very much.	43	40
I liked it a lot.	18	38
I liked it a little.	34	20
I didn't like it at all.	5	2
2. Was the program interesting?		
It was always interesting.	23	15
It was interesting most of the time.	55	72
It was boring most of the time.	21	13
It was always boring.	2	0
3. Did you learn anything?		
I learned a great deal.	5	18
I learned a lot.	39	44
I learned a little.	48	36
I didn't learn anything.	7	2
4. Do you think you learned anything which might help you get along better in the Institution?		
I learned a great deal.	16	5
I learned a lot.	11	26
I learned a little.	55	41
I didn't learn anything at all.	18	26
5. Do you think you learned anything which will help you get along better after you leave the Institution?		
I learned a great deal.	27	23
I learned a lot.	14	28
I learned a little.	45	31
I didn't learn anything at all.	14	15
6. How was this humanities course, compared to other courses you have taken at the Institution?		
It was much better.	84	92
It was a little better.	11	2
It was about the same.	2	2

It was a little worse.	2	2
It was much worse.	0	0

7. How was the humanities course, compared to other courses you have taken in high school?

It was much better.	64	67
It was a little better.	16	26
It was about the same.	16	5
It was a little worse.	2	0
It was much worse.	2	2

8. Has taking the course changed your mind about anything?

I have changed my mind on very many things.	16	10
I have changed my mind on many things.	25	28
I have changed my mind on a few things.	32	36
I haven't changed my mind at all.	25	26

designed to indoctrinate "good" values. Its intention was to expose its students to a wider perspective and to lead them to think about questions and issues they had never considered previously. Such exposure may not necessarily lead to more socially acceptable attitudes.

On the Rosenzweig Picture-Frustration test, for example, the humanities students became more extra-punitive (directing aggression toward the environment) rather than un-punitive (directing agression inward), more ego-defensive, at the expense of need-persistence, and less socially conforming in their response to frustration. Similarly on the Jesness Inventory the humanities students changed in the direction of greater alienation and repression, but exhibited less withdrawal, social anxiety, and denial of unpleasant realities.

The changes found in the scales of the Jesness Inventory present a pattern much in agreement with the objectives of the humanities program. The decrease in the withdrawal and denial scores suggest that at the end of the program the humanities students had a more realistic perception of themselves and their environment. The withdrawal scale reflects "... a tendency to resolve a lack of satisfaction with self and others by passive escape or isolation." The individual who scores high perceives himself as depressed, dissatisfied with

TABLE 2
ATTITUDES OF HUMANITIES STUDENTS
TOWARD THREE EDUCATIONAL EXPERIENCES
(in percent)

Question and Coded Response	Attitude Toward		
	Humanities Program	Prison School	Regular High School
	%	%	%
Do you think that you learned anything in this program?			
Yes	88	37	86
No	12	63	14
(Base number)	(33)	(30)	(29)
Chi square	24.81, p.		.001, df = 2
Did you like the things you studied in this program?			
Disliked	3	46	18
Neutral	9	21	29
Liked	88	32	53
(Base number)	(34)	(28)	(34)
Chi square	26.39, p.		.001, df = 4
Was there anything you especially liked about this program?			
Something mentioned	84	26	50
Nothing	16	74	50
(Base number)	(32)	(31)	(30)
Chi square	21.98, p.		.001, df = 2
Did you feel that any of the teachers cared about you, or were they just doing a job?			
Most really cared about me	93	8	54
Most were just doing a job	7	92	46
(Base number)	(27)	(25)	(26)
Chi square	37.28, p.		.001, df = 2

himself, sad, misunderstood; although preferring to be alone, he feels lonesome (Jesness, 1966: 14). The drop in scores for this scale indicates that the humanities program tended to decrease these feelings.

The items in the denial scale of the Jesness Inventory tap three areas: "About half of the items concern the individual's perception of his family, the high scorers seeing their parents without fault and admitting to no conflict with them; another group of items suggests denial of personal inadequacies or unhappiness; and a final group indicates unwillingness to criticize others" (Jesness, 1966: 15). The decrease in scores on this scale among the humanities students indicates that after the program they were more likely to admit to inadequacies, conflict, and personal unhappiness. Furthermore, given that the environment of a prison is not very pleasant, increased distrust and estrangement from others, especially authority figures, as indicated by the increase in the alienation score, seems a most natural result of increased awareness. Similarly, the increase in the repression scores can be interpreted as a heightened need to avoid a reality of which the humanities students have become more painfully aware.

The results of the Rosenzweigh Picture-Frustration Study support this interpretation. The humanities students became more extra-punitive and less un-punitive that is, more likely to turn the anger caused by frustration towards their environment and less likely to ignore or gloss over the frustration. The increase in extra-punitiveness was associated with an increased tendency to defend the ego from information that may be threatening. This increase in ego defensiveness is similar to the increase in the repression scale of the Jesness Inventory. Although these changes do not indicate positive personal growth, they do reflect an understandable reaction to the realities of prison life.

It should be noted, however, that all the data do not support these interpretations. The comparable ACL and MMPI scales did not relfect changes similar to the Jesness and Rosenzweig scales discussed above. Ad hoc analyses are, of course, very likely to lead to spurious conclusions. Nevertheless, the difficulties of assessing a project such as the humanities program suggest that the courage to draw plausible, but not definitive, conclusions may be more necessary than the safer course of displaying proper scientific caution. The pattern of changes which was found is so directly related to the types of changes the humanities program tried to bring about, and appears to be such an understandable reaction to the prison environment, that it seems overly cautious to dismiss the changes because all

TABLE 3
MEAN PRETEST AND POSTTEST SCORES BY GROUPS

Measure	Humanities			GED			Vocational		
	N	Pretest Mean	Posttest Mean	N	Pretest Mean	Posttest Mean	N	Pretest Mean	Posttest Mean
Rosenzweig P-F Study									
Extrapunitive	31	56.0	67.8**	8	56.6	65.6	18	51.7	56.6
Intrapunitive	31	21.3	16.9	8	22.6	17.1	18	22.2	20.7
Impunitive	31	22.7	15.4**	8	20.8	17.3	18	21.1	17.2
Obstacle dominance	31	16.0	17.2	8	16.1	15.4	18	12.6	13.5
Ego defense	31	61.8	70.0**	8	63.8	65.1	18	57.9	61.7
Need persistence	31	22.1	14.6**	8	20.2	19.6	18	24.5	19.3
Group conformity rating	31	59.2	49.2**	8	51.0	51.6	18	52.9	45.0*
Minnesota Multiphasic Personality Inventory (MMPI)									
Psychopathic deviation (Pd)	33	25.2	25.3	34	23.9	24.4	21	23.7	24.9
Social alienation (Pd_{4a})	33	7.9	7.7	34	7.6	8.2	21	8.0	8.1
Self-alienation (Pd_{4b})	33	8.0	7.6	34	8.4	7.5	21	7.8	7.5
Parole Violation (PaV)	33	13.4	13.4	34	13.9	13.4	21	13.8	13.8
Correction scale (K^1)	33	12.1	12.1	34	10.1	12.0*	21	11.8	12.7
Lie scale (L)	33	3.5	3.6	34	3.4	4.1	21	3.6	3.9
Jesness Inventory									
Social maladjustment	33	69.7	69.8	33	73.3	72.8	21	70.2	69.0

Value orientation	33	59.5	62.2	33	62.1	62.8	21	58.9	57.8
Immaturity	33	56.2	58.6	33	60.4	64.1	21	54.4	59.9
Autism	33	61.0	64.6	33	62.5	66.8	21	60.4	63.5
Alienation	33	59.5	63.7*	33	61.4	65.5	21	59.0	61.4
Manifest aggression	33	57.5	59.0	33	61.3	58.5	21	55.9	55.0
Withdrawal	33	55.6	50.3*	33	57.2	53.5	21	53.6	50.3
Social anxiety	33	47.2	42.3*	33	46.4	44.8	21	48.0	43.4*
Repression	33	50.8	55.2*	33	55.7	57.5	21	54.9	58.9
Denial	33	51.4	44.5*	33	44.7	44.4	21	49.1	50.1
Asocial index	33	68.8	68.3	33	71.9	72.6	21	71.6	68.6
Rotter's Internal-External Scale	31	70.3	9.4	7	11.0	12.0	20	10.3	9.3
Attitudes Toward Law	34	88.4	76.8**	34	89.2	77.5**	20	88.8	84.1
Adjective Check List (ACL)[a]									
Endurance	33	49.4	50.0	33	47.8	50.3*	19	49.2	47.5
Order	33	44.4	47.3*	33	44.5	47.4*	19	47.5	47.2
Nurturance	33	48.8	46.1*	33	45.2	46.2	19	45.1	43.0
Succorance	33	51.5	47.9*	33	53.1	46.6**	19	51.3	48.4
Unfavorability toward self	33	49.7	49.1	33	54.3	49.7*	19	51.1	53.7
Liability	33	49.0	47.0	33	51.2	47.3*	19	46.9	46.0
Standford Advanced Paragraph Meaning	22	7.5	8.9**	20	7.3	8.3			

* Pre to post change is statistically significant, probability less than .05
** Pre to post change is statistically significant, probability less than .01
a Seventeen scales without significant differences not reported

of the measures did not show a similar pattern. The changes that did occur indicate that the humanities students became more aware of themselves and the conditions in their lives, although this did not necessarily make them happier or more adjusted to these conditions.

Follow-up Phase

To determine the post-prison effects of the humanities program, its students, plus the inmates in the two comparison groups, were followed up at yearly intervals for almost three years. Each year they were interviewed about their work and vocational experiences and were asked to complete a confidential questionnaire containing measures of values, attitudes, and self-concepts. This section presents these results organized into recidivism, employment, and attitudes-values.

Recidivism. The major point of interest in any follow-up study of former prisoners is how many of them are able to lead a non-criminal life following their release from prison. Table 4 presents data on the subjects in the present study. These figures indicate that during the total follow-up period about half of the subjects were performing some role in regular society, including military service; 30 percent were fugitives or in prison; a few subjects were deceased; and data were not available on the remainder. The figures presented in this table are based on any available information concerning the subjects, but the primary source of information was personal interviews with the subjects themselves. Other sources were interviews with members of the family, reports from parole agents, reports of special commercial investigators who attempted to locate the hard-to-find, and reports from wardens of correctional institutions.

To test whether the percentage of subjects in prison or fugitive at the time of the interviews differed significantly among the three groups, chi square tests were run separately for each year. None of the analyses were significant. There was no evidence that particular educational experiences were related to the likelihood that subjects would or would not be in prison or fugitives from the law.

The percentages of fugitives or subjects in prison should not be considered as recidivism rates. The figures reflect the status of the subjects at the time of the follow-up interviews rather than the proportion convicted of crimes each year. The continuation of inmates in prison from one year to the next makes these figures higher than the recidivism rates.

In the present study, recidivism was measured by reports from

TABLE 4. CLASSIFICATION OF SUBJECTS AT EACH FOLLOW-UP INTERVIEW BY PROGRAM

	Humanities (N = 58)			GED (N = 58)			Vocational (N = 57)		
	% 1970	% 1971	% 1972	% 1970	% 1971	% 1972	% 1970	% 1971	% 1972
In society	54	52	51	51	38	36	69	61	58
Employed	33	28	28	28	22	21	39	40	37
Unemployed	16	12	14	21	16	12	28	17	14
Military service	5	2	9	2	—	3	2	4	7
In prison	31	41	33	21	33	31	14	21	23
Fugitive	2	3	2	2	—	2	3	4	—
	33	44	35	23	33	33	17	25	23
Deceased	3	3	5	2	3	3	—	—	—
No data	10	10	10	26	26	28	14	14	19
Total[a]	100	99	101	102	100	100	100	100	100

[a] Totals differ from 100% due to rounding

parole agents, rather than self-report, to avoid the possibility of distortion. The parole agent was instructed to record the most serious post-release criminal offense committed by the releasee. If the agent responded that the subject had no further record, a non-felony arrest with no conviction, or a misdemeanor conviction, the subject was judged to be a non-recidivist for that period. If the agent replied that the release was reported to be a parole or court release violator or to have a felony conviction with a sentence or probation, the subject was judged to be a recidivist for that period.

This classification system was admittedly arbitrary, and there were some problems associated with its use. Only subjects who were actually interviewed by parole agents were covered. Reports from family or friends or interviews conducted by the commercial investigators could not be included under this definition. It is also quite likely that some of the subjects who were not located for follow-up interviews were recidivists. Percentages of those subjects reported to be recidivists by the parole agents are shown for each year by group in Table 5. There were no significant differences in recidivism among the three groups.

TABLE 5. RECIDIVISM[a] REPORTED BY PAROLE AGENTS, BY GROUPS BY YEARS

		Humanities	GED	Vocational
1970	Percent	23	20	20
	Base Number	31	29	29
1971	Percent	13	20	21
	Base Number	23	20	24
1972	Percent	18	25	17
	Base Number	22	16	23

[a]Recidivism was defined as a parole or court violation or a felony conviction with sentence or probation

TABLE 6. LABOR FORCE PARTICIPATION AND UNEMPLOYMENT RATES AMONG RESPONDENTS AT TIME OF FOLLOW-UP INTERVIEWS

	Humanities			GED			Vocational		
	1970	1971	1972	1970	1971	1972	1970	1971	1972
Labor force participation (percent)	56	46	49	67	54	47	78	67	63
Base number[a]	50	50	49	42	41	40	49	49	46
Unemployment (percent)	32	30	33	43	41	37	42	30	27
Base number[b]	28	23	24	28	22	19	38	33	30

[a]Includes all respondents for whom data were available except those who were deceased.

[b]Includes only respondents in regular society from whom data were available. Respondents in military service, in prison, or fugitives were excluded.

Employment Experiences. The employment of released offenders is second only to recidivism as a measure of post-prison adjustment. Table 6 presents labor force participation and unemployment at each of the follow-ups.

The labor force participation rate is depressed, of course, by the proportion of incarcerated subjects. Their lack of labor force participation is not voluntary, but their absence still depresses the statistics. Among the subjects who were in regular society, the unemployment rates were quite high. For each group of subjects in each follow-up, about one-third or more of the subjects were unemployed at the time they were interviewed.

A number of indices were developed to compare employment experiences over the total follow-up period. These indices also failed to reveal significant differences among the groups. The former inmates were employed about two-thirds of the time they were available for employment, typically in low-level jobs for which prior skills were unnecessary. They reported they often left these jobs on their own initiative because of dissatisfaction with the jobs or working conditions or because of personal reasons not related to the jobs.

Attitudes and Values. The results for attitudes and values are in some ways even more disappointing than those found for recidivism

TABLE 7
ITEM MEANS FOR HUMANITIES-RELATED ACTIVITIES
SCALE BY GROUP
1970 FOLLOW-UP

Item	Humanities (N = 41)	GED (N = 36)	Vocational (N = 31)
Go to museum	1.20	1.22	1.29
See a live play	1.18	1.06	1.16
Hear a concert	1.20	1.17	1.18
Read a book	2.66	2.81	2.68
Do art work	1.55	1.42	1.63
Write poetry or an essay	1.48	1.34	1.47
Check a book out of a library	1.59	1.29	1.84

Note: Means calculated with "not at all" = 1, "once" = 2, "several times" = 3, "often" = 4.

and employment. Attitudes and values are variables that were susceptible to the influence of the humanities program. The evaluation of the experimental phase showed that some changes had been produced in the students. These changes, however, were not reflected in the follow-up data.

No differences were found among the groups even in the scale that was designed to measure the extent to which they engaged in the activities emphasized in the humanities program. The scale included the seven activities listed in Table 7. The respondents were asked to rate how often they had engaged in these activities in the year prior to the interview. Item means were calculated for each group, and the separate items were summed to yield a total score for each respondent.

All but one of the item means were below 2.0 indicating that the most frequent ratings were "not at all" or "once." The total respondent scores ranged from 10.22 to 12.17. Given the typical background and environment of most former inmates, perhaps higher scores should not have been expected. Unfortunately there was no evidence that the rather extensive exposure to the humanities resulted in any increased interest in such materials following release from prison.

A number of other standardized scales were administered to measure conceptions of best and worst "ways of life" and best and worst "ways to make a living" (Goodwin, 1969), social responsibility (Berkowitz and Lutterman, 1968), self-esteem (Rosenberg, 1965), personal competency (Campbell et al., 1960), personal control (Gurin et al. 1969), racial equality (Woodmansee, 1966), and psychological well being (Bradburn and Caplovitz, 1965).

All of these scales had significant test-retest reliability over the three follow-up periods, and inter-correlated in patterns that suggest the respondents answered them in a consistent manner. That is, respondents whose answers indicated general satisfaction with their lives also tended to have higher self-esteem and a sense of personal competence and were likely to reject illegal activities and government support. Individuals dissatisfied with their lives showed the reverse pattern. None of the differences in these scores, however, were related to participation in the humanities program or any of the other prison educational programs.

The one suggestion of possible follow-up effect from the humanities program came in response to a question on the usefulness of the education or training received at Camp Hill following release. The proportion of the humanities students who referred to that program as directly useful to them was only 4 percent. These students, however, were slightly more likely to report ways in which their time at Camp Hill improved them personally. Their comments usually referred to an improved outlook on life, to an increased ability to face reality, to better habits, and so on. Some of the answers that were volunteered by the respondents from the humanities group follow:

> "Taught me respect for my fellow man."
> "It has taught me to understand people and have patience."
> "How to avoid trouble and do better work."
> "To face reality and make it in life, whatever I decide to be."
> "I see things more clearly and am able to get along with people and can share their interests."

It is interesting to speculate whether any of these benefits were at least partly the result of experiences in the humanities program. This interpretation is not consistently supported by the data, for the proportion of humanities subjects who cited such personal improvement declined in the subsequent follow-ups. The first year following release from prison, however, was the time at which the program's effects would be most likely to be detected. Even though the overall distribution of answers does not differ significantly among the groups, if the proportion reporting personal improvement, increased interpersonal skills, and specific reference to the humanities program are combined, the total for the humanities subjects, 30 percent, is significantly higher than the total of these responses in either of the other two groups. This type of analysis is quite suspect, of course, for the investigator greatly increases his chances of selecting comparisons that will yield significant differences. Nevertheless, the results to this question are at least suggestive that the humanities program may have had some post-release carry-over among some of its students.

What Can Prison Education Do?

The five years that it took to plan, conduct, and report this study, June 1968 through May 1973, span a critical period in correctional thought. Two years before the study began Karl Menninger (1966) published *The Crime of Punishment*, which will probably be regarded as the last, eloquent statement of the rehabilitation approach. Two years after the final report of this study was published, Lipton, Martinson, and Wilks (1975) published *The Effectiveness of Correctional Treatment*, which will probaby be regarded as the death knell for rehabilitation. It was a knell that needed to be sounded.

It is my judgment, and I think it is shared by many who have examined correctional programs, that rehabilitation in a prison setting is an impossible task. Society has asked correctional officials to carry out a function in an institution that is antithethical to that function. The usual argument can be made that if adequate funding were provided, more effective treatment would be possible. I am very skeptical of that argument. As long as a prison is a prison, as long as its primary function is to confine convicted offenders, the type of personal development implied in rehabilitation is, in my judgment, impossible.

In saying this I am not implying either that prisons or education programs should be abolished. Much can be done to make prisons less detrimental and more humane, but incarceration will still be necessary for some offenders. Efforts must also continue to make the time spent while incarcerated as beneficial to inmates as they want the time to be. This means the provision of medical, educational, vocational, and even psychological services *if the inmates want them.* It does not mean the imposing of a treatment model under which inmates must demonstrate they have "rehabilitated" themselves to secure release, or as Chief Justice Warren Burger put it in a recent address "to learn their way out."

Such recommendations persist despite the lack of firm evidence that any type of prison treatment influences behavior after release (Hawkins, 1976). They persist because few people are satisfied to just "lock them up". Society wants offenders to be punished, but it also wants the punishment to make them better persons, persons who are less likely to engage in new crimes.

Most prison officials whom I have talked with recognize that the best they can do is provide opportunities. Some inmates will take advantage of these opportunities and others will not. Some of the experiences inmates have may help them once they are released, but in most cases the environments to which they return will overwhelm the effects of the prison's treatments.

Prison officials, however, do not control these environments. They can only affect what happens to inmates while they are assigned to their institutions. In light of these constraints, how should prison officials spend the money which they have for educational programs ? Which programs are likely to have the most post-release payoff?

In answering these questions I am relying more upon judgment than scientific findings. My answers are based on the belief, based on some evidence, that other things being equal, it is better to have a high school diploma than not to have a diploma and that it is better to have an occupational skill than not to have a skill. My priorities are based on the belief that there is likely to be more payoff from improving the literacy and occupational skills of individuals who already have some ability than from devoting resources to those who have the most severe educational problems. Accordingly, I would set the following priorities for educational programs in prison:

1. Programs to prepare inmates to obtain a high school diploma or its equivalent.
2. Programs to teach occupational skills.
3. Programs of adult basic education.
4. Other programs (avocational, values programs, college courses).

Further I would try not to set up complete occupational training programs in the prison itself. Where possible, I would attempt to use facilities in nearby public or private schools. The training is likely to be better and the costs of transporting and guarding students in these settings are likely to be less than the costs of equipping and operating training programs within the prison.

Some may be surprised to see programs such as the one I and my colleagues conducted so low on the list. My experience with that program led to this ranking and to my general skepticism about rehabilitation in prison. Prisons do quite well what society primarily wants them to do — confine inmates. Rehabilitation is not something that can be coerced; thus it is more appropriately left to other societal institutions.

REFERENCES

BERKOWITZ, L., and K. LUTTERMAN
1968: The traditionally socially responsible personality, *Public Opinion Quaterly*, 32: 169-185.

BRADBURN, N., and D. CAPLOVITZ
1965: *Report on happiness*, Chicago, Aldine.

CAMPBELL, A., CONVERSE, P.E., MILLER, W.E., and D.E. STOKES
1960: *The American Voter*, New York, Wiley.

GOODWIN, L.
1969: Work Orientations of the unemployed poor: Report of a pilot study, *Journal of Human Resources*, 4: 509-519.

GURIN, P., GURIN, G., LAO, R.C., and M. BEATTLE
1969: Multidimensional I-E Scale. In J.P. Robinson and P.R. Shaer, *Measures of social psychological attitudes*, Ann Harbor, Michigan, Survey Research Center.

HAWKINS, G.
1976: *The prison: Policy and practice*, Chicago, University of Chicago Press.

JESNESS, C.F.
1966: *Manual for the Jesness Inventory*, Palo Alto, Ca., Consulting Psychologist Press.

LIPTON, D., MARTINSON, R., and J. WILKS
1975: *The Effectiveness of Correctional Treatment: A Survey of Treatment Evaluation Studies*, New York, Praeger.

MENNINGER, K.
1966: *The crime of punishment*, New York, The Viking Press.

ROSENBERG, M.
1965: *Society and the adolescent self-image*, Princeton, N.J., Princeton University Press.

WOODMANSEE, J.J.
1966: Scoring instructions for the Reactions Questionnaire, Form C-2, University of Colorado. Mimeograph.

9. PRISON EDUCATION AND CRIMINAL CHOICE: THE CONTEXT OF DECISION-MAKING

Stephen Duguid

Few would deny the essential truthfulness of Emile Durkheim's profound conclusion that "...crime is normal because a society exempt from it is utterly impossible" (Taylor, 1973: 79). Violation of rules, laws, and customs is an essential part of man's life in societies and neither primitive communities nor anarchist attempts to exorcize crime through the elimination of private property will change that condition. From an Olympian perspective, this perception is quite comforting, calming our fears and obviating our sometimes irrepressible desire to create Utopia. From an 'on the job' perspective in the criminal justice system, however, this perception offers no paradigm for daily activity.

Working in a prison with apprehended offenders forces one to move beyond or avoid these Olympian rationales because one is confronted each day with individuals caught up in this social truth; individuals denied basic human freedoms, basic needs, and subjected to a variety of indignities, deprivations, and punishments which are offensive to any concerned observer. (The author is a teacher / administrator in a university program at a medium security Canadian prison). Given that the existence of crime and therefore criminals is not only inevitable, but necessary, what should be done with the individuals caught up in this system? They are, in most cases, intelligent, interesting, and vital human beings, full of aspirations, dreams and frustrations like their non-criminal peers—

This paper appeared in the Canadian Journal of Criminology, *23:4, 1981.*

many are in fact quite likeable to an outsider not irretrievably prejudiced by detailed accounts of their past activities. The social worker impulse in so many of us surfaces in this situation and the determination is made to do something, to save them, transform them or in some more modest way reverse the trend in their personal biographies which leads them repeatedly to incarceration. Beyond these liberal ideals, there is another powerful motivating factor: criminal activity tends to escalate in seriousness with successive offences. Thus, failing to act may create a more dangerous individual.

The record of such reformational attempts has not been marked with great success. While many individuals do manage to avoid further criminal activity after periods in prison (or at least avoid being caught), there is little convincing evidence that this accomplishment results from reformational or rehabilitative efforts on the part of society or its institutions. Most of these men return to crime and prison despite such attempts and despite the grim reality of imprisonment itself. This has prompted some to despair of all such efforts, claiming that 'nothing works'. Moreover, Durkheim's inevitable "laissez-faire" conclusion becomes operational, though in the tradition of Liberal ideology, it has a compassionate side. Thus Governor Brown of California calls for a rehabilitation of jails instead of people:

> ...human nature has some basic fundamental weaknesses that are always going to be there no matter what we do... I don't find much use or comfort for those great analytical studies of why crime is caused or how we can mold peoples' minds by various forms of treatment and government intervention. I think that they have very modest potential (1979).

Realism, or the ultimate cry of Liberal despair?

The cynicism, suspicion and despair so prevalent in contemporary judgments on rehabilitation and reformation of criminals is the inevitable result of the plethora of false prophets, town criers and travelling salesmen who have inundated this field so rich in government grants and social concern. Promoters of the work ethic, religious zealots, stern disciplinarians, transactional analysts, behaviour modifiers, Rogerians, Freudians and so forth have all played their cards and largely failed. Effects have been observed and measured but they have tended to be short term and non-universal. It is right, therefore, that further efforts in this field should be met with cynicism and suspicion, if not despair.

In proposing a further effort, I start from a simple assumption which lies at the base of the thought of Karl Marx, among others: "History is nothing but the activity of men in pursuit of their ends." More specifically: "Men make their own history, but they do not make it just as they please; they do not make it under circumstances chosen by themselves, but under circumstances directly encountered, given and transmitted from the past" (McLellan, 1971: 125). This image of people making decisions within a predetermined context of economic, social and political factors fits not only men in the 'macro' sense, but also the biographies of each of us as we act in daily life. Those who engage in criminal activity choose to do so; they are decision-makers. Not a new idea, of course. The Classicists argued the essential rationality of the criminal more than a century ago. What is new, however, is the tempering of this version of rational free will with the context within which that free will is exercised.

This paper is about education, specifically about how education can be utilized in the criminal justice system to persuade or enable the criminal to make different decisions in the future, decisions which will not lead to further criminal activity. The first step in making this argument is to demonstrate the validity of the decision-maker approach, i.e., the essential rationality of the object of our concern. The next step is more subtle and more difficult. Marx placed a crucial caveat on this rational man—the conditions in which he acts. Education cannot directly change such conditions as poverty, race, or class. I will argue, however, that there is a further condition or context which lies at the base of this decision-making, that being the range or repertoire of analytical thinking skills and moral paradigms available to the individual decision-maker and that education can most definitely affect this inner context. Thus in addition to possibly providing the means for the improvement of material conditions, education can completely transform the mental context in which all future decisions are made, irrespective of material factors. Finally, I will suggest specific ways in which an education program in a prison can be structured to facilitate cognitive and moral growth.

The professional criminal: free will or determinism?

It is a tribute to the complexity of mankind that the debate over free will continues to occupy such a central position among both intellectuals and laymen. Except for the demagogue, of course, there is no absolute answer, only leanings to one side or the other. As noted above, I see man as a decision-maker, exercising a kind of free will but exercising it within the confines of a variety of factors largely beyond his control. The early critics of Hobbes' atomistic philosophy of man and society stressed this problem, namely the persistent social inequalities which limited some men's ability to make decisions more than others. In comparing my own biography as an offspring of the North American middle class with the biographies of many of the prisoners I teach, these inequalities are immediately apparent. Not only was I encouraged and trained from youth to maximize my decision-making capabilities and opportunities, but the material conditions of my life were crucial in my ability to do so.

The limitations of class and personal biography obviously affect the range of possible or perceived alternative decisions and opportunities, but there is still choice within any range. Moreover, it is certainly possible through education, determination, or simple good fortune, to change those conditions, reassess biographies and thus broaden the range of possible decisions. While many prisoners readily don the mantle of victim, for others it is essential that the events and decisions that led them to prison were self-directed and not pre-determined by forces outside their control. They reason that if the decision to commit a crime was theirs, it remains possible to make the decision not to. Despite this will to change, these men all too frequently lack both the social reinforcement and the cognitive skills so necessary for these other decisions.

Generalizing about prisoners is dangerous, but then again, they are not a random group of individuals. In a recent study of the students in the University of Victoria Program at two British Columbian penitentiaries, we found remarkable similarities of educational, family and social backgrounds. As well, we discovered that the vast majority of the men shared a common record of consistent and escalating criminal activity. There were exceptions, of course: first offenders, some men from staunchly middle class backgrounds, stable family situations, and so forth, but they were clearly the exceptions (Ayers et al., 1980). While some of these men were clearly victims of specific situations or specific personal weaknesses, most were men who viewed their criminal activities as a vocation, what I have referred to as professional criminals.

The search for the origins of the decision to become a criminal is a noble quest, but one likely to give only individualized answers. I am less concerned with the origins of the decision than the fact of the decision itself, the element of consciousness involved in choosing a criminal career. This point is supported by Schmalleger who notes that "Most convicts are professional criminals... criminals out of choice and not out of necessity or unhappy circumstances" (Schmalleger, 1979: 50). Letkemann sees the professional criminal acting out of choice rather than frustration and as being "...committed to the illegitimate life style, as demonstrated in reliable and consistent behavior patterns" (1973: 20). Phelps, an administrator in the Louisiana Corrections Service, describes the professional criminal as a "...nobody who elected crime as an economic way of life" (*Angolite*, p. 44). From a different perspective, Manders describes both lower class and corporate crime as the "...perfectly rational response of a decision maker who actively violates the moral and legal codes of society" (p. 61). Taylor, echoing this view, argues that men "...consciously choose crime as one solution to the problems posed by the economic and social demands of society" (p. 271).

In my own work with the prisoner/students in the University of Victoria Program at Matsqui Institution, the prevalence of choice in the process of becoming a criminal has been evident from the beginning. In discussing their pasts, most men saw the initial impulse toward criminal acts in terms of a search for a role, for status they could not achieve in other ways. They also recall a sense of isolation as youths and used crime as an entry point to a peer group. They scorn the notion that drug addiction, weakness of will or personality defects 'drove' them to crime, especially subsequent to their first series of criminal acts. One man viewed his first prison term as resulting from an inability to compete in the normal world. His last term, a six year period, was spent "getting it together, trying to set some course in life, determine some sort of future, make up for lost time." The crucial difference seemed to be that decisions were being made consciously for the first time. "My decisions were tempered by a great deal of anger, but they were still my decisions."

Before discussing how education in prison might facilitate a more socially acceptable range of decisions, some further generalizations are in order concerning the affective and cognitive context in which the criminal makes decisions. The insight which I am able to bring to bear in discussing these individuals is largely impressionistic, based on my teaching in the prisons, informal conversations and work on a research study of the University of Victoria Program. While I started from no *a priori* assumptoins concerning criminals as a group, the common attitudes, thought patterns and assumptions of my students led me to accept, if not a criminal personality, at least a criminal world view.

The most pervasive quality of this criminal world view is the off-handed contempt most of them have for the average, honest, 'straight' citizen. Such people are regarded as weak, to be pitied and, among the more hardened, stepped on. Goodness, justice, humility, honesty and similar qualities are mere hypocrisy or the attributes of a fool. This surfaces in a kind of anaesthetized sensibility toward violence, a defence of violence as simply a tool of the trade, and the criminal's all too frequent stance toward the victim as someone who simply gets in the way (Hibbert, 1968). In this world of 'us and them', the relationship is inevitably hostile. One student recalled a conversation with a fellow thief who was quietly cursing people in a neighbourhood they were driving through. When he asked his friend why such venom, he replied, "Don't ever forget every one of those bastard square johns would take the stand and swear your life away."

In their attitude toward society, these men share many of the attributes of what has become known as the 'authoritarian person-ality', though as Greenstein notes, this may be a rational approach since the world of the lower class may in fact be a 'jungle' requiring such a stance toward authority (1965: 89). Kohlberg has argued that lower class children see the law as an external force which must be obeyed or rebelled against and Buck-Morss suggests that this rigidity of perception may reflect the reality of authoritarian or arbitrary enforcement of the law against that segment of society (Buck-Morss, 1975: 44). There is of course a political aspect in the criminal's condemnation of the rich and subsequent dismissal of any qualms about the consequences of big actions, but as most statistics show, crime is for the most part directed at the poor and working class segments of society. Behind these rationales and feelings of victimization is the view pervasive among criminals that society owes them a living (an all too common attitude) and when it does not deliver they are justified in simply taking it (a not too common attitude). With advancing age and persistent imprisonment, this becomes an imperative: "I'm too far behind to quit now, besides the system owes me."

Much of what is seen as common attitudes or in terms of a specific criminal personality in fact stems from cognitive factors and the associated level of reasoning ability. Perhaps the most salient characteristic of the criminal is a profound egocentricity, a characteristic of the pre-adolescent stages of cognitive-moral development. Samenow found this to be "...the most striking thing in their view of the world", that people are simply pawns on a chessboard, to be moved about at will. "The world had to suit them, rather than they the world... these are people who regard themselves as very unique, very special" (Samenow, 1979).

This egocentrism corresponds to Kohlberg's Stage 2 of moral reasoning ability in which "questions of right and wrong are answered only in terms of personal need and satisfaction" (Fishkin, 1973: 110). Simple reciprocity is the dominant interpersonal style, the equal exchange of favours, or blows, 'you scratch my back and I'll scratch yours' being the defining norm rather than loyalty, gratitude, conscience or justice. Kohlberg and others argue that in terms of cognitive and moral development there is a consistent pattern of underdevelopment among criminals, with Stage 1 or Stage 2 being the norm (Kohlberg, et al., 1972; 1974). A study of delinquents in the United States indicated that the 15-17 delinquents had a mean moral maturity like a 10-12 year old middle class child (Scharf, 1979). This immaturity is echoed in the realm of emotional development as indicated in these observations by a long-term prisoner in a U.S. prison:

> A prisoner who is not state-raised, e.g., serving only one or two short sentences, tolerates the situation because of his natural social maturity prior to incarceration. He knows things are different outside prison. But the others have no conception of any difference. They have no conception because they have no experience, and hence no maturity. Their judgement is untempered, rash; their emotions are impulsive, raw, unmellowed.
>
> There are emotions—a whole spectrum of them—that I know only through work, through reading and my immature imagination. I can only imagine I feel those emotions but I do not. At age 34 I am barely a precocious child (NYRB, 1980: 35).

Not only are social origins a factor in this cognitive, moral and emotional underdevelopment, but the prison itself plays a formative role. What we see in the adult offender as a fully developed criminal 'personality' is really a personality formed in large part by the prison itself.

The deficits outlined above when coupled with the subsequent egocentrism result in an inability or retarded ability to empathize, to see or take the roles of others, including those in authority. As Haan, Smith and Block note, this inability undoubtedly becomes an unworkable mode of operation for people as they grow older and can lead to anti-social behaviour (1968: 199). Kohlberg and others working with juvenile offenders and adult prisoners within a developmental program have thus emphasized role-taking opportunities as being crucial to producing movement through the stages of cognitive-moral development. Role-taking leads to empathy, "...the awareness of other selves with thoughts and feelings like the self... a critical aspect of social life" (Harris, 1976: 133).

Another concomitant of these cognitive factors is a lack of analytical skills, a tendency to view the world in an episodic way, not integrating past experience with the present nor anticipating and projecting for the future. Feuerstein sees this, plus a general impulsiveness, as coming from not having the proper distance between a given input and the act (1979). Spivak, Platt and Shure place great emphasis on these cognitive factors in their discussion of problem solving:

> to fully appreciate the efficiency with which the person navigates through the problem to a satisfactory solution, it is necessary to understand how well he thinks about and works through the interpersonal situation. It is this process, manifest in a set of cognitive skills, that defines his social problem-solving capacity. It is the manner in which he proceeds that largely determines the quality of the outcome. It is *how* he thinks it through, rather than what he might think at any given instant, that becomes the important issue in understanding the likelihood of long-range success or failure (1976: 4).

The central assumption of this paper could not be stated more clearly. The form is crucial in determining the nature of the content. Thinking skills and their corresponding stages of cognitive-moral reasoning are a major factor in establishing a 'predisposition to offend' among criminals and potential criminals. It is these skills and stages of reasoning which, when coupled with a moral/ethical framework, make up the crucial inner context for the decision-maker. It is this inner context which the prison educator must hope to affect through the mechanisms of development.

These cognitive and moral/ethical considerations do not, however, explain crime or the criminal. The predisposition to offend may have its roots in affective attitudes/feelings and cognitive/moral backwardness, but it only manifests itself as behaviour in particular situations. Motivational and situational theories of criminality have traditionally been seen as mutually exclusive, separate explanations for crime and the criminal (Gibbons, 1971: 272). In fact, they must be combined to make sense of either. There are criminogenic situations in society, as there always have been but not everyone when confronted with those situations behaves criminally. Clarke explains it as follows: "To understand why some do, we should not be obsessed by personality issues, i.e., one person's psychological prediliction to break the law. More likely, perceptual and cognitive processes are at work, i.e., how the individual perceives the situation and the various judgements he makes about it" (1977: 281). These judgments may in fact spring directly from the cognitive and moral factors discussed above or could be guided by an immediate personal crisis or situation: the individual could simply be bored, drunk, recently unemployed or broke.

So we have two major factors affecting our decision-maker: his internal cognitive and affective 'map' or level of development, and the social, economic and personal situations he finds himself in. The latter can to some extent be manipulated through social mobility or economic well-being, but it is largely beyond social or individual control. It is to the former inner context, therefore, that efforts must be directed to change the decision making process and finally behaviour itself.

The character of prison education

"Men who reason that theft is not a moral question, but only one of risk and consequence, will always take the risk."

This is in essence the central issue. For too many people, crime does pay and the risks and consequences are ineffective deterrents. The author of the statement is an educated man who, until quite recently, was a professional criminal, a career thief. The product of an education program in a prison, he raises the issue not just of education but of the type or character of the education program needed to elicit or facilitate non-criminal behaviour. In other words, to develop not just the structure of thought but the ethical framework of thought as well.

To attack the structural and ethical roots of the thought patterns and attitudes described in the first section of this paper requires more than a behaviourist approach which stresses overt behaviour or a therapeutic approach which probably raises more defences than it overcomes. The limitations of the "medical model" in corrections have become increasingly apparent in recent years (Kohlberg et al., 1974: 14-15; Ayers, 1979). The educational approach does not assume irrationality, sickness or the necessity to convert or replace, but rather assumes that most prisoners are simply deficient in certain analytic problem-solving skills, interpersonal and social skills and in ethical / moral development. Each of these deficits can be addressed most effectively through education, through a process of habilitation rather than rehabilitation.

Returning once more to the opening quotation, the character of the education offered in the prison is the central point. An educated criminal is not the desired product. The education program must go to the heart of the matter, to the thinking patterns of the prisoner / student and to the moral / ethical framework within which those patterns operate. As Samenow warns us:

> ...you need vocational training, you need educational programs, but its got to go beyond that because you know what you then have. You have a criminal with job skills or a criminal who can read, rather than a criminal who can't read. To help him read, to help him learn new skills does not change what he wants out of life. It doesn't change the thinking patterns of a lifetime... (1979)

Schmalleger likewise warns that education programs that focus on occupational skills and job placement are more likely to produce job-holding criminals than reformed criminals (1979: 53).

At whatever academic level, whether university, high school or basic upgrading, prison education must have two essential elements. It must first have a central concern with ethics or morality, that is, it must by its structure and content be dedicated to increasing the level of ethical knowledge and moral reasoning ability of its students. Secondly, prison education must have as a primary aim the development of thought itself, the facilitation of critical thinking skills through an issue-oriented curriculum, the encouragement of logical argumentation, and consistently high expectations of its students.

An education program centered on ethics or concerned with the development of moral reasoning is not a "moralizing" program, not simply the imparting of virtues. If carried on within the general framework of the approach outlined by Kohlberg and his followers, it is a program designed to advance the moral reasoning of the student through a series of sequential stages. The desired result is not a conformist but a more mature and ethical decision-maker:

> ...The aim of moral education, as opposed to moral training, is to produce adults who do not simply conform to the morality of their group, but are full moral beings, that is, persons who do what they believe is morally required of them. To produce such adults, moral education must foster in those to be educated three excellences. The first is the knowledge of what the group feels is morally required of one, together with beliefs as sound as possible of what is sound and what is unsound in the group's morality, and what deviations from the group's morality are therefore morally permitted to, or required of, one. The second is the ability to do what one believes is morally required of one. And the third is the willingness to do it (Baier, 1971: 10).

At the most mature levels, the individual sees morality in terms of a social contract, accepting the obligation to promote the interests of others in return for their agreement to promote his and acting in accordance with other's interests even when no immediate gratification or social approval is obtained (Maccoby, 1968: 261). Again in an ideal sense, the aim is moral decision-making. In the situational context described earlier, there should be an "evaluative assessment of the circumstances in which the action takes place, an interpretation of what the possible courses of action are in the situation... reflection about what ends are to be sought, what intentions are to direct behaviour, and what rules are to be followed" (Gustafson, 1970: 15). Most important, the actual behaviour or outcome of the situation is less important than the reasoning process behind the decision. It is this process that moral education hopes to affect.

There are several essential mechanisms for an education program with these lofty aims. Exposure to models, in the form of instructors, is an important factor, instructors who will challenge existing attitudes and moral stances and yet not be so distant as to be perceived as the "other". Interaction with peers is important since both growth and stagnation are in many ways governed by the nature and quality of such interaction. Above all, however, is conflict and the resolution of conflict. Tapp and Kohlberg see conflict and participation as the central feature of moral education:

> We would argue that experience-based activity involving conflict resolution, problem-solving, participation in decision-making and role taking opportunities beget compliance and independence of more than an

uncritical law and order sort. Educational experiences of conflict and participation extend the human's capacity to differentiate and integrate and to contemplate different points of view, in other words, to develop principles for evaluating "right" from "wrong" and perfecting a sense of responsibility, obligation, law and justice (1971: 86).

It is essential to create in the student a feeling of dissatisfaction with his existing concept of right and wrong or at least with the manner in which he arrived at that concept. That conflict must be amplified in discussions with teachers and fellow students, both in the classroom and outside, either directly or, more commonly, indirectly through the content of the academic curriculum. This conflict, a form of cognitive dissonance, opens the student to the opinions and ideas of others which can eventually be incorporated into his own thinking. "The advance from one moral stage to another is brought about by cognitive conflict, since resolution of conflict leads to a reorganization of structure" (Muus, 1976: 56).

The first part of this paper outlined the problem, the existence of individuals, who largely through choice, engage in behaviours seen as personally and socially harmful and labeled criminal. The behaviour leads to incarceration which leads in all too many cases to a repetition of the behaviour. The paper then proposes education as a means to break this cycle and outlines the goals of prison education. The goal is a developmental one, raising the level of cognitive development in order to affect perception and sophistication of analysis and raising the level of moral development in order to affect the way the individual uses and interprets the insights gained through cognitive development. It remains now to describe how these processes might actually work in a prison education program.

There are two aspects to a prison education program with the aims outlined above. The first is the environment in which the program operates and the second is the actual content and structure of the curriculum. For convenience they may be separated, but in practice they are inseparable. The success of each dependent on the other. Critical thinking and moral issues can only be meaningfully addressed in an environment that is supportive of that thinking in its praxis.

The environment most conducive to this kind of program has been described by Kohlberg and Scharf as a "just" or "democratic" community, a community run according to democratic norms with principles of justice as guides for interaction among students and between students and staff (Duguid, 1980). Formal, prescriptive classroom instruction is not sufficient for a moral education program. Hartshorne and May's studies in the 1930's showed that such efforts may teach specific moral or legal codes but do little to stimulate an understanding of the philosophy behind those rules. The latter step is essential if the learning implicit in the program is to be internalized and thus have a chance of affecting behaviour. The prisoner / students must be assisted in attaining a new perspective of the purpose of law, and empathetic "verstehen" (Jones, 1976) of the nature of democratic society and a more developed social conscience. These are all "social" developments in the sense that they occur in conjunction with others, not in isolation. Moreover, unlike the Freudian tradition, developmentalists see the evolution of a sense of justice as being autonomous, not something passed on from parent to child. While the parent or teacher plays an important role as the necessary model for more advanced reasoning, justice is only internalized through interaction with peers in the context of mutual respect and solidarity. (Craig, 1976; Maccoby, 1968; Tapp and Kohlberg, 1971). The approach is thus at base interactionist, requiring the individual's active intervention with his social environment. That interaction is mediated by a parallel process of cognitive development which in turn is mediated by the interaction.

The need, then, is for a community that is perceived as fair and legitimate by the prisoners and which would stimulate moral reasoning by creating a situation in which dilemmas evolving from conflicts of claims could be resolved collectively. The aim is the citizen, the individual who will act responsibly to protect and advance community interests without violating a set of principles which may at times conflict with their own interests or their perceptions of the community's interests (Duguid, 1980b). Assuming such a community is as democratic as is possible within the prison environment, the situations it confronts are neither artificial nor academic. Rather, they are as real as the men would confront in the outside world, involving rights, privileges, material interests and group welfare. The conflict, stress and passion implicit in these situations confronts each student with a series of decisions which require emotional, moral and reasoned responses, thus giving ample opportunity for the exercise of new and old problem solving skills.

Such an alternative community provides an ideal environment for moral development and training for increasing sophistication of reasoning and decision-making. It cannot exist alone, however. The base for such a community is the education program which makes it all possible. Without a parallel program of cognitive growth, the community would founder on the collective egocentricity of its members. So we must return in the end to the curriculum of the education program, the actual mechanism which begins the process of cognitive growth. That growth is the necessary base for a corresponding growth in moral reasoning ability which in turn makes possible the functioning of a democratic community.

Mathematics, the sciences and philosophy are effective tools for the teaching of logical thought and reasoning, but the liberal arts curriculum, especially English Literature and History, is more likely to couple such purely cognitive growth with the development of moral reasoning (Duguid, 1979; Kohlberg, 1975). Both English and History have the advantage of being broad-based disciplines, concerned with argumentation, philosophy, ethics, analysis of data and ideas, and both require the development of a strong sense of empathy. All of these characteristics are included in what Spivak, Platt and Shure see as the five essential cognitive problem solving skills:

> 1) Awareness of the variety of possible problems that beset human interactions and a sensitivity to the existence of an inter-personal problem or at least to see the potential for such problems whenever people get together.
> 2) Capacity to generate alternative solutions to problems.
> 3) Articulating the step-by-step means that may be necessary in order to carry out the solution to any interpersonal problem.
> 4) Considering the consequences of one's acts, in terms of their impact both on other people and on oneself.
> 5) Degree to which the individual understands and is ready to appreciate that how one feels and acts may have been influenced by how others feel and act (1976: 8).

These cognitive skills address themselves directly to the problems of egocentricity and impulsiveness identified earlier as key factors in the decision-making patterns of criminals.

It is argued by Yochelson and Samenow (1978) that such critical thinking skills can be taught directly through intensive individual therapy sessions where thought itself is analyzed, corrected and new patterns internalized. It is my argument that much of what we are talking about is in fact the very stuff of a liberal education and that the same or better results can be obtained through such an education. Moreover, as Giroux has observed, mere "communication" is not sufficient for learning of this nature, the student must write and writing is an inherent component of a liberal education program (1978: 296).

An education program with a multiplicity of courses and instructors has an added advantage of offering a wide range of vehicles for the delivery of ideas. Thus a student takes several courses at a time over several terms, interacting with different instructors and with different groups of students. Characters in novels, historical situations, psychological theories, and philosophical arguments all act in combination to produce the desired effect. Thus no one course or instructor is the key to the development process. Instead the education program as a whole is responsible for whatever development takes place and the primary cause or change agent may vary with each student in the program.

Besides offering a wide range of course material, emphasizing writing and issue-oriented readings and discussions, and encouraging conflict in the classroom, the curriculum used in the prison must have a moral or ethical component. This does not mean a required course in ethics but rather that within the context of the traditional liberal arts curriculum the role of values and moral reasoning must be present. Thinking is more than just a cognitive operation, it is also "...a process intimately connected to the beliefs and values that guide one's life" (Giroux, 1978: 299). Since the existing values of the students are the product of underdeveloped reasoning skills and unfortunate experience, the education program must not allow existing values to simply be reinforced through the acquisition of knowledge. Obviously, such a statement implies that ethical relativism has no place in prison education.

The teacher must start from the assumption that the values of the students before him are in part responsible for the commitment of certain acts which have led to prison. Further, he must accept the idea that these values are in fact unacceptable. He must not, however, become a preacher and impose his own values on the students. Rather, he must believe that the value structure of the students has its origins in large part in their cognitive and moral reasoning deficits and that by encouraging cognitive growth and by providing an environment both inside and outside the classroom for the development of moral reasoning, those values will change.

Initially, the instructor plays the key role in this process. Rather than allowing the students' value structure to impose an interpretation on a character in a novel or play that is clearly unacceptable, the instructor must argue his case. Interpretations of history and literature are not all equally valid but neither must there be one acceptable interpretation. What must be debated in the classroom are the parameters of interpretation, why some are acceptable and others not. Thus racism of the Nazi variety is not morally acceptable (though many students in prison will defend it) but other aspects of National Socialism may be open to more generous interpretations. Danto puts the moral component of such matters quite clearly in his discussion of violence, war and morality:

> ...the question of the morality of war is internally related to the questions of morality in war, and when violence in war becomes criminal the war itself is criminal, for no moral end can justify criminal means ...violence is not criminal as such and ...the use of it can be justified. But not *any* use. So it does not follow that once started on violence there is no justified stopping, no logical friction to keep us from sliding down the smooth slope to utter degradation (1978: 179).

Repeated discussion of such issues in an open manner but with a sense of moral / ethical boundaries can bring about the desired cognitive and moral growth.

Effects of prison education: impressions and evidence

The program described in this paper is based on the model program developed by the University of Victoria at Matsqui Institution. It has been in operation for eight years and I have directed it for the past six years. In assessing the actual and potential success of such a program in bringing about cognitive-moral development and in affecting behaviour, I have two evaluative tools: my own impressionistic views, and the results of a recently completed follow-up study of seventy five of the program's alumni.

I have in fact perceived a great deal of change in many individuals involved in the educational program at Matsqui. First and foremost is a tremendous growth in verbal and written communicative skills, along with a maturing of analytical abilities. Along with success in academic work comes a noticeable growth in self-confidence. The students take a great deal of pride in succeeding in what for most of them is an alien world. Another area of change is both intellectual and behaviouristic. It centers on the problem of polarization, the tendency among prisoners to see everything in good / bad, us / them terms, with virtually no shades of gray. It seems a truism that the effect of a liberal education is to accentuate the grays of life, to show that there are no simple solutions. In many ways this may be one of the most profound of the changes I have observed. It tends to inhibit old pre-university friendships, to draw students closer together as they share a common idiom which is increasingly distinct from that of the prison population. There are even attempts to come to terms with the institution, to see staff members as individuals rather than as a group to be indiscriminately despised.

Related to these changes is the emergence of a clear dual role or identity; the prisoner/student. An increase in verbal skills, more subtle and sophisticated thinking patterns, a somewhat more balanced attitude toward authority and an increase in self-esteem all work to change general attitudes, behaviour patterns in the institution and possibly lay the essential groundwork for similar changes upon release. It is also a fact, however, that these men must live and survive in a prison environment which has little in common with their student identity. Thus during the day the student role tends to be dominant — later, in another part of the institution the other role is dominant. Over the years, many students have perceived this duality themselves and have found in the student role an attractive aspect of their personalities which they wish to preserve upon release.

The follow-up study of the Matsqui Program conducted during 1979-80, confirmed most of my observations and added some new dimensions both in the area of cognitive-moral development and most importantly, in the area of post-release behaviour. Using a questionnaire and interview format, the study examined the attitudes and careers of seventy five students from the University of Victoria Program released from prison from 1976-1979. Each of the men had completed a minimum number of courses and remained out of prison at least six months.

In the area of attitude, striking changes were found in the men's thinking on law and politics, criminal behaviour, family and friendship. The responses on law and politics indicated a strong process of politicization at work within the program and a corresponding growth in a sense of political ideology. The men were "more aware" and had "greater insight" into politics and most important, have a much greater comprehension of the complexity of issues of politics and power as well as a new understanding of where the individual fits into that matrix. It is evident in the responses that the men are more able to see behind the superficial aspects of power (for instance, guns or uniforms) and begin to understand how it actually operates. Thus both sophistication of thought and empathy seem to emerge from the responses.

Prisoner/student comment on criminal behaviour ranged from definite rejection on reasoned or moral grounds to a relativistic attitude to finally a more basic conclusion that it just was not worth it, what the study called "enlightened self-interest."

There were definite indications of a link between increased perception and thinking skills and an improved ability to avoid criminal patterns. Thus:

> "I now have less of a conflict type perspective. I can be "the other person" and know that legal and right are not the same but recognize the right of society to make laws."

And:

> "As I am able to evaluate myself better and to have a better understanding of why I do things, it is easier to avoid the pitfalls that led me to do the things that led to my problems."

The comments and many others indicate that perhaps the most important benefit to be derived from the education program is an ability to analyze life situations from a reasoned perspective.

The effect of both the cognitive development and the dualism implicit in the alternative community emerged most clearly in the men's attitudes toward friends and friendships. There was a clear movement toward new friendships after release and a corresponding difficulty in maintaining old ties:

> "It is difficult now to spend much time with a lot of ex-friends. I like some of them but find at times that I risk being dragged into the "old life style". It seems hard now to spend a lot of time with someone that is not doing something meaningful."

Most of the men stressed a new ability to choose friends more wisely and a general expansion of the range of possible friendships. Again, this was indicative of the program affecting both the decision-making process and the range of possible decisions.

Taken as a whole, the attitude change evidenced in the study indicated a movement away from the "moral alienation of the criminal from society and its institutions," (Scharf 1976: 107) toward an understanding of that society and the position of the individual. As one respondent to the questionnaire said:

> The knowledge that through education, an individual is doing something

positive to help himself cannot but instill a feeling of self-worth and relative well-being. At least the time is not being wasted as it is in so many other places in the prison.

The program teaches students to think in many different ways, and about many different subjects. Discussion with professors on a person-to-person basis and reading and *understanding* texts stimulates a positive feeling towards other people, and life in general. This is something which has been sadly lacking in the prison population. Without this feeling, a prisoner feels — correctly — that he has been "warehoused" as a useless article. This is not conducive to rehabilitation, or anything save a "prison mentality."

The results of the study were particularly significant in the area of post-release behaviour. Virtually all of the men located and inter-viewed (45/75) were employed or going to school full-time. While a full range of occupations was represented, there was a definite indication of upward mobility among the students who had completed more than two years of university courses. Several men remained dissatisfied with their current employment, but expressed a willingness to wait for better opportunities. This seemed to indicate movement toward what Bettelheim described as the keystone of middle class morality, "...the conviction that to postpone immediate pleasure in order to gain more lasting gratification in the future is the most effective way to reach one's goal" (1970: 88). Likewise, Forster in his study of education in British prisons noted that immediate satisfaction is one of the characteristics and attractions of crime and that a major reforming effect of formal education was the "...realization that things come in time" (1977: 23).

While only 30% of the group credited the academic program with help in obtaining employment, the contributions of improved cognitive and social skills was clear. One respondent was quite specific:

> I benefitted greatly from the program, though I didn't really realize it until after I was released. I found that I knew how to plan and set up a series of goals, knew how to set up a job search, write a resume and how to present myself as employable, no mean feat with my record.

Finally, besides the specific learned skills, the new goals and more articulate manner, the success of these men in the job market and in their family relations may be in part attributed to the increased sense of self-worth evident throughout the study. Cynicism, defeatism, bitterness and low self-esteem are all too characteristic of men in prison and lead to an abysmal record of self-fulfilling prophecies upon release. Any program which changes that generalized attitude will have an impact on not only employment but on all other aspects of the individual's life.

The ultimate test of a prison program is, of course, its success or apparent success in inhibiting reincarceration. Most professionals in the field question the validity of this type of measurement, seeing recidivism as one of the least understood and elusive of measures (Gendreau, 1978). All the same, Parlett's point remains a compelling one:

> In the final analysis, the function of prison is primarily, by consensus, the protection of society. Society is not protected in the long run if the products which the prison turns out have not attained a sense of reason and proportion and revert once again to criminal activity. It is, then, insufficient to show paper and pencil growth; freedom from crime and non-return to prison must also be shown (1980).

To arrive at some kind of comparable data concerning reincarceration, the group of seventy-four ex-students was compared to a matched group of other ex-prisoners who were at the same Institution, released during the same intervals but who had not taken part in the university program. Of the university group, eleven (15%) were reincarcerated during the three year period, while thirty five (48%) of the non-student group found their way back to prison.

The low reincarceration figures are a powerful argument for Kohlberg's position that "...persons reasoning in a more morally mature way act in a more mature way" (1974: 27). The results are supported by a separate follow-up study of an earlier group of students from the University of Victoria program (Linden, 1980). Conversely, an extensive study of several prison education programs in the United States which did not include an orientation toward moral education concluded that education was not a significant factor in reincarceration (Seashore, 1976).

There is convincing evidence that criminals are different in significant ways from other citizens and that these differences, while they manifest themselves in terms of behaviour, have as their base deficits in cognitive development and moral reasoning abilities. There is evidence that the traditional prison environment only serves to exacerbate these differences and that the medical/ therapeutic model of treatment has not been effective. Rather than being a corrective problem requiring transformation or cures, the problem is one of development and can be logically addressed through education. Criminals act by making decisions in specific situations and those decisions are in large part formed and determined by the cognitive, ethical, and attitudinal make-up of the individual. Change that, and different decisions should follow. Evidence has been offered of one prison education program which seems to change that "inner context" of decision-making and does in fact result in significantly different behaviour. All that remains is for others to attempt similar education programs to verify the universality of the model.

REFERENCES

ABBOTT, J.H.
1980: In Prison, *New York Review of Books*, June 26.

AYERS, J.D.
1979: Education in Prisons: A Developmental and Cultural Perspective. Paper presented at Canadian Learned Societies Conference, Saskatoon, June 79.

AYERS, J.D., DUGUID, S., MONTAGUE, C., and S. WOLO-WYDNIK
1980: Effects of University of Victoria Program: A Post Release Study. Prepared under contract with the Ministry of the Solicitor General of Canada, May 1, 1980.

BAIER, K.
1971: Ethical Pluralism and Moral Education. In C. Beck, *Moral Education*, University of Toronto Press.

BETTELHEIM, B.
1970: Moral Education. In J. Gustafson et al., *Moral Education: Five Lectures*, Oxford University Press.

BUCK-MORSS, C.
1975: Socio-Economic Bias in Piaget's Theory and its Implication for Cross-Cultural Studies, *Human Development*, 18.

CLARKE, R.V.G.

1977: Psychology and Crime, *Bulletin of the British Psychological Society*, 30.

CRAIG, R.

1976: Education for Justice: Some Comments on Piaget, *Contemporary Education*, 47 (2).

DANTO, A.

1978: On Moral Codes and Modern War, *Social Research*, 45 (1).

DUGUID, S.

1979: History and Moral Development in Correctional Education, *Canadian Journal of Education*, 4 (4).

1980: Post Secondary Education in a Prison: Theory and Praxis, *Canadian Journal of Higher Education*, 10 (1).

1980b: From Prisoner to Citizen: Theory and Practice of Moral Education in the Prison. Paper presented at conference in Chorley, England, Positive Aspects of Penal Education, June 80.

FEUERSTEIN, R.

1979: Transcript of videotaped interview by Dr. D.K. Griffin, "Crime and Reason". Available from Education and Training Division, Ministry of Solicitor General, Ottawa.

FISHKIN, J.

1973: Moral Reasoning and Political Ideology, *Journal of Personality and Social Psychology*, 27 (1).

FORSTER, W.

1977: The Higher Education of Prisoners. University of Leicester, Dept. of Education, Vaughan Paper 21.

GENDREAU, P., and M. LEIPCIGER

1978: The Development of a Recidivism Measure and its Application in Ontario, *Canadian Journal of Criminology*, 20.

GIBBONS, D.

1971: Observations on the Study of Crime Causation, *American Journal of Sociology*, 77 (2).

GIROUX, H.

1978: Writing and Critical Thinking in the Social Studies, *Curriculum Inquiry*, 8 (4).

GREENSTEIN, F.

1965: Personality and Political Socialization: The Theories of Authoritarian and Democratic Character, *Annals of the American Academy of Political and Social Science*, 361.

GUSTAFSON, J.

1970: *Moral Education: Five Lectures*, Oxford University Press.

HAAN, N., SMITH, M.B., and J. BLOCK
1968: Moral Reasoning and Young Adults: Political-Social Behavior, Family Background and Personality Correlates, *Journal of Personality and Social Psychology*, 10 (3).

HARRIS, S.
1976: Some Cognitive, Behavioral and Personality Correlates of Maturity of Moral Judgment, *Journal of Genetic Psychology*, 128.

HIBBERT, C.
1963: *The Roots of Evil*, New York, Minerva Pr.

JONES, C.
1976: The Contribution of History and Literature to Moral Development, *Journal of Moral Education*, 5 (2).

KOHLBERG, L., et al.
1972: The Justice Structure of the Prison: A Theory and an Intervention, *The Prison Journal*, 51 (2).
1974: *The Just Community Approach to Corrections*, Harvard, Moral Education Research Foundation.

KOHLBERG, L.
1975: The Cognitive-Developmental Approach to Moral Education, *Phi Delta Kappan*, June 75.

LETKEMANN, P.
1973: *Crime as Work*, Englewood Cliffs, N.J., Prentice-Hall.

LINDEN, R., PERRY, L., AYERS, J.D., and T.A.A. PARLETT
1980: An Evaluation of a Prison Education Program, Report prepared under contract for the Ministry of the Solicitor General of Canada.

MACCOBY, E.
1968: The Development of Moral Values and Behavior in Childhood. In J. Clausen, *Socialization in Society*, Boston.

MANDERS, D.
1975: Labelling Theory and Social Reality: A Marxist Critique, *Insurgent Sociologist*, 6 (1).

McLELLAN, D.
1971: *The Thought of Karl Marx*, London, Macmillan.

MUUS, R.
1976: Kohlberg's Cognitive-Developmental Approach to Adolescent Morality, *Adolescence*, 11 (41).

PARLETT, T.A.A.
1979: Education — A Necessary if not Sufficent Modality in the Correction of Offender. Unpublished paper.

SAMENOW, S.
1979: Transcript of a videotaped interview by Dr. D.K. Griffin, "Crime and Reason". Available from Education and Training Division, Ministry of the Solicitor General, Ottawa.

SCHARF, P.
1976: The Prison and the Inmate's Conception of Legal Justice: An Experiment in Democratic Education, *Criminal Justice and Behavior*, 3 (2).
1979: Law and the Child's Evolving Legal Conscience. In R. Sprague, *Advances in Law and Child Development*, New York, John Wiley.

SCHMALLEGER, F.
1979: World of the Career Criminal, *Human Nature*, March 79.

SEASHORE, B.
1976: *Prison Education: Project Newgate and Other College Programs*, New York, Praeger.

SPIVAK, G., et al.
1976: *The Problem-Solving Approach to Adjustment*, San Francisco, Jossey-Bass.

TAPP, J., and L. KOHLBERG
1971: Developing Senses of Law and Legal Justice, *Journal of Social Issues*, 27 (2).

TAYLOR, I., et al.
1973: *The New Criminology*, New York, Harper.

YOCHELSON, S., and S. SAMENOW
1978: *The Criminal Personality*, New York, Jason Aronson.
1980: The Career Criminal, *The Angolite*, Jan.-Feb. 80.

10. ON THE PLACE OF VALUES EDUCATION IN PRISONS

Lucien Morin

Introduction

Oratorical precautions, except when they are mere formalities are an indication of prudence and politeness. They introduce the quality of the speaker and assuage the apprehensions of his audience.

One precaution that I decline to take today is to warn you that the topic "The Place of Values Education in Prison" is a multi-faceted, complex and difficult one. Common sense alone is sufficently persuasive to convince even the most sceptical on this point. One precaution that I insist on taking is to forthwith state the two points of reference which guided the choice of my arguements in treating this question.

Concerning the theoretical foundations and assumptions, one of my major concerns has been to never lose sight of the eminently ethical dimension of the question of values education in prisons. First, because moral education is unquestionably one of the most significant aspects of any values education. But there is another and, I think, more profound reason. The ethical connotation here seems to draw its permanence and ultimate justification from the very roots of criminality. Before being a juridical question, or the subject of some particular science, criminal conduct is moral conduct. Much is said and written today to explain or qualify crime, criminal action, and criminal thinking. In the majority of cases, the unassumed

Paper presented to the Learned Societies Conference: Canadian Educational Research Association Symposium on Education as a Cultural Alternative for Prisoners and Delinquents, Saskatoon, Saskatchewan, June, 1979.

premisses (that is, always implied but rarely stated) refer to crime as an act or omission forbidden by law and punishable upon conviction. Originally, however, the Greek word for crime, *crimen*, meant *fault*. This fault was related to evil, and referred primarily to some serious offense against morality. Crime, therefore, must unquestionably be considered a matter of ethics. It is extremely important that we make these basic assumptions very clear, if we are to develop for criminals, a system of values education which has the potential to succeed.

With respect to practical possibilities, I have tried to focus my attention on measures that could, concretely and comprehensively, serve a values education program in the prisons. This is important because comprehension of a problem is only a beginning. It is always necessary to subsequently define precise strategies of action. Here again the course of proposed action is acutely demanding since we are dealing with prison environments, where life itself is defined as a continuum of actions and reactions which are more or less controlled and predictable, and where also each human gesture is observed with quasi-microscopic scrutiny.

In a prison, the slightest detail of a human act takes on primary significance and even the smallest gesture can become — at any given time — a ritual of extreme symbolism and consequence. The stakes, as we can see, are high. For this reason, the practice of values education in a prison should be carefully planned and implemented with caution. New and experimental projects in prisons are scrutinized with such suspicion that a partial success might well be interpreted as total failure.

By now you will have undoubtedly guessed the two major issues that I wish to discuss with you: first, the theoretical base for values education in the prisons; second, the elaboration and implementation of a viable, realistic, values education plan.

I — Reasons for Values Education in the Prisons

On a question like values education in the prisons, no theoretical justification can ever be formulated that will satisfy the intellectual doubts and preoccupations of all the protagonists. Nor will one theory ever be able to adequately examine all the aspects of this extremely complex problem. Yet rational convictions are indispensable, because one instinctively believes in Truth and will consequently lend his consent to that which he can recognize as true and rationally valid. How then shall we proceed? I believe it is best to bear in mind our ultimate objective: the construction of something useful and practical. We are far more likely to obtain consensus on what should be our objective for the student, than we are to agree on the nature of values education, the nature of criminality, or of man and the universe. Our efforts will be much more productive if we concentrate on achieving some clear, practical objective. In order to design a workable program, we will have to use the common element of our theories, and to set aside those differences which would impede action.

Even if this were granted, we do not wish to shy away from our duty to formulate a sound, theoretical justification — a justification which will involve not only our pedagogical and scientific convictions, but the entire gamut of our moral and metaphysical certitudes.

In this perspective, I will examine the three following propositions: 1. from a moral point of view, values education is a being-becoming fulfillment affecting the entire person; 2. from a logical point of view, values education exhibits polarity and polarization, allowing for the contrast required in adult reasoning; 3. from an educational point of view, no education makes sense if it isn't first of all values education.

1. Values education as a being-becoming fulfillment affecting the entire person

Behind any values education concept there lies the fundamental principle of bipolarity. Simply stated, values are not created, but are recognized. Values take on real significance through existential embodiment. On the one hand, a value is not, properly speaking, the product of some arbitrary choice nor the result of some mental caprice or fancy. Value is not really man-made. It would be more accurate to say that it is man-recognized, something which imposes itself upon man's faculties and to which he can only respond. On the other hand, value cannot be said to have real meaning unless and until it is incarnated, invested with human form; embodied in the daily routine of being, and acting, and becoming. There is nothing mystical nor abstract about this. An incarnated value is one with existential being and living: tell me what your values are and you will tell me who you are.

This second element of the principle of bipolarity (I will consider the first in my logic argument) is of capital importance when it comes to education since, obviously, one does not inculcate values as one teaches mathematics. Because it must be invested with flesh, so to speak, that is, integrated in and personified through behaviour, value is quite distinct from a scientific aptitude, habit, or power — or any cognitive disposition for that matter — developed through a formal educational process. First, for its development and acquisition, value implies the energetic commitment of the entire person — which is not usually the case when competence in a particular science is the objective. Second, contrary to science, whose more immediate result consists in perfecting the learner *qua* learner an incarnated value affects the fulfillment and amelioration of the entire person. Briefly stated, through science, knowledge arises. Through value, man emerges. Let us consider these two propositions in more detail.

i- Values education implies the total commitment of the person

Concrete incarnation being its destiny, value requires the contribution and collaboration not only of the cognitive powers of the mind but all the energies and vital capacities of heart and soul. Through and because of value, these various manifestations give structure and unity, orientation and meaning to man as being. As such, value is the connecting element producing wholeness or completeness. Let us examine this a little more closely.

Men are usually detached from scientific truths, and can know different kinds of facts independently of each other. Even though common first principles underlie all scientific investigation, the content of one science can be intellectually separated from the content of another without mental anguish. The definitions proper to each individual science are not interrelated or mutually connected: as "per se notae" propositions, that is, as lacking a unifying middle term, they cannot share an inter-causal relationship. This is not the case with values. Values adhere together, and produce a total world outlook. Values cannot be freely detached from each other, and held in comfortable isolation, as can scientific facts. Values cling to one another in an inseparable whole. This is what best reveals the difference between science and values.

Incarnated values are totally interdependent, regarding both their acquisition and maintenance. An intimate connection unites them in their matter and in their principles. Regarding matter, for example, a narrow, naturally "unbreachable" contract with the concept of good practically cements their family ties. Concerning principles, the degree of integrity required for a value to be fully incarnated is so imperious and intense, that each value demands of the entire person that he act according to the highest standards, at all times, in all circumstances, and notwithstanding any and all inclinations to the contrary, no matter how compelling. For instance, the generous person must be ready not only to confront and dominate the petulant passions of avarice and egoism, but he must also be able to surmount the obstacles that can arise from his respect for others, his striving for excellence, his openness to beauty etc. The same must be said of every value. When it comes to incarnated values, a firm and total commitment of the person in one sector of human action presupposes a like commitment in all related sectors. Good intention, which serves as a principle in the election of incarnated values, cannot be partially realized. The whole person, with all its faculties, is at the root of each incarnated value. Specialization, here, is hardly possible.

It seems to me that the corollary to this first conclusion is of particular importance when values education is talked about in reference to prison education. Unless I completely misread the actual situation, a new school of thought is gaining rapid popularity among prison officials. Its basic claims suggest that the development of good reasoning suffices for good action to ensue. Since this is an important supposition, directly related to our question, please allow me to briefly detail my objections. If it is understood that a *science* of value can automatically *cause* an incarnated value, then there is no point in pursuing the type of values education that I have been advocating up until now.

In the Preface to the second edition of his influential work, *Toward a Psychology of Being*, Abraham Maslow observes that the creation of a better world ("the construction of the One Good World") will come about through "knowledge" and that the demonstration of good action ("how to be good", "how to love") will generate from science ("I am convinced that the best answer is in the advancement of knowledge"). Further on, Maslow admits his profound belief in the promise of "a scientific ethics" (p. 4) according to which man will better know and understand his "natural tendencies". In turn, this knowledge will "tell him how to be good, how to be happy, ... how to respect himself" etc. Still more precisely, he says of this "scientific ethics" that it will induce the "automatic solution" (pp. 4-5, 149) to problems of personality. In chapter 5, he succinctly states his ideas:

"Knowledge and action are very closely bound together, all agree. I go much further, and am convinced that knowledge and action are frequently synonymous, even identical in the Socratic fashion. Where we know fully and completely, suitable action follows automatically and reflexly". (p. 66)

There is no doubt in my mind that the philosophy of inmate education referred to above directly reflects Maslow's position (taken at face value, of course). And what exactly is its unavowed ambition? The antiquated, deeply entrenched and almost sacrilegious dream to abolish once and for all the irritating antinomies between what is and what ought to be. The means chosen to attain this end consist in a kind of circulary conversion where knowledge causes action or, stated differently, where science of the good automatically causes good action. It is assumed that between the science of value and the incarnation of value, there is identity and reversibility.

This ideal, as we all know, is not new. To briefly reminisce, already in the 17th century the influences of Cartesian "mathematism" are strongly felt. Descartes himself, in his *Regulae ad directionem ingenii*, wishes to extend the process of mathematical or scientific reasoning to all human knowledge. In his *Recherche de la vérité*, Malebranche bluntly asserts that "we can express all relations through numbers and represent them to the imagination through lines". A similar propagation of the *mathesis universalis*, extended to all human experience, is to be found in Leibniz' *De arte combinatoria* and Hobbes' *Logic*. The most representative figure of this movement is probably Spinoza. In a fundamental passage taken from his remarkable treatise on ethics (the title speaks for itself: *Ethica ordine geometrica demonstrata*) where his brilliant mind searches desperately for rigorous ways to eradicate the deficiencies of human action by scientific demonstration, he writes:

"Beatitude (happiness) is not the price of virtue but virtue itself. And this development is not obtained by the reduction of sensual appetites. On the contrary, it is this very development which renders possible the reduction of our sensual appetites". (*Ethique*, prop. XLII)

Having previously identified happiness with science (prop. XXXII), Spinoza concludes that intellectual growth can, by itself, automatically correct passionate inclinations.

This excursion into the past (and I hope it wasn't too long) seemed necessary if we wanted to better understand the impact of the present revival and resist it, if it is our wish to do so. It is mine. A rational adhesion to value interests reason and only reason in the sense that the science of value, as such, is exclusively pre-occupied with truth. Now truth is not a prime mover, does not trigger automatic action or conduct, does not effectuate instinctive reaction. "Potest grammatica perfectissima blasphemare Deum" — Even the most perfect of grammarians can swear to God. Furthermore, the science of value is, in large part, measured by things, by reality: it is not because man wishes it that moral conscience is a value. Basically, the truthfulness of a value is established by referring to something which is outside of the knower.

To move toward action, the agent or operator must claim value as his good, desire it with all his might and adhere to it in concrete ways. Thus, the sphere of incarnated value is not the sphere of scientific knowledge but the sphere of total desire and engagement where man does not aspire to some universal, abstract object, good only for intellectual jugglery and delectation. Rather, an incarnated value means a value that I love for me, that has meaning for me, to which I commit my entire person. One can easily see that this particular interpretation of values education is extremely difficult and demanding, especially as regards prison inmates. But also extremely beneficial. For inmates especially, a conversion to incarnated value is much more laborious and painful than an intellectual conversion to truth (which can satisfy logic alone without changing behaviour). Only the former implies a reshaping, a refocussing of the total being. To summarize, values education implies the commitment of the entire person.

ii- Values education effects the bettering of the entire person

Having briefly seen how, for its acquisition, value depends on the total energies of man, I wish now to show how the effect of an incarnated value betters not the mind alone, but the entire person.

An education centered principally on intellectual or cognitive learning would not necessarily lead to a bettering of the total man. On the contrary, it would essentially mean the progress or amelioration of man in one of his "parts" — man in his function as knower. For instance, if it is man who mends my shoe, we nevertheless call him a cobbler. It is also man who treats my sick liver or stomach, but he is remunerated as doctor, not as man. So that John-doctor, for example, is not the whole man John, does not exhaust all of John's qualities and, more importantly, John-good-doctor is not identical to John-good-man. Said differently, when what is at stake concerns the goodness of the man John, his fullness and perfection as man, "all" of John is involved — the bettering is not, cannot, must not be partial. Giving with the hand does not make a good hand: it makes a good man. On the contrary, when it comes to medecine, if John-learning is always man, it nevertheless is John-doctor that results in the acquisition of medical qualities and aptitudes. So that, no matter how good he is as a professional, John-doctor could stay John-good-doctor and at the same time be John-bad-man.

Clearly, limiting the education of the prisoner to intellectual learning or development is not sufficient. Only value can better the entire person. We might go further and suspect that sheer intellectual concentration could even have negative effects on an inmate's total well-being. For example, does it not happen that the same object, while a principle of intellectual delight for the mind, can, considered in itself, be a source of repugnance for the bettering of the whole man? This is because the intellect can take great pleasure in cogitating evil — for all knowledge, as such, rejoices the intellect. But who would say that, under the pretext of rational development, an inmate should be encouraged to amuse himself in imagining and planning a perfect crime of murder. This is clearly one case where the good of intelligence is not good for the whole man.

Finally, as we have already seen, values share natural cohesion and complicity. One cannot be just if he is not, at the same time, honest. Of course, one can, without possessing the incarnated value of honesty, feel a strong, natural inclination to do justice to one's brother. But basically, if one is not at the same time honest, if one is incapable of controlling himself when temptations of calumny or slander arise, one will forever remain exposed to difficulties when facing the problem of being just. The converse is also true. The interdependance of values is such that any incarnated value, because of its causal influence on the others, contributes to the betterment of the whole person. Values education betters the entire person.

2. Values education allows for polarity and contrast indispensable to reasoning

If my observations are correct, a considerable amount of recent research has been putting much emphasis on the logical or cognitive deficiencies of the inmate. Insufficiently aware of the substance of these new affirmations, I will espouse nor reject them. I will be content to retain them as useful hypothetical material in reflecting upon the place of values education in the development of reason. Two propositions will be examined: 1. inmates do not think like adults but like children; 2. values education acts as a useful contrast in the development of logical thinking.

i- Reasoning like a child and unlike an adult

a) The first presumption is that an inmate reasons like a child. And how does a child reason? For one thing, a child does not reason with reason alone. The genesis of his intellectual progression reveals that the child has little autonomous reasoning, that is reasoning transcending globalistic confusion. He is part of the things that he judges, things which, in turn, are undistinguishable emanations of the self. In the light of the principle that knowledge progresses from the imperfect to the perfect, from the less known to the more known, Piaget describes the penomenon with adroit sophistication:

"Assimilation and accomodation proceed from a state of chaotic undifferentiation to a state of differenciation with correlative coordination". (*La construction du réel chez l'enfant*, p. 309).

In less technical terms, he adds:

"Intelligence does not begin through knowledge of the self nor through knowledge of things in themselves but through knowledge of their interaction. And it is by simultaneously orienting itself to the two poles of this interaction that it organizes the world by organizing itself". (*Ibid.*, p. 311)

To be sure, this integralistic undifferenciation is not reducible to the biological. It is part of egocentrism, a well-known characteristic of the child's cognitive process, and, as such, an epistemic phenomenon. We might add that although it is a distinctive mark of the child's thinking process, this phenomenon is not confined or restricted to childhood. It can appear, and does appear, at all ages in the individual whose mental structure has not developed. Let us once more quote Piaget:

"It is, as it were, the sumtotal of pre-critical — and, accordingly, pre-objective — attitudes of knowledge... It is a spontaneous attitude which governs the psychical activity of the child from the outset and exists throughout his life in states of mental inertia". (*Le langage et la pensée chez l'enfant*, p. 69)

I shall assume that it is through this undifferenciated, egocentric reasoning that the similitude is established between the reasoning characteristics of inmates and children.

b) The second presumption is that inmates do not reason like adults. And what do we mean by adult reasoning? As far back as the pre-Socratics, valid reasoning has been identified as the instrument by which reason draws from objects of seemingly contrasting nature, common and invariable elements of unity. The rational is community inherent in contrasting objects. A rational principle is one that allows the construction of unity out of a plethora of contrasts. This construction is produced by the insistance upon common characteristics shared by the opposing objects.

This simple definition dominates the history of Occidental thought. It is important to our topic for three reasons. b-1) First, no matter the nature of the unitary theories, no matter their methodology, it seems obvious that the reason for Reason is the connection of disparate items. Reason must recognize contrast before it can manifest principles of similitude; that is, before it can make the distinction between things as they are in themselves and the affirmations and negations that reason says of them. Practically, Reason presumes that differences exist, differences which she has not caused to be differences, and which are independent of and anterior to her own existence. Finally, every man, precisely because of his rationality, must tackle the laborious task of discovering and elucidating principles of unity in order to escape the insignificance of a world of plural contrasts.

b-2) Second, because the rational relates to the discovery of similitudes, the concept of measure has always been closely associated to the rational process.

As Cassirer says of Cusanus:

"All knowledge presupposes comparison, which, in turn, more precisely understood, is nothing but measurement. But if any contents are to be measured by and through each other, the first, inevitable assumption must be the condition of homogeneity. They must be reduced to one and the same unit of measure; they must be capable of being thought of as belonging to the same quantitative order (Ernst Cassirer, *The Individual and the Cosmos in Renaissance Philosophy*, 1964, p. 10).

Said differently, all similar objects, and only similar objects, can be measured. Accordingly, if reasoning is essentially a process of comparison or measurement, every act of judgment will imply necessarily two things; that which is judged, and that by which we judge it. In other words, what is common to all cases of judgment is that there is something which is taken as a principle, i.e. as something first, by which we measure something else. Moreover, this something first, this principle, must be known before it can serve as a measure. Thus, whoever does not know what the length of a yardstick is, can not judge whether the object in front of him is or is not, say, three yards long. The major problems of reasoning are always to find what is this something first, and secondly, to apply it. We judge of length by using a length as measure; we judge of art by principles of art. This is the problem of the homogeneity of the measure with the thing measured.

b-3) Third, the ultimate argument is a practical one. Man feels a moral obligation to reason, an obligation which is little more than the instinct of survival and self-preservation. The failure to be rational results inevitably in alienation from the world structure and, thus, a rational man is one who sees and follows the regularity and order of the universe, one who has discovered and lives his life within the laws prescribed by nature. Passing those bounds is an act of the irrational. The moral meaning of reason illustrates thus the essence of the rational as the discovery of order based on similarities.

To summarize, if the criminal mind is to be accused of child-like reasoning, this is probably due to undifferenciated globalism or egocentrism. If it is to be associated with un-adult thinking, this could be explained by the incapacity or unwillingness to recognize logical contrast.

How then can values education contribute to any of this? This is the next question to be examined.

ii- Values education as contrast useful for logical thinking

Let me recall the first element of the bipolarity principle. A value, we said earlier, is not the product of some arbitrary choice nor the result of mental invention. Rather, value is something which imposes itself upon man's faculties and to which he can only respond. After what we have said about reason in the child and the adult (with special reference to inmate thinking) this principle sheds new light on our problem. As an imposition from "elsewhere", value expresses reality as existing outside the self. As such, it means opposition, polarity, antithesis. It offers an alternative to subjective egocentrism by introducing within the epistemic structure of the mind, the possibility of "objective" consciousness. From a strictly logical point of view, reason is doubly served here. For one, it is forced into submission by accepting that many worlds exist which are not identified with, nor caused by, the self. For another, it is brought to realize that continuous, subjective affirmation is not conducive to progress. Development of the rational powers comes about only through dialectics that is, through the consideration and use of contrasting views. It is in this sense, probably, that values education in the prison can be said to help a prisoner's thinking process. For an inmate, values education represents a world totally different from *his* world. Once he recognizes this, he knows that he cannot avoid dealing with this existential contradiction. Hopefully, he will benefit in the process.

What follows is an effort to better articulate this argument.

When investigating truth — and values education, is committed to such an investigation — what comes first is doubt. The real beginning of knowledge is not acceptance but negation. And investigating truth is no more than the careful examination of the reasons for negating or, said differently, the finding of proper solutions to the doubts anterior to intellectual consent. Thus, true education always takes into consideration the necessary first condition of doubt.

As an agent generating doubt in the mind of the inmate, values education could produce attentive listening to contrasting opinions and the respectful consideration of their premises. And as long as values are not simply presented in an enumerative, juxtaposed, or uncritical fashion, as long as they are not condemmed beforehand to the realm of gelatinous relativism, they entail the kind of adversity indispensable to intellectual growth. There are at least two important reasons why the perception and analysis of contrast and adversity require intelligence. First, the matter out of which values are made, their very substance, is of such complexity that no one can advance sure-footedly without an awareness that many possible interpretations can exist. Secondly, it is by reason of the inherent weakness of intelligence itself that this precautionary inquest is rendered necessary. Otherwise, if our major difficulties came from things themselves rather than from intelligence, wouldn't we better know those objects that are most abstract by definition? Of course, experience testifies to the contrary.

To summarize, knowledge of truth grows in proportion to the effort of reason in studying the origins of doubt or contrary opinions. In this sense, values education can be a most valuable contribution to logical development.

And what precisely are the benefits to logic? We could think of a few. For the purposes of the present paper, I will discuss only the beneficial effects of prudence to be gained through the training of logic.

History is full of examples we could borrow from to illustrate our point. With your permission, I will take my inspiration from Plutarch. In one of his remarkable essays entitled "On the utility of one's ennemies", he points out a very interesting ingredient in man's intellectual evolution. As regards their contacts with wild animals, primitive men, says Plutarch, were satisfied not to be killed or mamed by them; consequently, they devoted their energies to simply hiding or running away. The idea was to avoid predatory beasts in any possible way. But as time went on, men grew wiser. For then, not only did man avoid being harmed by savage beasts, he discovered ways to profit from his natural ennemies; by learning to eat their flesh, to cloak himself with their skins, to create protective shields out of hides, even to use parts of the animals as medicinal treatment. Man became so dependent upon them, that if the animals were to become extinct man would also inevitably disappear, depending as he did for his existence on those very beasts that he had once so feared. Similarly says Plutarch, there are some men who content themselves with running away from their enemies. Others, much wiser, know how to utilize them and profit from them. The fact is, Plutarch continues, a smart enemy will only attack our faults and weaknesses. So that enemies can be real beneficial in so far as they oblige us to constantly be wary, to avoid drastic action or unprepared commitments. Enemies make us prudent.

Isn't this an enlightening way of stating it? Just as the enemy can invite prudence and, by the same token, moral regeneration, so too, logical contradiction can generate intellectual prudence in the examination of truth. Intelligence needs to fortify itself through opposition in order to grow to perfection. This is a sign of education and wisdom. As Montaigne writes:

> "Contradictory judgments neither offend nor distrub me; rather, they arouse and exercise me... When someone contradicts me, he arouses my attention, not my anger. I search for my contradictor, he who educates me" (*Essais*, "De l'art de conférer").

Another aspect of this benefit in prudence comes from the time factor related to contrast. Because of its inherent weakness, intelligence proceeds slowly. It cannot jump from principles to conclusion, from ends to means but must, for long periods of time, remain within the shaded boundaries of ignorance and half-truths. One could say, I imagine, that this is one point where similarities between inmate thinking and "child-like" logic are more of an obvious nature. Both are intellectually imprudent, inclined to precipitation, rapid and peremptory certitudes, equal only to their degree of ignorance of whatever question they are debating. Now it is only with time and through exercise in listening and examination of the other's position that prudence is developed. Value provides an opportunity to observe contrasts. By fostering the discussions of adverse opinions and positions, it brings one to realize that until he had actually studied all the aspects of a question, his point of view may have been not only weak, but — perhaps — false.

Rational negation then, is a constant prelude to rational affirmation. Practically, value as contrast will serve this function of rational development. Even if it shows up to be a "bad" value, reason will be able to give reasons for its inadmissibility. In short, value should encourage in the mind that looks at it with close attention, uneasiness and a certain anxiety, the beginnings of sound, intellectual prudence.

3. Values education gives meaning to all education

Although the role of value theory in education is a complex matter, this is not the time nor the place to present ours. For the purposes of this paper, it is assumed that the bipolarity principle can again serve our argument. And the argument is that values education is the ultimate aim of all education.

Though the Canadian Correctional Service has clearly stated the purposes of incarceration, its position on the aims of penitentiary education seems very confused. Great attention is paid to security problems, administrative planning, pedagogical testing or methodology and taxonomies of objectives. But there are some educators who hold jobs of influence in the system for whom talk about purpose appears boring and useless. This of course, should not come as a great surprise. Reflecting upon the aims or the goals of education is not a popular pastime even among professional educators. Nevertheless, whether one likes it or not, questions about aims neither disappear nor resolve themselves by simply being ignored, they are always just beneath the surface whenever important issues arise. For instance, if it is true that the purpose of education is self-realization or self-actualization, to borrow Maslow's expression, what is understood here is not so much the self one is as the self one ought to become. And it is while focusing on issues of this nature that great educationists such as John Dewey come to the conclusion that the "moral purpose is universal and dominant in all instruction — whatsoever the topic" (*Moral Principles in Education*). Now this is not to say that education is or ever should be moralistic. There is a world of difference between "moral ideas" and "ideas about morality". The purpose and task of education is to convert "ideas about morality" into "moral ideas".

What this means is that educational aims serve two functions; they give fundamental direction by stating highly desirable ideals and they provoke internal motivation by showing why these ideals are desirable for me. The etymological origins of the world already contain the essence of what we are trying to convey here. Education comes from *educo, are* which means, literally, to feed, to nourish. *Educat nutrix*; the nurse breast-feeds the baby. The child is given something of intrinsic value, which he does not possess but which will become part of him, of his total being. But education also comes from *educo, ere* which means to draw away from. *Educit obstetrix*; the mid-wife helps the baby come into the world. In this sense, the child is expected to be the principle agent of his being and becoming. The process of maturation starts within the living, creative energies of the living being — the child. From our point of view then, the aims of education are that someone become someone of quality or value by incorporating quality or value into his being. The more value an item has, the more being it has. Now man, as a human being, has numerous potentialities. The more education contributes to his actualizing these potentialities, the more a human being he will be. The more he realizes himself, the more he makes of himself, the more a valuable person he becomes. The measure of his value then is not in his doings or makings of things, not even in his contribution to society, but in his self-fulfillment or in the self-actualization of ideals.

Let us return momentarily to our bipolarity principle where it was shown how values represent, on the one hand, an objective pole of intrinsic worth, *per se*, and, on the other hand, how they need to be inculcated or activated in some incarnated way. The connotation is clear. Values are aims and the bipolarity principle proves it. Values do not originate from private experience or individual preference, that is, from biologically or psychologically endogenous sources. They are more than the product of native impulse; they are purposeful in themselves, in other words, worthy enough to be pursued as ends. Conversely, values cannot be equated to the objective striving for some permanent residence "outside" of the beholder. More awkwardly said, values are not known by being "known about". They must be felt internally. Thus, if education expects to teach the truth about value without teaching value itself, it is nonsense. Besides being purposeful, values need to be personal. In short, the objective pole of the bipolarity principle can be interpreted as the claim of the ideal and the subjective pole as the recognition of necessary internalization.

But this acknowledgement of basic, one could almost say "banal" verities, is not enough. It is one thing to say that education must have purposeful end-values; it is another to say what those end-values should be. How do we know value when we see it? How do we distinguish value from disvalue? Undoubtedly, if we were ardent disciples of St. Augustine, the answer would be simple. In his *De Magistro*, the famous philosopher writes that it is God Himself, while operating through human educators, who is the teacher of mankind, giving direct light on human values. But, of course, modern education operates on the theory that God does not ordinarily give this direct light. The question then remains; how are we to know the end-values of education?

Again, for the purposes of this paper I will limit myself to the following remarks; i- end-values must be clearly enunciated; ii- end-values must refer to ideal meaning.

i- End-values must be clearly enunciated

If it is true to say that fundamental values are not created but recognized, it is no less true to add that a minimum of effort is needed in order to articulate one's response. This is what we call naming or enunciating end-values.

Now the obstacles to this undertaking are considerable, both in number and importance. For one, we lost the habit of this sort of activity long ago. The kinds of questions that educators are worried about today have little to do with aims and ends and purposes that give meaning to educational practice; they are avowedly unphilosophical in scope and content, and relate more to managerial interests and preoccupations — taxonomies of objectives, for instance.

For another, the pretext of cultural pluralism presents strong resistance. Undoubtedly, one of the riches of our contemporary society has been to discover the value of variety *qua* variety and respect for difference. The great danger with such high standards of generosity, however, is the fear of indoctrination, that is, the apprehension that forceful and opinionated, publicly stated convictions can only be liberty-destroying impositions. So that in the realm of ends, our eductionists have often manifested unwarranted silence, timitidy and even scepticism.

For yet another, enunciating end-values means cultural and historical regression in the sense of suggesting that elitist aristocrats of the mind resort to antediluvian and dogmatic ways of imposing ideals of thinking, doing and being.

But we have to overcome these difficulties. First we must make clear what enunciating end-values is and is not. To be sure, enunciating end-values does not mean drawing up a sort of catalogue or shopping-list of value objects. Such a list would be nothing more than a series of high sounding words or vague generalities. Enunciating is meaningful only when the current connotation, the most profound meaning, the concrete implications of the value-words are made clear. Naming end-values is not, then, an exercise in rhetoric. It is the expression of the educational ideal itself. More so, it is the concrete incarnation of this same ideal. In short, it should be a way of developing the type of thinking that can express an educational ideal.

Enunciating end-values does not imply creating a totally new set of values without regard for the wisdom of the past, nor does it signify establishing any exhaustive and definitive philosophy of education. A never-ending task, it is an attempt to strike a balance between the comfortable old frames of reference and all that challenges these. To enunciate end-values is not so much to find or to claim to have found, as to continue seeking.

Naming end-values means trying to identify, not particular objects of desire, but rather the main currents and the central ideas which can inspire personal lives as well as collective educational aims. There is no question of pursuing the pipe-dream of a single value which would cover all aspirations or the totality of an educational project. It would be unrealistic and indeed too simple to cling to a single "super-value" such as tolerance, autonomy or justice. Real life requires a more extensive vocabulary, a closer and more detailed examination of man's needs for man is both a personal and social being of whom any one-dimensional portrait would be inadequate.

We cannot name end-values without having recourse to the tried and true words — freedom, love, beauty, truth, justice — which have perenially been used. But our aim should be to lay bare their meaning rather than to repeat them; we want to enable them to speak to us today; we want to explore their content. Must words be renewed? Perhaps. But the important thing is the reexamination of our ideas and of those essential questions which enable us to determine what the important human values are. Naming end-values is thus the exact opposite of making cut-and-dried intellectual judgments.

And who, precisely, should be doing this naming? All of us should be. The construction of the ideal man is a collective enterprise and responsibility. We cannot leave to any one particular group the entire task of deciding the ultimate values that should motivate education. People must therefore find the courage to speak out and state their values. Leadership must be exercised. Where people's daily lives are intimately tied up with an educational project, such a sharing of responsability is indispensable. Naming end-values implies the conscious participation of students, teachers, administrators.

ii- End-values must refer to ideal meaning

Fundamental end-values cannot and must not be infinite. Were they indefinitely numerous, end-values would lose their ideal element. The reason for this is simple: the world of ideal is the world of utopia, of metaphysical questioning, of ultimate meaning. Material wealth is value, so are good apparel, fast trains and straight highways. No sound axiology would ever consider them as ideal meanings for human growth. The realm of ideal meaning is the realm of knowledge without proof, the realm of absolute truth in absence of absolute knowledge. Thus, we can judge when end-values are fundamental by their claim for this place for ideal meaning. For "men live not of things", writes St-Exupery, "but of the meaning of things" (*Citadelle*). In the unfolding and uplifting of interior being through the "meaning of things" end-values imply at leas two things.

Firstly, their major task is to provide men with a sense of purpose or, if you will, with a philosophy of education that is never completely finished. On the one hand, this means developing the ability of individuals and their desire to think seriously, deeply and continuously about the purposes and consequences of what they do and ought to do. On the other hand, this means that end-values in education can never be proclaimed once and for all, in an absolute or abstract manner. They need to be ever present in the minds of students and educators alike, constantly recalled and reexamined in the light of everyday experience. For all practical purposes, the school must see them as prevalent over didactics, objectives, reports, notes, percentages, regulations and the like. They may seem boring and useless at times, unpractical and contradictory. Yet, without them, education is an overwhelming confusion of insignificance.

Secondly, end-values try to express what it is to be man. They are fundamental because they help him to be, when they "fit" man and come up to this essential concept "man". For some, this is understood as their justifying all of man's various and manifold activities; for whether man seeks to nourish and preserve his life, to prolong and perpetuate it in his descendants, to grow more conscious of it through science and art, or to give it roots in faith and love, the end still remains the mysterious unfolding and uplifting of his being and becoming. Said differently, end-values let it be known that to be man is to be more than just man. Man is more than the sum of his knowings and actings and doings, and being human surpasses human conscience and human consciousness. Proof of this lies in human ignorance itself. In the recognition of human limits, lies the intuition that existence is possible beyond these limits. End-values introduce and sustain questions about "being" beyond human limits, questions about ultimate meaning.

More important still, this kind of investigation does not have to be a sort of monastic meditation causing withdrawal from normal functioning. It can be, and must be, a very day-to-day thing within existing structures and behavior. Program content, for instance, no matter the "grade" level, can and should always serve as a path leading to end-values. Excellence, moral conscience, the will to truth respect for others, interior discipline, etc., are the values that should be the ultimate outcome of academic and vocational training — not learning grade 10 mathematics or welding. Of what good is any learning if the inner man feels no joy in moral goodness, in self-actualization, in respect for his fellow man, in the appreciation of a beautiful poem or painting? This is the kind of being that end-values promote. Anything less is not human growth but stagnation.

II — Implementing Values Education in the Prisons

Justifying theoretically the place of values education in the prison is one thing. Showing how it can be done is quite another. At this level of intervention, the difficulties no longer concern intellectual comprehension but the much more demanding affective participation and commitment of the whole person.

Here again, I must warn you that my general lack of experience in a prison setting particularly hinders me and obliges me to be prudent while examining this crucial practical aspect of the question. I will limit myself to the two following topics: 1) values education and formal education or training; 2) an institutional plan for values education.

1. Values education and formal education or training

We are refering here to activities pertaining especially to the penitentiary school and workshops, momentarily leaving aside the prison as a whole. Although the situation is extremely complex, it is not unrealistic to suggest that something, and something important, can be done within the present framework, that is, without having to upset or change the entire system. In this respect, there are at least two areas where immediate action could enhance the introduction of effective values education in the prisons: i- by forcefully declaring human growth as the major aim of penitentiary education and training; ii- by helping teachers see themselves as philanthropists.

i- Human growth as the major aim of education and training

A quick look at the expectations of education and training in the prisons produces stunning revelations: for some, education and training are poorly conceived as cheap and effective means of keeping inmates occupied and under close surveillance — "killing time" is a well-known expression. Others see in education and training a therapeutic method of rehabilitating sick individuals — crime is seen as an illness, the causes of which can be identified and remedied. For others, education and training are considered as the indispensable preparation to employment "outside" — it is assumed that to function in society one needs to know a trade or have a high school diploma, or both.

This hasty resumé does not do justice to the arguments presented above. Nevertheless, it is not unfair to say that each one of them falls short of a sound, defensible philosophy of education for none of them actually desires to educate, that is, to foster the promotion of human development through respect for human dignity. Now in my mind, there is absolutely nothing one can do or plan to do in a prison that is of much worth until the principle of the inmate's human dignity receives profound attention and religious respect. Values education starts not with the changing of the guards, or with the better meals served in the cafeteria or with production or social-ization or whatever. It is rooted in the basic assumption that no matter who he is, what he's done, where he comes from, what religion he practices, what his political beliefs are, what the color of his skin is, the inmate is a person whose dignity is intrinsic to his being. "So act as to treat humanity, enjoins Immanuel Kant, whether in thine own person or that of another, in every case as an end withal, never as a means only" (*Metaphysics of Morals*). There is no hope for and no use in hoping for any form of decent education if the principle of human dignity is not clearly stated at the outset.

My second contention follows directly from the first. It is that human growth can only mean the promotion of the inner man. Not intellectual man as learner, not practical man as doer but inner man as total being-becoming person. Who cares whether an inmate learns his ABC's or a welding trade if the occasion is never given him to discover his inner self and worth as a person? Who cares if an inmate obtains a high school diploma or even a college degree if he is not introduced to the meaning of human culture and civilization? For the deepest need of the inner man is to feel himself a benefactor of manking and only as he identifies himself with the most sublime interests of humanity does he find thoroughly, complete self-actualization. Even when social harmony is desired (as is clearly the case when rehabilitation is aimed at), let us not forget that the qualities that make for a good man come before those that make for a good citizen. All men who have attained a high degree of order and justice and peace will tend to produce, in their social relations, outer order and justice and peace. Self-cultivation is the root, social harmony the fruit. To be sound, a person must begin with himself and progress towards self-fulfillment. He must become a valuable man before becoming a social man.

Finally, human growth means aiming to achieve the mental, physical and moral integration of the individual: a quality of being, ordered, unified and integrated, which is peculiar to an integrated personality. If there is one thing that must stand out prominently here, it is that the development of integrated man is a process of self-actualization, self-education. No man can cause inner growth in another. No mere reading of books, no passive listening to lectures, no indifferent production in workshops will achieve it and no discourse in absolute truth or goodness will effect it. The interior development of being and growing and becoming is a process of the most intense, concentrated and energetic self-activity, requiring the united and cooperative effort of all the powers of the individual. Practically, having lofty goals is not sufficient: one must also be extremely demanding of the inmate, requiring of him, so to speak, interior striving and commitment.

ii- Teachers as philanthropists

After positing human growth, the second most important element in the process of implementing values education in a prison is developing the quality of the teachers. In this particular situation (the argument would be similar if the context involved small children, mentally retarded or handicapped individuals) the primal quality expected of the teacher is a moral quality. By "moral quality", let us understand, not pedagogical skills nor specialization in subject matter. The latter are essential but, alone, of little use. And that is because the teacher must be first and foremost an educator of men — not of learners and doers — a promoter of human vision and hope. Literally, he is a philanthropist (*philein*, to love, *anthropos*, man) a lover of mankind, a professor of humanity. And values education has little future in any setting if the teacher, as indispensable artisan, has little belief in the high values that make man a superior, spiritual being. How does this teacher-philanthropist operate?

First, let us state briefly what he isn't. For sure, he is not a galloping, short-winded, short-sighted activist, puffing away at multi-directional doings, undoings are redoings. Beyond caricature, he is not bent on wasting all his energies on method or technical gadgetry or immediate skill.

"For immediate skill", as John Dewey writes, "may be got at the cost of the power to keep on growing. The teacher who leaves the professional school with power in managing a class of children may appear to superior advantage the first day, the first week, the first month or even the first year. But later "progress" with such may consist only in perfecting and refining skills already possessed. Such persons seem to know how to teach, but they are not students of teaching" (*The Relation of Theory to Practice in Education*).

So that, for the teacher-philanthropist, "the power to keep on growing" refers less to exterior display than to continual interior acquisition and advancement. The teacher-philanthropist is an unfinished man who shares with his students his human efforts for human perfection.

Second, the teacher-philanthropist is willing and capable of carrying his student inmates, through the use of any subject matter, to fundamental depths of questioning and interrogation. Not every man needs to learn how to weld or how to use a typewriter. But it is every man's job to learn his job of being man. In this respect, the teacher-philanthropist has to show the way. To illustrate, he is capable of making it understood that between him and the inmate there is the same kind of mysterious, almost mystical relationship as between man and his world. For between man and his world there is more than face to face observation. To borrow Levi-Strauss' expression, "there is much more in the exchange than what is exchanged" (*Les structures élémentaires de la parenté*). This "much more" is precisely the order of meaning, of ultimate significance, the order of spiritual attributions that give reasons for being and becoming. The teacher-philanthropist unglues inmates from their egocentric problems and conveys them to the unpolluted atmospheres of significant and meaningful resolutions. This is not rhetoric or metaphysics: this is being profoundly a questioning human being. Properly speaking, the teacher-philanthropist is not an answering machine but an educator with meaningful answers; more specifically, a teacher of meaningful questioning.

Third, if the teacher-philanthropist presupposes encounters of spirits before confrontation of minds, he is, more basically, a dialogist with his own inner conscience. The relationship of one with another rests upon the internal maturation of the relationship between the self and the self. The progressive elucidation of his secret motivations is part of the essence and the quality of the philanthropist's philosophy of man and, concomitantly, of the meaning he attributes to educational practice. In short, the teacher-philanthropist is not an unconscious amateur of human affairs. It is assumed of him that he has confronted the obstacles and overcome the barriers of the *gnoti seoton*, the know thyself, before he can even think of leading others on the same path. He knows that the idea which man shapes of himself, justifies his existence, gives meaning to his everyday living and determines, in large measure, his human conduct. The teacher-philanthropist has registered this truth not only in his pedagogical vision but, initially, in his heart and conscience.

Fourth, the teacher-philanthropist does not consider himself primarily as a teaching specialist. Of course, if he has to teach grade 12 mathematics or grade 10 history, it is expected that he will know, and know well, his subject matter and all related questions, but most important, he must understand the deeper needs and wants and interests of his student inmates and be able to answer to these. Now, this range of qualities is not the fruit of specialization. It belongs to a world called culture or liberal education or the humanities. The teacher-philanthropist has standing and class on all important issues pertaining to man, be they philosophical, political, aesthetical, ethical, anthropological, etc. His only true specialization, we might say, is man himself.

Finally, the techer-philanthropist knows that he needs to know these things. He knows that he needs more than knowledge of subject matter and methodology. He knows that he needs to know about knowledge and the ramifications of subjects to life in general and to the meaning of life in particular. He knows that he needs insights into the purpose of teaching and learning and being. He knows that he needs to understand the kinds of questions that his teaching will raise and to have some sense of where to turn for further understanding. In his soul, he knows that he has to be a philanthropist.

2. An institutional plan for values education

The idea behind this last commentary is to explore how, not only formal education or vocational training, but each penal institution, as a whole, can participate in values education. For this, I wish to submit the concept of a values education plan in each institution.

First, the term of plan is preferred to the term "program" which is more commonly equated to schooling and school subjects. Now values are simply not the exclusive province of particular subject matters or particular teachers. Values such as autonomy, beauty, respect for others, moral conscience are the concern of everyone. Furthermore, values education is a compelling force calling on and involving all the powers of the individual — his feelings, his passions, his emotions, his imagination. It does not fall principally within the sole domain of formal education or vocational training. Finally, if values education underscores the ultimate aim of human development, it has to be a collective concern. A values education plan will meet this demand by involving the participation of the entire institution.

Second, what would be the major characteristics of this institutional plan? As defined in the dictionary, a plan is a "detailed project, comprising an ordered series of operations directed to a particular end". A "detailed project" because action supposes clear orientation. But more importantly because the project would be expected to become the central focus, the pivotal axis of penitentiary life in the institution. This has already been noted with theater at Matsqui Institution and with the Olympiad at Collins Bay. These projects became so pregnant with value connotations and meanings that they monopolized and polarized the total energies of the institution for weeks, even months. The same would happen with a music project or with handicapped children, I am sure. It could be yet another idea. I am thinking of some form of yearly publication prepared by volunteer inmates and, why not, by volunteer security people and teachers and administrators and clerical personnel. Call the project *Issues*, for lack of a better name. Simply stated, it would consist in identifying a number of major issues — political, educational, ecological, religious, cultural, social, international, economical, etc. and having interested inmates express their views. Imagine all the stimulating possibilities involved. They are almost limitless, from collecting information — reading, research, visiting lecturers, setting up seminars, discussion panels and debates — to personal critical analysis of one's chosen topic. Now, there are scores of ideas germinating in my mind at the present — and in yours, I am sure — on ways that could be developed to exploit an Issues project. But we need go no further. I think I have made my point. Besides being a detailed project with high value content, such a plan would specify strategies for promoting specific tasks and sharing particular responsibilities. Since the idea would also touch the whole life of the institution and the responsibilities of all personnel, common strategies could also be invented which would foster and facilitate the multi-disciplinary approach. In this way, the plan would become an important source of cohesion in the development of values education for the entire institution. The director, especially, should be a man of great intelligence, culture and energy. The main tasks of this committee would be: to suggest or receive projects, submit guide-lines and ideas for their development, arouse interest and promote the participation of everyone, follow the project through to completion.

Finally, the institutional plan would have to be at the center of the institution's preoccupations. The center is both a point of convergence and a point from which things diverge; we can think of it in terms of both centripetal and centrifugal forces. An institutional plan would therefore have the true power to attract and be a place for revitalization. Now it could only attract everyone and help everyone if it had undeniable intrinsic worth. In other words, it would not be enough to arouse brief interest in a project or initiative with little promise. Those involved would have to be permanently drawn by a force capable of uniting them around a common idea and of providing inspiration for their work. An institutional plan must not be a gimmick. It must have solid content. After all, what is at stake is human life.

11. SOME THEORETICAL ASPECTS OF CORRECTIONAL EDUCATION

T.A.A. Parlett

I have read the papers presented by Dr. Morin and Dr. Duguid *
with a great deal of interest and I cannot but agree with the
sentiments expressed therein. However, I have some difficulty in
accepting either paper from the point of view of the expression of a
theoretical basis. I have difficulty in accepting the definitions of
morality given by both writers when they assume that the prisoner,
because he is in his present plight, is necessarily not fully morally
developed. That is to say that they have not differentiated between
the two sorts of evil — those which are termed a matter of *mala in
proprium*, and *mala in se*. Such an exercise may have shown that the
prisoner is not more immoral, amoral or less moral than others from
his social class who are not prisoners. Perhaps such an elucidation
would be of little worth, perhaps it does not alter the case. Perhaps I
am asking for a return to the criminal causation model and perhaps I
am hair-splitting. Whatever the case, I feel that the basis of a sound,
empirically based, judgement should be factual in nature. As it is, I
feel that both of the papers are presenting to me that same case which
I presented to myself some dozen years ago and out of which the
Matsqui project evolved.

If I may pray your indulgence, I would go back in time some
twelve to fifteen years before values education, the remediation of
retarded moral development, and so on, struck me as arguments for
the expansion of education in prisons to the University level and of
the necessity for a hidden agenda which in some way would effect

*Paper presented to the Learned Societies Conference: Canadian Research
Association Symposium on Education as a Cultural Alternative for Prisoners and
Delinquents, Saskatoon, Saskatchewan, June, 1979.*

changes in the underlying mental structure of the prisoner and in that way modify his behaviour so that he would no longer return to prison.

In taking a body of inmates in a school in a minimum security Institution and teaching all of them three subjects at the Grade Thirteen level regardless of the educational level attained before-hand, (English Literature, English Composition, World History), I discovered many of the same characteristics which Dr. Duguid has spoken of in his paper. I would point out that in this particular case I had also to deal with the deficiencies in the whole educational background of my students and this was done with the aid of rather extensive programmed instruction.

Now, at that time I was not of the opinion that the higher level education which I was offering would moralize the prisoners. The Grade Thirteen subjects were being offered on my own rather immoral assumption that it is of more commercial benefit to an inmate applying for work to be able to say and to be able to present a document which set out that he had failed Grade Thirteen rather than proof that he had passed Grade Six or Seven or so on. I was rather shocked to find that most passed rather than failed. However, I did not attribute the changes observed in behaviours as a result of the Grade Thirteen exercise, but rather as a result of the massive programmed instruction which has given them the skills to even deal with the Grade Thirteen material.

It is well to recall that at the time of which I am speaking, the medical model was the one which was most frequently used in discussing criminality and the results of various treatments on the prisoner. It was pre-eminently the era of the treatment model. It is quite understandable, then, that I attempted to subsume the changes which I saw and the changes which Dr. Duguid reports as changes in underlying personality constructs.

The first attempts then, to clarify in terms of theoretical models, the results of correctional education at a high level was in terms of changes in personality as measured by Cattell's 16 P.F. Inventory, despite the recommendation of Cattell that the instrument was not to be used with criminals. It is of no little interest to observe that the changes which were postulated in that early research did occur. It was hypothesized that criminals would show deviations from the norm on Factors C, E, G, I O Q 3 and Q4, and that the results of exposing the prisoners to rather massive upgrading through programmed instruction would be to change these factors to a more pro-social personality level. The data derived is given below:

TABLE 1
Analysis of Covariance on 16 P.F. for Four Groups

Factors	1 pre post	2 pre post	3 pre post	4 pre post	F	P
C	4.6 6.1	4.3 4.4	4.0 3.6	3.7 3.6	6.02	.002
G	3.5 5.0	5.0 3.6	3.5 3.9	3.5 3.8	3.82	.02
O	6.8 4.6	7.1 6.7	7.3 6.2	6.0 5.7	4.65	.01
Q3	5.1 6.5	5.7 4.4	5.1 5.0	4.9 5.5	3.52	.05
Q4	5.5 4.4	6.5 6.5	7.0 7.1	6.1 6.2	3.83	.02

Means for Groups

(Data from Parlett and Ayers, *Canadian Journal of Corrections and Criminology*, April 1972)

In the above table the educational group is number one and further analysis of the data reveals that the significant differences all stem from group changes.

In this same research, an interest in the cognitive style of prisoners was pursued. It was presumed, and has been found to be true on a number of occasions, that prisoners fall within the global end of the spectrum on the Hidden Figures Test. A number of speculations have been made on this matter which will be dealt with later.

It was presumed, and admittedly on a rather sketchy basis, that education would modify the cognitive style towards the more analytical end of the spectrum. The researchers involved in this project have never really been able to grasp the mechanics of what happens to the cognitive style of prisoners during an educational process, and it has thus remained a peripheral area of interest to them. So much has this been so that we have only used one form of the test for both pre and post measurement. This allows for memory to increase the scores somewhat. The data derived from the same groups mentioned above is given below.

We will deal with this matter of personality factors and hidden figure scores later in the paper but I might say that an area of concern to us and one which we do not appear to be able to control is the question of whether the changes attained are an artifice in that the educated inmates have had more time spent on them and more humane treatment and as a response they take more care in answering questionnaires and tests. That is to say that the changes which we perceive in inmates may only be a change in perseverance at tests. Stated another way, the attitude change may only be towards compliance stemming from liking.

This, of course, is the core difficulty we encounter when we deal with the aspects of behaviour of which Dr. Duguid speaks. Is he speaking of an actual moral development, or is he rather observing facets of compliance or at best identification? Does he, indeed, have internalization of moral structures and if so, can it be demonstrated?

As may be observed, these early postulations on the effect of correctional education were naive and probably ill formulated. This matter was brought to my attention by my friend and mentor, Dr. Doug Ayers, from whom you have already heard. Perhaps his most telling comment was that I had not demonstrated that the programmed instruction was instrumental in the changes which I had delineated and that, further, I had not dealt with the fact that any changes which did occur were not functions of the teacher and the teacher's style. It was further brought to my attention that what may very well have happened was that some cognitive deficiencies, particularly in the area of moral development, may have been touched.

TABLE 2
Analysis of Covariance — Hidden Figures Test

	1 pre post	2 pre post	3 pre post	4 pre post
X	14.6 21.1	11.7 13.1	7.6 7.9	9.1 12.4
s.d	8.4 9.7	7.9 8.5	6.5 5.5	7.5 7.6
AdjX	18.13	12.48	10.77	14.07

Adjusted $F = 5.053$ p .005

This, of course, was the commencement of the Donner project. The project being of a multi-disciplinary nature led to the inspection of models of which I had before been ignorant. Not only did the matter of cognitive retardation open up in so far as moral development, but the area of attitudes, and attitude change and the concept of morality as being a concatenation of attitude structures. There were also areas of peripheral interest yet remaining. Personality, cognitive style, subjective probabilities and so on, each of which positions had to be looked at, and to be kept or discarded as proven or disproven.

As always is the case, many of the factors were neither proven nor disproven for a variety of reasons. Theoretical positions had to be discarded because there was no evidence that the prisoner subjects differed from the norm in any way. Such was the case with Eysenck's much touted claims on the personality of criminals and the measurement of those personality variants as measured by the Eysenck Personality Inventory and the Eysenck Extraversion, Neuroticism, psychopathy scale. We found no evidence at all for any variation from the norm in the case of prisoners when we used these tests. In fact, the mean scores which we derived were the same as the mean scores reported by Eysenck for North American College students.

We had some difficulty in obtaining figures which matched the reported data for Attitudes to Law, Courts and Police and Morality scores reported for Canadian prisoners by Reckless and others. Particularly, we found no significant differences between Canadian prisoners and Canadian policemen in the morality scores attained on the Crissman scale.

Unlike the previous experiment, we were unable to demonstrate that the educational programme made any significant changes in the scores obtained on the dimensions of Cattell's 16 P.F. which had been of such interest in our earlier work. The differences between the first and second attempt with this instument probably indicate that the matter of educational programmes making a difference in certain constructs should be re-examined using a different test than 16 P.F. in view of the fact that the test's author has recommended that it not be used with criminals.

Once again in this study the quite important matter of cognitive style emerged as quite interesting in light of our earlier findings. The data is given below.

In this matter it can be seen that as we used the same test at both pre and post testing some learning occurred for both groups and accounts for a proportion of the gain scores in both cases. The gain score for the experimental group as much higher leads us into some speculation as to the reasons for such a gain.

There appears to be no *prima facie* case for expecting the course offering English, History, Psychology and Sociology to bring about such changes. One would make easily believe that the program was responsible for the changes if we had been offering geometry or mathematics or some subject which would allow us to say that we

TABLE 3
Pre-Test / Post-Test Means, Standard Deviations and
Univariate Analysis-Hidden Figures Test

Experimental Group			Control Group			P
N	$\overline{X}$	s.d	N	$\overline{X}$	s.d	
		Pre-Test				
17	8.94		19	7.27	6.41	.73
		Post-Test				
14	25.56	6.48	10	16.90	9.53	.01

had taught analytic skills. The task is much harder if we take the subjects which were in fact taught.

There is a further possible explanation for the high gain scores in the case of the experimental group. One could propose that because we had given so much time and had been so close to the subjects, they responded in kind and paid more attention to our tests and tried harder to please us, for as well as being a test which is presumed to measure an aspect of personality, this is also a test which requires effort and patience. This whole matter of cognitive style is one that needs further attention, both in terms of how it occurs, why it occurs and what it means if it can be shown to occur. Does it, indeed, show that significant changes in this test are indicative of significant changes in thinking patterns? One thing that we do know from our previous studies on the subject is that embezzlers return perfect scores after spending only a third of the allotted time for the test. We have further found that the "big con" criminal also does better than the general inmate, intelligence as measured by the standard tests held constant.

The results of the Crissman tests left us a little disappointed both in the fact that the pre-test did not differentiate our population from normal subjects and in the lack of significant difference at post test. At the end of the experiment, however, we became aware of the Defining Issues Test (a form of the Kohlberg Dilemma Problems Test). It seemed reasonable to us to suppose that if we took a sample of the inmates who had completed the prescribed course of studies and compared their scores with a group of inmates who had volunteered to enter a following course, that we should have some basis for comparison of before and after situations.

Additionally, we thought that it would be a fair and revealing operation to take two dissimilar groups and compare them also to the two groups of prison inmates we had available to us. The two groups we used were a group of armed services Warrant Officers from Her Majesty's Forces undergoing training at H.M.C.S. Naden in Esquimalt and a group of school teachers involved in an educational philosophy course at the University of Victoria.

The results of the comparison are given below:

Analysis of Variance, Morality on Rests Defining Issues Tests, Educated Prisoners, Uneducated Prisoners, Armed Forces Men, Teachers (M and F)

SOURCE	SS	DF	MS	F	P
Total	428.664	182	—	—	—
Between	63.052	3	21,107.3	10.28	.001
Within	365.632	179	2,042	—	—

Scheffe Comparisons of Means, Educated Prisoners Uneducated Prisoners, Armed Forces Men, Teachers (M and F) on Rest's D.I.T.

Comparison	F	P
Educated Con vs Uneducated Con	14.35	.01
Educated Con vs Armed Forces	23.01	.01
Educated Con vs Teachers	.38	—
Uneducated Con vs Armed Forces	3.31	—
Uneducated Con vs Teachers	9.99	.05
Armed Forces vs Teachers	10.14	.01

An interpretation that may be derived from this is that if Rest's Defining Issues Test does measure Moral Development, then the educated prisoners are more morally developed than all groups except the teachers. Further, one may see that the uneducated prisoners are more morally developed than all groups except the teachers. Further, one may see that the uneducated convicts are more morally developed than the armed forces personnel.

One may rationalise this by saying that the nature of the training of a Warrant Officer or, indeed, any member of the Armed Forces, is such that heteronomy is induced in that the soldier must do without question that which he is told on the basis of reward and punishment. The inference being that the training of a soldier is such that a moral regression must take place. The writer would not care, however, to make this statement aloud in the Sargeants Mess late on a Saturday night, even in mixed company.

Attitude Measures

As others have found before us, the measurement of a wide range of attitudes was found to be a difficult task, although one member of the interdisciplinary group (Hoppe, University of Victoria) attained some very interesting results on the Rokeach instrument. The writer finally (and one might say, almost in desperation) constructed a number of Semantic Differential Scales which produced some results which may be of interest to others who wish to duplicate some of our findings.

The writer, however, was content to assume that the scores on the defining issues test were indicative of at least expressed attitudes.

In addition to the measured responses, we also had similar subjective feelings about the inmates as Dr. Duguid has reported in his paper. They indeed did seem to have changed; they were more reflective and spoke about their changed perceptions. They, in fact, at that time, in a Maximum Security Institution, the very harshest surroundings, made similar subjective responses to those which Dr. Ayers has witnessed and reported from the alternative community of which Dr. Duguid speaks.

If what I have said is true and that moreover the only criteria we use is the clinical analysis of responses and that those responses are similar in both a Medium Security Institution with the best possible facilities which can be obtained in a prison setting and with the alternate community, and in a Maximum Security Institution with minimal conditions and after only six months of a very limited offering, it may not be demonstrated that an extensive foray into University Training up to graduation level gives any more than an initial small treatment program. Can it not be demonstrated that the changes take place in the first few months and continue without any further interaction and without the alternate community?

Herein lies my criticism of the lack of what I would refer to as empirical evidence in both the paper delivered by Dr. Morin and the paper by Dr. Duguid. It is not in my opinion sufficient, although it may very well be necessary to put forward a philosophical position without supporting it with a theoretical rationale which informs in some way, however meagre, what the curriculum taught should look like and what methods of presentation are best suited to attain the results desired.

In the multi-disciplinary research discussed earlier, which was carried out under the auspices of the Donner Foundation, there was a clear understanding of why we taught what we did and the way in which we taught it. Attitude change theory dictated that the source of attitude change must be prestigious and it was for this reason that a University was used. There is no evidence, however, that attitude change cannot be attained by a Penitentiary staff teacher, teaching at a lower level than University courses.

We further proposed that the material presented must start off at a primitive level; i.e. that it should deal with the literature and the history of the Ancient World because the subjects with whom we deal are at that level of development and that it is necessary to come gradually to the intricacies of modern literature and modern history which reflect the social conditions with which our subjects have had difficulty in dealing. This is a postulate derived directly from the work of Sherif and Hovland's Contrast and Assimilation Theory, which, as you will recall, states (if one may encapsulate such a profound theory in a few words) that in order to get assimilation, the point of attack must be at the point at which the subject is, and that departing from that point or close to it will make change more difficult.

Intuitively, and in response to some of the statements that the students have made, Dr. Duguid has come to the conclusion recently that modern history is not the subject to teach in the prison, for the prisoners tend to admire the least desirable models. An inspection of the Theory of Change would have revealed that truth to him at an earlier date than did intuition and the analysis of subjective responses. It might be said that an analysis of certain responses to a quite simple paper and pencil test might reveal with a fair degree of accuracy the areas which should and should not be pursued.

I do not disagree with Dr. Duguid in stating that the alternate community is of great value, but I would not accept that it is necessarily of great value because it is a part of a University program. It is highly likely that if we separate out the Carpentry Shop and imbue the members with a sense of *krugovaya poruka* (group solidarity in the Soviet manner) we will get very similar results. The initial research stated that such a process of separation should occur, not on the basis of Bem's Hypothesis of Self Perception. Indeed, there is sufficient research to indicate that propinquity and some level of isolation will bring about the goals which the manipulative experimenter wishes to attain.

I do not wish to attack the program which Dr. Duguid directs in any way. It is an excellent program and it seems to me that it produces all the responses that Dr. Duguid speaks of and more, of which, I suggest, he is unaware.

I make a special pleading, however, for a more scientific approach to the matter at hand, a matching of what theory has found with what he presumes to have found. I even make some small plea for some numerical, statistical data to substantiate what is happening or what appears to be happening.

Speculation, subjective data, and so on, may very well lead us into following the excellent fopperies of our age: Belief in Pyramid Power, Astrology, the Tarot pack, the Bermuda Triangle, Mind Power, and so on. Like Hamlet, I would have evidence more relevant than "*seems*".

I will close by quoting a short excerpt from one of William Thompson's (Lord Kelvin) remarks from one of his popular lectures of 1891:

> "When you can measure what you are speaking about, and express it in numbers, you know something about it; but when you can not measure it, when you cannot express it in numbers, your knowledge is of a meagre and unsatisfactory kind: it may be the beginning of knowledge, but you have scarcely, in your thoughts, advanced to the state of science."

NOTE

* See articles 9 and 10.

12. CORRECTIONAL EDUCATION AS PRACTICE OF THE JUDICIAL APPROACH: A CONTRADICTION

Lucien Morin

"Ye have heard that it hath been said, An eye for an eye, and a tooth for a tooth: But I say unto you, That ye resist not evil: but whosoever shall smite thee on thy right cheek, turn to him the other also. And if any man will sue thee at the law, and take away thy coat, let him have thy cloke also."
(Matthew 5, 38-40)

"Ye have heard that it hath been said, Thou shalt love thy neighbour, and hate thine enemy. But I say unto you, Love your enemies, bless them that curse you, do good to them that hate you, and pray for them which despitefully use you, and persecute you; That ye may be the children of your Father which is in heaven: for he maketh his sun to rise on the evil and on the good, and sendeth rain on the just and on the unjust."
(Matthew 5, 43-45).

Paper presented to the World Congress in Education: Values and the School; Symposium on Prison Education, Université du Québec à Trois-Rivières, July, 1981.

1. To introduce

The history of our prisons is sufficiently littered with projects for reform based on utopian dreams. To place a new candle of the same nature on a cake already well decorated with potential solutions would serve in no way to resolve the enormous problematics which the penitentiary system represents. While it is important to push back the boundaries of the unknown, the essential need now is for doors to be opened to new possibilities. This approach will perhaps produce results less rich in analytical decantations, and limited too in terms of exhaustiveness and "definitiveness". Yet it will have the virtue of suggesting concrete possibilities, of pointing the way to horizons where effective action seems within reach. To achieve this end, we must refuse to admit that all truths are equal and that all possibilities are solutions. The solutions which emerge from our analysis of the penitentiary system will thus attempt — a colossal task, but one as aware of its limitations as it is of its aim — to put meaning into a universe which has long been abandoned to the ravages of the meaningless and, even more important, to offer hope which is both realistic and realisable.

"Why educate in prison?" This, very clearly, is the question which summarizes our project. It has served as a stimulus and polarization for all our thinking and questioning. It is by clarifying this question that we shall come to grips not only with its scope and extent but also with the obstacles, the complexity of the relationships, the theoretical and methodological demands which it entails.

Our inquiry, modest as it is, does not entirely escape the problem of where to begin, at least to the extent that it implies a certain determination, a certain approximate definition of its objective.

Now, and herein lies the astonishing singularity of our problem, the suppositions and presuppositions behind the question "why educate in prison?" have always been just that: suppositions, unexplained and unanswered. Otherwise, why this lively, concerned, radical questioning in 1981 of the reason for education in the prison environment? Why, after two or three centuries of attempted reform beating constantly and with almost predictable regularity against the walls of penal thought, why, especially, given a certain institutional educational practice — rarely displaced by these same projects for reform — why have these efforts never succeeded in winning education an official position, a recognized rank in the vast array of preventive and curative measures? How is that, on the nature, place, role and scope of education in prison, no position has ever been taken other than a timid suggestion of progress, soon absorbed and swallowed up by the banal ideologies which justify usage?

All these considerations suffice to explain the enormous and very eloquent silence surrounding our question. Yet many other reflections could be added to accentuate the difficulty which marks our point of departure. For example, we might investigate teaching strategies as subversive strategies for the training and discipline, classification and arrangement of so-called dangerous and marginal individuals, for the control and supervision, then, of those "naturally" lacking in one virtue or another. We might examine in depth the meaning of the double trilogy of "work-morality-education" and "work-economics-education", to learn the reasons which have helped to prevent an intelligent understanding of the educational function *in* prison which is more than an expanded concept of the educational function *by* prison. We might take a look at the lack of elevation in the arguments apparently in favour of penitentiary education or, inversely, the lack of seriousness in many of the negative positions. We might also wonder at the almost total absence of studies on this question in this, the twentieth century.[1]

But the essential point of this introductory analysis is not, however, to exhaust the problem through the etiology of what we do not know about it. For us, the question of why to educate takes precedence not only over that of how but over that of its "preferability" to all the other so-called "rehabilitative" activities. Naturally, it would be possible, and some might even say desirable, to base our study on an analysis of educational practice in prison, as exemplified in the work of Michel Foucault. For various reasons, we cannot limit ourselves to this approach.

On the one hand, the question of penitentiary education, at least as an historical fact, does not appear to fall into the same category of significance as the history of prisons and hence does not lend itself to analytic isolation or to comparable treatment. The history of prisons is an integral part of the history of civilization. The memory of human justice, of its development and its many profiles, its aspirations and its shames, its oscillations and its adjustments, its penalties and its punishments, is a remembrance and a reminder of the fact that respect for human dignity is born of uneven proportions of love and hate. Prison history constitutes one kind of particular account of this birth. Penitentiary education, on the other hand, has served rather to illustrate *one* of the modes of articulation and execution of the penal system. It has never been taken seriously, by which we mean as a non-etiological vision of the human being or as a non-utilitarian and non-rehabilitative view of deviance or criminality. Even today, penitentiary education is seen as a way of operating the prison, as one of the many tools of incarcerational technology. While its institutional presence is more than sporadic, its traces, in terms of effectiveness, are sediments with no evident persistence in the stratum of the various serious attempts at reform, moments of no lasting impact in the confusion of the heterogeneous and discontinuous efforts at change. As a result, any attempt to speak of the practice of penitentiary education amounts, in fact, to speaking of incarcerational practice, quite simply. And any attempt to analyse education in the prison environment as an isolated phenomenon leads inevitably to failure, to the identification of a work in dissolution and infinite dislocation. This explains the barrenness of data on the history and the significance of education in prison. It is also what defines the inner circumference of the demands imposed by our project.

On the other hand, penitentiary education is not simply part of a whole, the substructure of a much wider and more general reality; penitentiary education can only be explained, can only be understood, can only be justified in, by and through the complex area within which it exists. More specifically, a clear idea of the judicial system and of its corollary, the penal system, not only as symbols but as actual functions of a society, appears absolutely essential to an understanding of education in the prison environment. It is because they have not understood this requirement that many modern theories become lost in a maze of trivialities and repeated frustrations. We hasten to reassure the reader! We are fully aware of the pitfalls and enormous demands of such a project. We know that penal justice is not born in prison, any more than psychiatry is born in the asylum. We know too that the basic core of the philosophy of penitentiary education arises elsewhere, is rooted in a philosophy of general education, by which we mean a concept of man, God, nature, society, learning, etc. It would be madness to try to deal with these enormous questions. On the other hand, our analysis has led us to evidence of the vital necessity of examining these questions in their interdependence, and has convinced us that the dissatisfaction and contemporary epistemological failures in this field are due almost entirely to a misinterpretation or unawareness of this interconnection.

Obviously, given the complexity of our problematics, no one

would attempt an exhaustive treatment of all its aspects. It is the definition of the essential, in fact, which weighs upon us here. As Lucien Goldman observes in his introduction to *Dieu caché*, some minimum level of erudition seems essential to any serious work of philosophy, or, perhaps more accurately, analysis. However, no one has sufficient mastery of his subject to dare say how far the knowledge of his own lack of knowledge meets this terrible require- ment. The even greater risk of having to brave the suspicion of the fashionable forms of knowledge, the knowledges in power. The arrival of a new form of knowledge always represents a certain threat, that of overthrowing, to use Valéry's expression, the estab- lished "politique de l'esprit", the policy of the mind. Substituting one idea for another is called education. Substituting one idea for another established idea is called revolution.

Because the prisons are, after all, better prepared to deal with revolts than with revolutions, our effort to develop a synthesis has been a modest one — a rough draft, a sketch which will require continual improvement. Yet the effort is marked by a feeling of openness, a feeling which, it must be admitted, flows less from the meritorious virtue of courage than from innocence. We shall make no attempt to hide, for example, what we believe to be one of the most valuable discoveries of this study: a political, or moral, or criminological, or psychoanalytical interpretation of the peniten- tiary problem is not a sufficient or adequate interpretation. It merely emphasizes, in its progress from one speculative disaster to the next, its inability to offer any real explanation of a complex and still unanswered question. Too much time has been spent in the habit of seeing in narrations of the genesis and morphology of our insti- tutions, in etiological descriptions of the criminogenic or in prescriptions of curative therapies, their symbolic and "representa- tive" nature. As a result, the prison universe, so vast as to be almost beyond comprehension, has experienced the passage in recent years of a nameless plethora of theoretic meteors, with infinite variations and unlimited, interchangeable aims. Result: the mystery of the penitentiary has remained almost intact.

Given these conditions, instead of criticizing the scientific inade- quacies currently fashionable in the analysis of the penitentiary environment, it is essential that we act positively. To do so, we have borrowed our method of analysis from an hypothesis skillfully developed and brilliantly implemented in the area of fundamental anthropology by René Girard.[2]

It is now for us to judge its effectiveness in answering our initial question.

2. To understand

> "Why should we hate one another within the same camp? None of us has a monopoly on purity of intention."
> St-Exupéry,
> *Lettre à un otage*.

It is true for science as it is for justice: the courage to affirm implies the courage to denounce. But how to describe the delicacy which must mark the progress of the intelligence that assumes the responsibility for dealing with the error of another mind? What intellectual diplomacy will succeed in showing that the promises of penitentiary education rise up continuously like some enormous Nietzschean deception, "the illusion of a prophecy biting its own tail"? This is the first challenge facing our study: to say only what is, and, in so doing, to denounce its failings. Immediately, this means recognizing that the mind which "knows" the judicial system, the penal system, and, particularly, penitentiary education is first and foremost a rectifying mind. For an accurate reading of the present situation in the penitentiary environment leads to an immediate conclusion as to the existence of a vast universe of accumulated misunderstandings and superimposed frustrations. Perhaps more significant, the usual approaches in this area, particularly in their rehabilitative intentions, are astonishingly synchronic, full of locked doors, curled up on themselves like the "illnesses" they describe. Any attempt to understand the why of education in the penitentiary environment implies not only the recognition of a legacy of failings — every acquisition of knowledge is first of all a successor to incomplete knowledge — but the anticipation of a response and of a meaning beyond criticism of its past and its origin.

Like hungry vultures, specialists have invaded the penitentiary. But their respective victories, which clearly involve the staking out of territorial boundaries, advance from implosion to implosion, setting aside in the progressive narrowing all possibility of an overall view and solution. The criminologist buries himself deeper and deeper in his ever more "explanatory" etiology, the psychologist takes refuge behind his ever more "effective" therapy, the sociologist spins out more and more projects for reintegration, all of them more and more "in keeping with the needs and abilities of the prisoner". The attentive observer watching the field with any honesty soon discovers a cacaphony of words no longer directed at anyone, no longer heard, in outright but unremarked contradiction. Problems arise and fall, indifferentiated, in total disorder. Each problem with its own area of expertise, as if it were the only one, as if it were an end in itself; each with its own policy for organizing and enshrining the insoluble; each with its own technique of intervention, to the point that it begins to seem that strategies are based, in this area, on a refusal to think. It is no wonder that what we call the problematics of the penitentiary system, in which the judical and penal systems are merely the two poles of an extremely complex reality, is perceived only as an amorphous collage of isolated problems. It is a curious phenomenon that these "specialisms", even as they claim to be extending their grasp of reality, seem to be growing ever less meaningful. One fact remains: no matter how the specialists attack it, the problem of the penitentiary remains untouched. For anyone in full possession of his faculties, there is no need for special approaches or profound views to recognize that this situation is a disturbing one: it is one of those facts which not only arise out of the problematics of the penitentiary, but which create it.

What to do? Obviously, we cannot simply offer yet another theoretic opposition and continue the absurd scenario of symmetrical contradiction. If we are to seize from the problematics of the penitentiary even the shred of a solution, another approach must be considered, another level of discussion must be attempted, another credo of the mind must be sought for hope of a solution. The problematics of the penitentiary system, as we envisage it, cannot escape the complexities of the contemporary epistemological labyrinth. Although the study of the problem and the search for solutions lie beyond the quarrels of ideological sects, a number of difficulties remain. More specifically, there are four which must be clarified immediately in order to appease the insatiable appetite of the functionaries of the true, by whom we mean these specialists in "manner".

i —*The question of meaning*

Until very recently, for example, the relationship between the signified (concept) prison and the signifier (auditory image) prison could imply several different meanings for the word prison, but none would have any "meaning" at any given point without some reference to reality. But this is apparently no longer the case since Lacan developed the idea that "the signifier, by its very nature, always anticipates the meaning, unfolding, as it were, its dimensions before it."[3]

In another context, can the meaning of the penitentiary system be reduced to that of the epistemological explanation? Under the circumstances, to choose sides would be to resume the cycle of exclusivist antinomies. Might the innocence of a "possible meaning" not disarm the hardened soldiers of truth? For to appreciate the difference between meaning and truth, we must re-read Claudel's "Parabole d'Animus et d'Anima".[4] "Things are not going well in the home of Animus and Anima, the mind and the soul." Despite "his true nature, vain, pedantic and tyrannical", Animus cannot live without Anima. "After all, was it not Anima who provided the dowry and supports the household?" The penitentiary world reeks of truths, as Animus's literary meetings "reek of vomit and tobacco". What it needs is a little higher lucidity, a vision of the soul, the soul of some wisdom: a question of meaning.

ii —*A unifying knowledge*

Over and above all that has been said of it, the history of human reason remains a history of unions, of correspondences, of connections. The first task of rational knowledge is an effort to discover, in the most disparate objects, what it is that joins them, what is common to them — whether function or structure, behaviour or end, cause or genesis, appearance or change. Now, the human sciences have recently been invaded by specialists with the mentality of specialized insects, whom Castoriadis describes as "diverters" and who delight in knowledge which is splintered, discontinuous, disunifying, infinitely mediatized by the subject. Curiously, this knowledge persists in affirming itself through the negation of the possibility of knowledge, a sort of eschatological anti-knowledge in reverse, a knowledge which defines itself by the entropy which consumes it, a knowledge more at ease in the commerce of ruptures and breaks than in the search for inclusiveness and meaning, a knowledge turned in upon its genesis and the already symbolic traces of its origin, a knowledge almost indifferent to its own direction, dried up by its anaesthetizing analysis, resistant to any possibility of surpassing and transcendance.

The problematics of the penitentiary system, with the disappointments which it has already produced and the subterfuges which it pretends not to see in order to hide the impasse which it has reached, cannot be abandoned to a form of knowledge which is yet more obscurantist, more nihilistic. Rather, we must assume that any knowledge which hopes to study its various facets and determine its meaning is based on the desire for an authentic and total analysis.

iii —*An understanding through reversal*

Some types of knowledge are content with voyeurism. Others are preoccupied with engineering. No one ever fully escapes the old progressionist myths of a causal equivalence between intellectual power and wisdom in life.

In the problematics of the penitentiary system, both camps are well represented. On the one side, solemn analysts, uncontaminated by correctional intentionality, devote themselves to discussions of justice and the penal system, or guilt and etiology... all in the name of Science. The essential point here is finding categories of intelligibility in which understanding — "making intelligible that which is obscure" (Littré) — is less important than classifying, organizing, arranging, "parameterizing". On the other side, there are the practitioners of infallible cures, a whole army of dealers in guaranteed Magianism. As a former prison administrator once remarked, with perhaps a touch of cynicism, the important thing for these people is finding diseases to match their cures.

And what if the answer to the problematics of the penitentiary system is hidden somewhere behind the two extreme viewpoints which we have just caricaturized? What if, instead of marginalizing the questions, the problems and the individuals; instead of viewing the penitentiary system as a wart or abscess on society, the ordinary question: what can society do for the penitentiary system? were to become: what can the penitentiary system do for society? We must learn to see in suffering, in conflict, in human rejection a path to humanity as revealing as the idiosyncratic disturbances of the individual. Was Sophocles interested only in Oedipus' pathology or in every man's struggle to find his own identity? Perhaps it might not be inappropriate to establish a profound analogy between the "criminal mentality" and the artist's inspiration: to recognize both as the "antennae of the race". In both these universes, we are "beyond cause and effect", as Merleau-Ponty says of Cézanne and his schizoid world: to enter them is to know the realm of possibility.

iv —An hypothesis as method

With few exceptions, among them Michel Foucault, discussions on the problematics of the penitentiary system begin from some difficult point outside — theory, method, approach, strategy — which is continually excusing and justifying itself as the objectives are attained. A child needs no method to talk to God. It is the grownups who lack simplicity. In other words, the higher the stakes, the more ridiculous and sterile it is to quibble over manner. What purpose is served by these quarrels between "ologists", fighting over the prisoner's intelligence with their contradictory theories or dividing up his soul on the pretext of validity, empathy, active listening and who knows what else? No one is improved by polemics on method, and anyone who is obliged to impose his knowledge by means of method bases it on bitterness and indignation, that is, on submission. Truths which are worthy of interest are not conquests achieved through the humiliation of the ignorant. Indeed, ignorance lies not in the absence of genius but in the vanity of the claimant. Truths which are worthy of interest are gifts which enrich both the giver and the receiver as they are shared.

In our analysis, then, of the penitentiary question, instead of following the common practice of announcing our preference for one of the reigning, and for that matter disciplinary, methods, it may be of some benefit to leave the beaten paths.

Because it explains, better than any other theory, the origin of rites, myths, religion, society, in short, the origin of civilization (the genesis of the significant systems), because it casts a unique light on man, on his relationships with God, with others, with nature, with himself, this hypothesis releases the problematics of the penitentiary system from its prison, as it were, and offers hitherto unsuspected hope. In the following paragraphs, we shall attempt to describe, adapting it at the same time as far as possible to our problematics, the hypothesis of René Girard.[5]

More than ever before, we find an expansion in the number and variety of "discussions on man", involving questions from various disciplines and thus constituting so many individual anthropologies.

Even more significant than the proliferation of contradictory approaches is the crisis of man which plagues our era, and which seems more serious than all the rest, since it is the crisis of the "death of man". For to dispossess man of his hope in man is at the same time to swallow up the future of humanity, along with the stores of hope which constitute the fundamental guarantee of its life force. Perhaps most difficult: to have to admit the powerlessness of a prodigious reserve of knowledge about man. "No era has accumulated more extensive and diverse knowledge about man than our own. Yet no era has known less of what man is."[6]

We must protest and resist this peculiar habit of seeing, in the legacy of our predecessors, only the debit column and the dead ends. And cease dividing man up into his differences. It is difficult, certainly, to visualize, to articulate, to express man, and to resist the ultimate temptation: to install him and lock him up in logics, words, languages. By locking something up, we believe we have caught the essential. But the caged stag is not the stag. Incarceration of the criminal does not chain the man. The true stag is a creature of freedom, of grace, of movement, of impulse, of silence, of fragility. The essential nature of the stag will always escape the bars that seek to hold it. The essential nature of man eludes man: we stubbornly attempt to seize it with our pincers of words and concepts, the better to divide it into separate pieces, when we should be content to express it, to find a meaning for it.

This is the first merit of René Girard's anthropology: an unconditional valorization of the question of man. "No question holds greater promise today than the question of man." He is right. In a world where God is still a matter for "holy wars" and diplomatic manœuvres, for shame and muffled whispers; in a society where truth is plural or nonexistent and morality relativist or ridiculed, man's last, man's only refuge remains man. Indeed, when all doors seem barred and hope of no avail, only man can take on the responsibility of man, can establish and accomplish him against the weight of meaninglessness and indifference. In its almost masochistic distress over the death of man and the "age of ruptures", to use Jean Daniel's phrase, our era has almost forgotten that no one can be a man without knowing man, without becoming fully aware of his situation in existence. "Start by loving the man you are before criticizing the man you are not" is not a moral precept. It is an existential slogan. For the idea that man creates of himself justifies his existence, gives meaning to his life and determines, to a large extent, his conduct and his behaviour. Let us examine more closely then the thesis which will be our guide.

Two precisions by way of precautions. First, for all it is extremely simple — too simple, in fact, according to some critics — Girard's position is developed at great length and through numerous examples, no doubt in at least partial response to the habits and demands of intellectual comprehension of an era which is no longer interested in anything but the complex and the complicated. We shall have to limit ourselves to the essential, that is, to the hypothetical nature of the hypothesis: "We must emphasize the hypothetical nature of the hypothesis. It must be judged not on its immediate plausibility but on its power to explain."[7] Secondly, in applying the hypothesis to the examination of the problematics of the penitentiary system, we have deliberately chosen to accentuate the positive and revealing scope of this exercise. As for the limitations and weaknesses of this type of contribution, they will be examined elsewhere.

All human conduct and training are learned, that is, they are all based in one way or another on imitation, on mimicry. Here anthropology overlaps not only ethology but disciplines as varied as biology and child psychology as well.

For his acquisition of being and becoming, man, like the animal, is basically an imitator. "If men suddenly ceased imitating, all cultural forms would disapear. Neurologists frequently remind us that the human brain is an enormous imitating machine..." It is only by understanding this mimicry of appropriation and its repression, Girard tells us, that it is possible to achieve any real understanding of the source and genesis of the major cultural traits of humanity as a whole. This is because the mimetic behaviour of acquisition or appropriation is also and inevitably conflictual behaviour, mimetic rivalry behaviour. Faced with the same object, two mimetic beings will fight for possession of it because they both see it as desirable. In other words, recognizing man as a mimetic being means seeing him too as a creature of conflict, rivalry or violence. Reciprocity of mimicry, reciprocity of rivalry and reciprocity of violence — they are all identical in meaning. The astonishing thing in conflictual behaviour is the implacable symmetry of the antagonists. Each one imitates the other imitating the other to the point that each appears to be a reflection, a perfectly orchestrated double with his mimetic response. Thus there is no victory in mimetic violence but rather reciprocity, that is, infinite reprisal. Everyone emerges the loser in vengeful repetition to the unbounded mutualist crescendo.

If, then, man's relations with one another and with the world are regulated and governed by a mechanism of imitation and rivalry which is constantly giving rise to violence, a question naturally arises: how has man succeeded, over the ages, in channeling the reciprocal violence, the reprisals of infinite vengeance, and surviving? How has man been able to emerge — grow, achieve, build — from the crushing violence which threatens him with extinction at every moment of his existence? How can violence be at once constructive and destructive, unifying and disintegrating, the source and cause of order and disorder, purifying and contaminating, liberating and ruinous? Since man, unlike animals, has no instinctive restraint on mimetic violence, he solves his problem through the religious, Girard tells us. Now, the religious system is based essentially on two pillars, taboo and ritual, which exercise the dual function of eliminating violence and maintaining peace and harmony within the community. Taboos, on sexual objects for example, or dietary taboos, are intended to repress and control mimetic conflicts by preventing anything which may provoke them. The taboos "always relate to the closest, most accessible objects, those which belong to the cohabiting group, the women produced by this group, or the food accumulated by this group. These objects are taboo because they are always available to all the members of the group: they are thus the most likely to give rise to rivalries which can threaten the group's harmony and even its survival." In short, the taboo is not a symbolic function but a custom, an extremely "functionalist" tradition of regulation, a sort of catechism of social peace which teaches by rote and by decree the articles of community faith, the severity of the transgressions between pure and impure, what is permitted and what is forbidden. In addition, the taboo is an indication of a profound recognition that the most serious threat to community harmony comes not from an outside enemy, from some maleficent god or natural cataclysm, such as flood or plague, but from the mimetic violence present in each of the members of the group. The antimimetic taboo is a prohibition which is much closer to lucidity than to mad authoritarianism.

Ritual, on the other hand, is a mechanism for doing what the taboo normally forbids. When the crisis of violence is no longer controlled or controllable by means of taboos, the community reverses the procedure and encourages the prohibited behaviour in order to channel and eliminate it. It achieves this end very concretely by diverting the violence of all against all (reciprocal violence) into a communal violence of all against one (unanimous violence). The sacrifice of a scapegoat-victim thus re-establishes the threatened order and reconciles the community. It is because he is "unable to defend himself and incapable of vengeance" that the scapegoat-victim plays such a fundamental role. Through him, another violence can be performed and justified in the hope and conviction that it will be the final violence, the violence which will put an end to the cycle of all violence. The fundamental unity of all rituals thus concludes mimetic violence. "There is a unity not only in all mythologies and all rituals, but in human culture as a whole, both religious and antireligious, and this unity of unities hangs wholly on a single mechanism which is still operative because it is still misunderstood, the mechanism which ensures the unanimity of the community against and around the scapegoat-victim."

It should be noted that no one is responsible, a priori, for the origin of mimetic violence. Any attempt to find an origin here is properly mythical. Since violence makes uniform, that is, since each individual is pitted against all other individuals and vice versa, there is nothing to prevent any one individual from becoming, at any given point, the double of all the others, that is, the object of universal fascination and hatred. In fact, the time always comes, who knows how or why, when a victim is designated and substituted for all other potential victims and the hostility of the community converges on this victim, whom it charges with and accuses of all evil. This single victim, the scapegoat-victim, calls up and suffers the violence of all because he is "responsible" for all the misfortunes of the community. But just as he is reviled, hated, immolated, this victim also attracts admiration, the "supernatural" respect of the group, since, through his own expulsion, he restores the harmony of reconciliation, peace and order. To the extent that he brings a return to marvelous calm, the scapegoat-victim becomes sacred, holy. In this sense, as Durkheim suspected, the religious is the basis of all societies, civilizations, cultural institutions. A strange phenomenon and one which is difficult to accept since it signifies, among other things, that the social state does not arise, as Hobbes or Rousseau assumed, from the will of the social contract. "There is always human death at the origin of the cultural order", Girard says, and this is true even for the most advanced democracies: "Men murdered themselves into democraty", wrote D.H. Lawrence.

We should add that the mechanism of creative violence appears to be all the more effective when its true meaning remains hidden from those who use it. "Men cannot face the senseless nakedness of their own violence without the risk of abandoning themselves to this violence; they have always misinterpreted it, at least partially, and the possibility of properly human societies may well depend on this misinterpretation." But how far must we go to maintain such a fragile and precarious peace in human communities? If the violent expulsion of original violence and its recall by cultural rituals are essential intermediaries in man's accession to being and meaning, can we continue to ignore the meaning of the sacrificial mechanisms? Are they not becoming less and less effective? Is the difference between legitimate violence and illegitimate violence not being dangerously eroded? The substitution and generalization of the judicial system as a transcendant mechanism for the prevention and correction of violence (we shall return to this point later) are certainly signs of great progress. But is justice enough? Has it the means to suffice?

For René Girard, there is only one answer: love. Man's salvation lies in love, in reconciliation without rivalry, without violence, without the sacrifice of a victim. There is a real New Testament epistemology of love, which shows it in its unique demystifying and revealing role. Naturally, at first sight, reticence and resistance are strong, almost visceral. And it is certainly no easy task to urge contemporary men to an "anthropological" re-reading of Judeo-Christian texts and at the same time to avoid the prejudices of apologetics or of ridicule pure and simple — Christianity itself having become the scapegoat for our civilization. It is clearly a radical reversal which is required, a sort of "one-dimensional" leap involving the destructuration of our most profound existential habits. "To escape from violence, it is evidently necessary to renounce the idea of retribution; it is therefore necessary to renounce those forms of conduct which have always appeared natural and legitimate. It seems just, for example, to respond to good with good and to evil with evil, but the results are obvious..." We must realize, then, that if man persists in using evil to resist evil, he closes and locks himself within the Realm of cyclic violence. Only the Realm of evangelical love can liberate man from the slavery of violence. "Only love is truly revealing, for it escapes the spirit of revenge and vengeance... Only the perfect love of Christ can achieve, without violence, perfect revelation."

3. To judge

> "Therefore thou art inexcus-
> able, O man, whosever thou art
> that judgest: for wherein thou
> judgest another, thou con-
> demnest thyself; for thou that
> judgest doest the same things."
> *Epistle to the Romans*, 2, 1

Girard himself touches the very root of our problematics when he refers to the emergence of the judicial system as a highly developed mechanism for the control of violence. Let us examine this more closely.

Whatever its form or means of expression — imitation, appropriation, threat, persecution, vengeance, crime — violence is resolved only by violence. A violence of control or prevention, the incest taboo, for example, or a violence of punishment, the family vendetta, for example, are always perceived as inevitable responses or replies to an earlier violence, and on and on. In other words, there is no difference between the violent act which the violence is intended to prevent or punish and the violence itself. Man is so constituted that the social order, society, civilization imply, a priori, a founding violence; peace is merely the difficult fruit of a liberating violence, the legitimacy of which, we repeat, is presented less as a moral obligation than as a duty of self-preservation. It is within this context of avenging contagion with its irremediable expansionist destiny, only occasionally delayed by sporadic sacrificial immolations, that the judicial institution has established itself as a discovery of unequalled effectiveness.

Thus, before it is seen as being of metaphysical or moral significance, the discovery of the judicial system seems, to the piercing gaze of fundamental anthropology, the logical conclusion of an effort to survive. The judicial system responds to a primary need for protection and is justified first as a mechanism of prevention, as a force of negation: "it helps man to respect vengeance". We must stress this point. It is because he is losing ground to his own violence that man is forced to accept justice. Justice is the consolation prize, the forced promotion. It prevents men from surrendering to private vengeance and taking the law into their own hands, that is, from killing one another to the point of extermination. Which does not mean that violence is thereby prevented. On the contrary, it becomes all the more efficient as it is rationalized, transcendentalized, raised to the level of abstraction for a greater effect of domination over the entire community. To say that the judicial system rationalizes vengeance is to say that it distributes it as it chooses, manipulates it with impunity and without dispute, transforms it into a curative and preventive technique. Let us say it at once: the origin of the judicial system as a social function has nothing to do with the romantic notion of humanization by the spiritualizing Word. The judicial function is the deserved product of a desperate search for supreme and sovereign power. "This rationalization of vengeance", Girard says, "has nothing to do with a more direct or profound rootedness in the community; it is based, instead, on the sovereign independence of the judicial authority, which is sanctioned once and for all and whose decisions, in principle at least, cannot be questioned by any group, not even the community as a whole. Representing no particular group, it is thus in the service of all and all must bow to its decisions. Only the judicial system need never hesitate to strike violence in the heart, because it has an absolute monopoly on vengeance. Because of this monopoly, it usually succeeds in snuffing out vengeance instead of exacerbating it, instead of causing it to spread and multiply as the same type of conduct would in a primitive society."

Thus revealed in its functionalist and pragmatic essence, the judicial institution shakes the almost mythic belief in a basic goodness in the heart of man. The desire to mimic is both cause and support of mimetic violence. Man is not good by nature. Nor is he violent by instinct. In revealing the genesis of the judicial mechanism as a concrete mechanism for limiting violence "by violence", fundamental anthropology forces us to re-examine and rethink questions which have never been answered: what is crime, evil, the criminal, punishment, rehabilitation, expiation, correction? Is the criminal a "good" being whom society has corrupted or a "freak of nature" barely manageable by medicine, psychiatry, group dynamics, self-education? In particular, it suggests not only the limitations but the near-futility of these kinds of questions. The record of the judicial system shows a varied and complex range of possibilities, but since it is made of the same fabric as that to which it is opposed, it remains a closed system. We must turn away from justice if we are to go beyond it, and appeal to something other than the judicial system to open the necessary door.

This demythologization of the judicial system applies as well to its finality. Preventive or curative, the judicial system is still an essentially channeling taboo. It does not eliminate violence, never suppresses it once and for all. As a response to and reprisal against violence, it is symmetrical with vengeance, however legal, legitimate and pure it may be. Hence, it may require a given activity, a given form of conduct, a given behaviour, but it cannot require good. Paradoxically, justice is designed to achieve, not peace, order or equilibrium, but non-violence. The worthy man, the morally good man, cannot be a product of the regulations of the Code. The purpose of correctional rehabilitation as established by our penal laws is not to convert the criminal into a good citizen or a good person but to produce an individual who is capable of abstaining from violating the law. The command of justice, in the simple fact that it commands, remains a command of poverty and privation.

Moreover, while they arise as processes designed to ensure greater effectiveness, the mechanisms of the judicial system are marked for life with the sign of violence. "The procedures which permit men to moderate their violence are all similar, in that none of them is foreign to violence." To judge is to do violence, as Hobbes has said. To judge is already to punish, as the precedence of retibutive justice over distributive justice in the child demonstrates. The infiltration of etiological rationalism, that permanent apanage of contemporary criminology, into the administration of justice sheds a special light on violence as the logic of the judicial system. From the preliminary investigation, designed to collect the first facts to justify the validity of suspicion, directly through to the accusation and verdict of guilt; from the unbridled curiosity of the judge, protected by the truths of the specialists in judicial circumstances — psychiatrists, psychologists, physicians, sociologists, etc — preoccupied as much with an individual's qualifications as with the condemnation of an act, buried in the genealogical exegesis of his past life, the better to understand his present state; from the standard pleas to sentencing, to execution of the penalty; in short, a whole panoply of permissions accompanies, as if to justify, the exercise of justice. "If our system seems to us more rational, it is in fact because it is more strictly aligned with the principle of vengeance. The emphasis on punishment of the guilty has no other meaning." Violence clings to justice with the appetite and patience of a cancer.

The judicial system is still represented as an example of real progress in that it displaces the axis of violence from the victim to the culprit, that is, in that it centres on the culprit and the principle of guilt. Among primitive peoples, all the interest is directed towards the unavenged victim, since he represents the greatest threat to community harmony. "Untreated" violence is a source of impurity and contamination and incalculable repercussions. The response must therefore be rapid and appropriate: it is important to be able to assess and measure the crime and the evil it has done and to respond in due proportion — an eye for an eye, and a tooth for a tooth. Judicial intervention against the guilty party thus liberates the community from the terrible duty of unending vengeance. But essentially, is etiological analysis of the criminal so different in its consequences and its precise instructions from the proportioned measurement of primitive reciprocity; is it not in fact superior in terms of effectiveness of vengeance? And what are we to say of the practically institutionalized efforts to separate the guilty from his guilt? Seeing the criminal as a victim to be spared and protected or as a scapegoat to be punished and purified reflect the same malaise: the profound inability to escape from the cycle of violence.

In this logic, to conquer evil, justice must be superior to it in strength. Hence the basic injustice of justice, its natural imbalance. "Nothing is further from this thinking, consequently, than the idea of justice as a scale always in perfect balance, an undisturbed impartiality. Human justice is rooted in the differential order and fails with it. Wherever the interminable and terrible equilibrium of tragic conflict becomes established, the language of just and unjust is absent. What are men to be told, indeed, when they come to this point, except to be reconciled or to punish one another?" The equalizing function of the judicial apparatus is a lure, a deceptive deviation; and its curative and rehabilitative ambition a powerful technique of sacrificial diversion. Most astonishing of all, the more effective it becomes, the more the judicial system wraps itself in mystery and hides its true function from human eyes. "Centuries go by before men realize that there is no difference between their principle of justice and the principle of vengeance." We can illustrate this point through the example of a primitive society.

The Chukchi, anthropology tells us, displayed a curious form of behaviour when one of their number committed an attack of any kind against a neighbouring tribe or family. In contrast to the common practice of the clan protecting its members at all costs, as, for example, among the Ifugao, they refused to intercede on behalf of the aggressor, that is, to give the supporters of the victim of the aggression the signal to embark upon an inevitably endless series of reprisals. But their reaction did not centre, as we might easily assume, on the aggressor, that is, on the guilty party. Their repression of criminal violence did not give way to condemnation of the person "responsible". It did not give way to justice, in short, for what is justice without a guilty party, without some awareness of the necessary correlation between guilt and retribution?

But this is not all. To do justice to their adversaries, the Chukchi would choose from among themselves an innocent victim, someone totally unconnected with the crime committed, and sacrifice him as an offering in reparation. But this is the height of injustice, any child today would protest! Indeed, such behaviour is astonishing. Justice is not justice when it punishes the innocent. Thus we find a limitation, indeed an impasse. The extensive confusion as to the role and place of the prison system in our societies is based, certainly, on the very logic of the institution and on its contradictory objectives, from its most sacrosanct imperative of retribution to its impossible wager on reformation and rehabilitation. It is rooted even more deeply in the very heart of the judicial power, which is, in reality, merely the power to prevent and constrain, a permanent measure of calculated suppression, an asymptotic movement of perfect, and hence impossible, deviations and balances. The judicial system is not in itself generative, vivifying; it is not life-giving. Bergson was right to see, in humanity's ascending history, in its passage from the closed to the open, a series of leaps forward by the creators of justice. And Durkheim was right to support him by stating that the noble consciences opposed by fashionable opinion in any moral conflict move more creatively to the profound truths. In *Sociology and Philosophy*, for example, he maintains that "Socrates expressed more accurately than his judges the morality appropriate to the society of his time". But creative justice invents only out of indignation, only through imagination directed against injustice. While it extends the field of the possible and expands the circle of collective security, the judicial system still belongs to a closed system, that of preservation. The most it can do is to fulfill, with wavering effectiveness, its function of maintenance. Simply to exist, it needs an artificial "oxygen", with which it cannot be confused but without which it would die, according to Jankélévitch.[8] Thus, in revealing some of the intrinsic limitations of the judicial apparatus on which the modern concepts of incarceration are grafted in one way or another, together with their ascetic and aseptic appendages — punishment, supervision, correction, normalization, rehabilitation, therapy, etc — we are working towards a specific end: to demonstrate the futility of any proposal for penitentiary education which is locked onto the projections of the judicial system.

There are a number of concepts of the place and role of education in the prison environment: a privileged technique of moral correction; an a posteriori naturalization and legitimization of the power to punish; a calculated justification of the policies of confinement; a studied pretext for establishing criteria of normality; a "scientific" classification of deviations and a gradation of differences; a unique opportunity for experimentation in the human sciences; a concrete introduction to social reintegration; a training of tendencies and discipline of attitudes; an identification of lacunae and isolation of their causes; an application to the secret soul of the criminal of the old ideology of control by panoptic surveillance, exculpatory compensation, pity, economic strategy, etc. All are linked to the primary orientation of the judicial and penal systems, from which, in fact, they can be separated only as extensions and variants. Certainly, the solution is not to eliminate the judicial function entirely. The failure of the experiment attempted in Denmark, during the German occupation, is sufficiently eloquent. In an age when the transcendencies which normally play the role of the supreme judge — God, morality — are disappearing, the judicial institution appears to be not merely useful but essential. Nor do we advocate abandoning ourselves to the evasions of the demanding subjectivisms. A civilization based as firmly as ours on the ideology of right already represents a world-scale menace; it would be senseless to crush it with legalized mimetic demands. On the other hand, an attempt to fill the gaps in a thesis does not refute its partial validity. Now, "impeccable, inexorable justice has no intention", Jankélévitch reminds us. The answer to the question "why educate in prison?" will never go beyond the judicial approach except by actually leaving it behind. And our discussions on correctional justice should lead us to replace the traditional arguments with that of "reconciliational education".

Dedicated as it is to the incomprehensible violence which commands it, justice appears to be not only a virtue of observation but a virtue of necessary contention. In other words, when it is proposed that justice is conformity to the right or conformity to the law, the consignment clearly does not flow from any imperative of nobility, dignity or sharing. Judicial architecture is totally foreign to fraternal construction. Justice which judges is limited to and bounded by what is: violence. It does not settle it, does not eliminate it. Here, the most rational of the virtues reveals its impotence. It is not that it is indifferent or evasive. It would prefer to understand, to know the secret causes behind man's violent acts. It is the old mythical dream of overcoming, through science, the imbalance between man's strength and his wisdom. "Knowledge is power". Occasionally it even believes that it has grasped the secret, but its illusion is shortlived and the "causes" prove to be incomplete, circumstantial, casuistic. See the judge and the justice he renders, feeling that he must go outside the judicial system to give a better judgment, consulting specialists in evidence before the evidence — psychiatrists, psychologists, criminologists, etc; or see him reducing the opportunities for judicial decision-making by extending the authority of investigative curiosity up to the intervention of the police officer. "It is the criminal who is judged, rather than the crime. As evidence, we call in psychiatrists, character witnesses, we ask the defendant's little sister whether he is kind, we question his parents about his early childhood. And it is the knowledge we gain about the criminal which determines whether or not we inflict a given punishment on him."[9] The calculations and perfect demonstrations of our extra-judicial authorities are utopian dependencies, imaginary museum pieces. In short, the certainty of violence is the first and only constant. The second act is the act of justice, an act neither of submission nor of expulsion but of compromise and elimination through tidy organization and constraint.

If justice does meet a need for knowledge, it must be in terms of manner. How to control, channel, supervise reciprocal violence? How to manipulate, organize, situate? How to distinguish pure violence from impure violence, legitimate violence from illegitimate violence? How to forbid, prevent, differentiate? How to rally by dissociation, unite in division? How to deviate without deceiving? How to camouflage and disguise without forgetting? How to compel in order to liberate? How to condemn to duty? How to punish while making amends? How to judge without judging? How to judge without doing violence? Justice has become a mechanism of restraint.

"When I name justice, I name at the same time the sacred bond of human society, the necessary restraint on licence, the sole basis of repose, the equitable temperament of authority and the gentle support of subjection. When justice reigns, good faith is present in treaties, security in commerce, clarity in business, order in goverment; the earth is in repose and Heaven itself seems to shed its beams more pleasantly upon us and to send us gentler influences ... (Justice) encircles all men within its limits; it sets up an invincible barrier against the violence of enterprise and it is not without reason that the Sage attributes to it the glory of being the support of thrones and the defence of empires."[10]

Bossuet's synthesis summarizes perfectly the instrumental scope of the Chukchi diversion. Mimetic violence, contagious and infectious, is a fact. To respond to it with further violence, like the Ifugao, even in the hope of putting an end to it, is senseless. It is the custom? And can custom not be senseless? Why not seek another solution? Punishing an innocent victim is not primarily a crime against humanity, it is a cry of hope and despair, a tactic for survival. The Chukchi know perfectly well what they are doing. In exchanging the purity of innocence for impure blood, it is the pestilential defilement, the murderous contagion which they seek at all costs to avoid. And thus the tactics of digression and camouflage etch the order of the natural strategies of justice, the very first of which, which we may call the essential strategies, are inevitably exercised through prevention, control, surveillance and sanction. Those which our modern society defines as the indelible mark of justice and which it has baptized strategies of equilibrium, equity or equality are in fact superfluous strategies. Justice is not just and it is not in its nature to be just. Justice makes use of violence because it is against violence. Contrary to the popular and expansionist ideologies of our times, hatred, struggle and conflict embody neither the ideal of justice, nor even its method — they are its primary enemies. It cannot be stressed strongly enough, justice concludes a procedure commanded by the instinct for self-preservation, the objective of which is non-violence and the peace which is its counterpart.

The task is clearly no easy one. The end always justifies the means in questions of survival. For this reason, something always seems false in the proper, dressed-up manners of justice. Even in its most laudable efforts to meet the needs of others, it acts unequally, that is, in accordance with due proportion. "All the moral virtues applied to operations are combined in a certain general concept of justice under the title of the debt to society, but are distinguished on the basis of the various reasons specific to each one... But this debt does not have the same significance in all cases. A thing is due in one way to an equal, in another to a superior, in another to an inferior. It is due in one way as the result of an agreement, in another as the result of a promise, or a previous favour."[11] In short, if justice cannot eliminate natural injustice, how can it do more for the other form of injustice? Very clearly, it will not learn to serve anything higher than itself.

On the one hand, it cannot permit itself the slightest error in its identification of the guilty party. Otherwise, it is an abominable catastrophe, a mixture of pure violence and impure violence, a destructive and disintegrative failure to differentiate between them. Etymologically, justice means to take just or accurate aim. Consequently, the better it fells its victim, we might say, the more effective it is. The right to shape and distribute differences by means of the violence of control or taboo remains a right to violence. Hence, its paradoxical discomfort when faced with the guilty party, who is to be touched as little as possible, as we see in the Chukchi's total unwillingness to deal with the aggressor. Is it ashamed of itself? Is it ashamed of the criminal? Of his disgrace or of his similarity?

Primarily, it is afraid. Afraid, first, of making a mistake, as we have already pointed out. Missing its victim or hitting too many — the effect is the same. Afraid too of being contaminated. This is probably one of the hidden and unacknowledged meanings of the etiological efforts of contemporary criminology to separate the guilty from his guilt. But the truth of justice cannot bury itself in the labyrinths and interstices of an exogenous causality. Since evil generates evil and justice must do violence to eliminate violence, its aim, quite simply, is to do evil without the possibility of response. In order to do this, it must select a victim, or, what amounts to the same thing, make the culprit into a victim incapable of defending himself, that is, one foreign to contaminating reciprocity. Afraid, finally, through enforced meditation, through inner uncertainty. Innocence adds spice to judicial error. By making the culprit into a victim, we lay the ambush for the final guarantee. The supplication of despair, to be honest. Justice is never sure of itself. Like Sisyphus, it must imagine itself happy.

At the same time, its precautions are self-directed efforts to guard against its own ambiguities and possible excesses. For example, its transcendant authority is to relieve the community by exercising surveillance and control over the individual oppositions to each of its members. Yet any error in degree or judgment in the execution of its powers sanctions either officialized injustice or reciprocal violence. In the first case, it could take the form of oppression of the poor and weak. The result: the organization and orchestration of the judicial system around material possessions, that is, around the constituted property of the "dominant classes": "To protect their property, the rich have invented courts, judges and the guillotine, like a flame that draws and consumes the ignorant", Gobsek oberves in Balzac's *César Biroteau*. Or around cultural attainments, against the original, the marginal, the "modern", so regularly threatened with perpetual exclusion, against poetic genius, artistic genius.

In the case of reciprocal justice, judicial ineffectiveness is equivalent, for all practical purposes, to the primitive regression of the primal cry — every man for himself, and devil take the hindmost. Today, this stirring mimetic temptation hides easily behind the popular banner of the rights of man, for everyone has rights, as universal justice in particular must recognize, since its role is to give everyone his due. Despite our visceral attachment to the question of human rights, it is important to recognize something which no one wants to admit, the fact that a justice which yields blindly to the law of rights is destined, little by little, to disappear, purely and simply. Plato pointed out long ago the profound significance of a collective justice which can be borne only by the man who is himself his own master. Hence, the right to justice is a right to mastery, not a right to some absolute claim. Otherwise, we have destruction through excessive power. In Lord Acton's elegant phrase, "power tends to corrupt, and absolute power corrupts absolutely". In other words, if right decides on the basis of what it is, it destroys itself. If it decides on the basis of what it wants, it destroys others. In short, there is absolutely no difference between a justice of rights and a justice of mimetic appropriation, symmetrical mutilation, rejection, expulsion. "And he who departs alone saying 'I, I, I' is as if absent from the kingdom."[12]

What can we say then of the ambiguous and strained correspondences between justice and equality or justice and freedom? The fact is that men no longer know that perfect equality is nothing other than perfect rivalry. Identical beings experience identical mimicry, that is, a situation of perfectly symmetrical conflictual violence. Justice suspects this, and sees in the equality of the majority of men a store of provisions to be accumulated rather than a springboard to brotherly sharing. Strangely enough, the equality acquired and established by judicial logic makes men resemble one another; it never brings them together. Occasionally, equalitarian justice will succeed in uniting men whom equality has divided; their union is known as alliance, agreement or mutual surveillance. But justice is too concerned with what they do not have or what is due them to educate them. It has no idea of what they are and what they can give, that is, receive.

As for freedom, "one of those wretched words", as Valéry says, "of more value than meaning", its relationship with justice is scarcely more impressive. This is due largely to the fact that justice has said everything when it says that man is not free before the law. Rebellion, constraint, protest, autonomy, struggle, pressure, conquest, authority, will, etc, no matter: when freedom and its kin are introduced by justice, belief in it has ceased. Essentially, freedom which is maintained by justice is weakness, whereas the only possible freedom is defined as strength, as a centre of inner strength. The only freedom which justice can affect is a superficial freedom, the freedom created by the influences and conditioning of the environment, or a stiff, ceremonial freedom, smothered under legal prescriptions. The just man is not free, he does what he must.

In short, justice is neither creative, nor liberating, nor critical; its role is to pacify. Moreover, whether preventive or curative, its function consists of a single power, a single prestige, a single status: effectiveness. In its name justice exists and progresses, but without it it would crumble. And it is in obedience to its dictates that it constantly perfects itself by appealing to the most refined of tools — judgment. In the judicial order, to judge is to accomplish the very act which vengeance demands, it is to yield to the urgings of the violent spirit. The judicial effort is neither an ideal nor a solution: at best is is prophylaxis; at worst, a crime like the rest.

For those who have eyes to see, the answer to the question "why educate in prison?" will come not from the judicial approach.

"Judge not, O man, for thou that judgest doest the same things."

4. To punish

> "Punishment is an Evill in-
> flicted by publique Authority,
> on him that hath done, or
> omitted that which is judged by
> the same Authority to be a
> transgression of the law; to the
> end that the will of men may
> thereby the better be disposed
> to obedience."
> Hobbes, *Leviathan*, II, 28

Clearly, positions and counterpositions could easily be amassed, and all the writings on the question of the punitive function would fill many library shelves. We shall not be so foolish as to attempt to synthesize them all, nor even to list their principal facets. Our efforts shall be directed primarily at pointing out, through the diversity of structures and the complex modalities of genesis and transformation, the lack of variation in the human function of punishment. Now, this function of punishment is rooted in the preventive and curative functionalism of the judicial system, to which the penal system is grafted as its ultimate instrumental extension. As its symbolic exaggeration, we might say. There is a hidden significance to punishment which is never seen, or, at least, never pointed out by the experts, which has nothing to do with its chronic and congenital inadequacy. Rather, it is in the scope of its ambiguous radicalism that the punitive function becomes singularly revealing, and only a close examination of this radicalism will enable us to understand the dual contradictory role which retributive justice has always played — that of the expiatory sanction of "punishment", and that of the corrective sanction of "compensation".

The criminalist Beccaria described the malaise quite bluntly in the mid-eighteenth century. "What", he wrote in his *Of Crimes and Punishments*, "is this right which men assume to slaughter their fellow-men?" And as Foucault's analytic genius has demonstrated, the problem has become an unbearable trauma, one of the great and apparently insoluble anguishes of our time. If we examine it closely, and set aside simplistic and redundant arguments, the frustration can be readily understood: no one has ever successfully justified a phenomenon in which inflicting evil on another person is accepted as a good, as a cause of well-being, as an obligation, in fact, and a duty.

Yet the problem has long been part of our collective memory. God punished Adam and Eve by turning them out of an earthly paradise, that is, by condemning them to humanity. The Romans and the Jews punished Jesus by crucifying Him, while the Athenians punished Socrates by forcing him to drink the hemlock. Hitler punished children who dared to be born of Jewish parents with extermination, and American Southerners punished the hazards of skin colour with slavery. How strange is humanity, that does not yet understand what it has always done best! Where shall we begin?

A return to etymology through our anthropologic hypothesis may place us on fresh trails. First, we must consider the idea of sanction, since it covers all the rest: punishment, penalty, expiation... all are forms of sanctions. The concept of sanction comes from the Latin "sacer", or sacred, and "sancire", to make sacred or inviolable. The "sanctio", or sanction, is the act by which a person or thing is made sacred or inviolable. To use the word only in the sense of condemnation, correction or repression distorts the dual reality which it expresses. Moreover, all dictionaries agree in accepting the French Academy's definition: "A penalty or reward intended to ensure the execution of the law". Hence when modern analysts of the idea of punishment claim to be distressed by the ambiguities of the term — for example, to punish a criminal, the law provides for imprisonment and correctional education — the antinomic connotations of the word sanction may help to dissipate the original contradictions. However, they alone will not solve all the difficulties. Correctional education is not immediately considered a reward in the sense of a prize won for a good action or for a service rendered.

But let us consider for a moment the major elements of the sacrificial mechanism. A community which is unable to control the violence of its members by means of taboos and social rules makes use of ritual as a device to transform violence by all against all into violence by all against one, the scapegoat-victim. But the scapegoat-victim, as we have learned, fulfills a dual function: by him and through him, the evil afflicting the group is expelled, with the immediate effect of producing and establishing peace and order. This dual antinomic role naturally gives rise to two categories of opposite feelings. First, feelings of hatred, rejection and condemnation, because the scapegoat-victim combines in himself the evils and vices, the impurities and weaknesses which have brought about the community's misfortune and despair; secondly, feelings of admiration, respect and adulation, precisely because he re-establishes harmony and calm within the community.

In a profound sense, the same is true of the criminal recognized as a scapegoat-victim. The legal penalty dispels the evil by punishing the evildoer, as, in the past, the rite of sacrifice expelled evil-generating violence by immolating the scapegoat-victim. At the same time, the removal of the criminal, that is, his physical exclusion from society, either radically by means of the death penalty, or temporarily by means of imprisonment, constitutes a true restoration of peace and order. And while it confuses the issue to some extent, the additive "correctional", so dear to our society in its efforts to liberate the penal function by camouflaging it behind a rehabilitative function, is not a new one and in no way modifies the significance of the punitive ritual. On the contrary, it actually sharpens its hidden and forgotten meaning. For the problem, basically, is still one of effectiveness in terms of eliminating violence. In fact, since the sacralizing certainty of sacrificial immolation is absent from the modern penalty, the problem is one of ensuring, with as many guarantees as possible, that the *arrest* of the criminal will not only halt an evil but will in fact replace it with some good. Correcting the criminal or killing the scapegoat-victim are thus identical. The correctional efforts of our modern criminology all amount to updated processes of saving sacralization.

Yet, and strange as it may seem, our society is still perplexed and lost before the significance of its punitive prescriptions. In vain it substitutes for the analysis of ideologies that of strategies; its one great certainty is that of having reached an impasse, with no possibility of escape. In vain we reason about the mournfulness of the right to punish or the subtle degrees of punishment, the proportions which can never be finally adjusted or the manner of execution, in vain we compare the desired effects with the results achieved: the discomfort persists. It is the impression of being unable to touch the essential which is the most difficult to bear, for man retains something of the significance of punishment, as the clay statue retains something of the god it represents. And this terrible weight of impotence, in our opinion, relates to the fact that penal practice represents the ultimate measure of the judicial function, as we have described it above. Punishment is justice in the hangman's hood.

In essence, the explanations of the penal system which we have had the opportunity to examine, including some which are extremely brilliant, seem to be based on the preventive and curative functionalism of the judicial system. We punish because someone has committed a crime and because we do not want him to commit another, that is, because we want to prevent him from continuing or resuming his acts of differentiating defilement. All the arguments about the penal system, even those most generously imbued with philanthropic suggestions, converge on this evident fact as if drawn by some blind force. As one random example, Jacques Léauté defines the four aims or functions of punishment as follows: expiation, intimidation, elimination, correction. Almost certainly, all the known ideas on the penal system could be classified under one or the other of these concepts. Each of them is, in our opinion, one variant in the invariant armature of the judicial system.

Expiation, as its etymology indicates, seeks to make amends by repaying evil with evil. The penitentiary services, we must remember, are in the service of penitence, in the service of suffering legally imposed in the guise of appeasement and cathartic purification. And for all it prides itself on wiping out the past, expiation remains nonetheless a policed conciliation; it refuses to forget the offence. Intimidation, on the other hand, is intended to frighten, to horrify, to terrorize. Of the four, it is surely the harshest, the closest to the barbaric, for it alone can bear to confuse the force which crushes with that which elevates. Elimination comes from the arsenal of biological alibis. The strong exist to eliminate the weak, it believes, just as the good exist to drive out the evil. While it is convinced that lucidity is its strength, everyone knows that it is based on error, for it has always confused certainty with truth. Correction is the failure of the final threat. To dare to claim that another human being stands tall only when he raises himself to the height of his master may be the sign of divine privilege. As seen by ordinary mortals, it is the command of contempt.

Everywhere the parallel is the same. Someday we shall have to see that punishment is rather like nothingness offered as a remedy for chaos.

With the exception of Kirschheimer and Rusche, whose work pioneered this field, no one has done more than Foucault to reduce the "whys" of the penal system from its "hows", to expose the secret tangles of punitive intentions through demystifying analysis of penal practice, to see in the details of the act of punishment the features of the punishing spirit. But even Michel Foucault's extraordinary analyses fail to escape the verdict of the anthropological approach.

Punishment is justice in the grimace of its final duty. It is justice *in extremis*, its final act, its last chance. Once the penalty is exacted, justice has no further obligation, nor is it expected to, for the choice, if any, of the penalty is limited to questions of modality or morphology. In terms of intention, it has been assigned one absolute and brutal commandment: to succeed, as the sun has been commanded to shine and the lungs to breathe. To succeed, that is, to put a final end to mimetic violence. Here is the drama! The penalty, by the very fact that it is punishment, a necessary evil, can neither close the cycle of violence nor create a new order of existence, that of a good dissociated from the memory of its origin. In one way or another, even a penalty established on the highest of hopes advances from nostalgia to nostalgia, its eyes turned towards the past. What we might call exemplarist punishment, which attempts to protect against evil, cannot act except by imposing a greater evil — a kind of pride, arrogance and presumption. What we might call rehabilitative punishment, which claims to lift men up out of evil, is obliged to exercise its evil inwardly, so to speak, somewhat as the rapist strikes at his victim's dignity by arrogating to himself the right to handle her body. But evil can only generate evil, just as violence, in primitive man, can only give rise to violence. In the closed universe of justice, evil is root and base, foundation and support. The moralists have attempted to teach us to distinguish vengeance-punishment as revealed by a certain ethnology from the punishment of justice, the only acceptable human punishment because of its medicinal justification. All punishment is a remedy, Aristotle claimed in his *Nichomachean Ethics*. And the moralists have already taught us to condemn the vengeance-punishment of the ethnologists because of its arbitrary nature and its laws of reciprocity, and, in particular, because of its dedication to the production of evil. But only the punishment of justice, they continue, is legitimate and legal vengeance, permitted and committed in the name of good, in the name of the conservation of justice ("ad justitiae conservationem"). The old principle of inversion applies here as elsewhere and soon reveals that punishment as a technique of conservation is itself the hostage of justice.

More profoundly, punishment not only fails in its effort to effect a radical break with evil, but it manages to separate being and existence, little by little, in a sort of pollution by omission. Although it is defined as a tool against evil, punishment remains, first of all, an evil, in that it is directed essentially against. Because it introduces itself into existence by way of opposition, punishment is declined in the indicative of the diminished, or, more precisely, in that of diminution, because giving and fullness cannot arise out of denial or prevention. Yet giving and fullness are the conditions of being, for being is constant enrichment or it is not. In its first sense, creation means being for, for life, for being, for the expansion of being. And punishment is against, against evil, an evil against. And evil — violence, crime, sin, punishment — is thus de-creation, to use Simone Weil's term, that is, the contrary of creation, indeed, the inversion of creation.

Punishment does not go beyond evil, as is frequently suggested by the judicial process, but actually implies that one who surrenders to it surrenders to evil, contaminates and is contaminated, is himself diminished and diminishes others. If only punishment used its power to raise up the criminal. But it cannot, set as it is in its mounting of justice. Its territory is not that of reconciliation. Its camp is always pitched amidst the dissensions to be hated, or, at least, to be put in order. It is already apparent that the opposite of punishment is neither weakness, nor anarchy, nor indifference, but growth, creation, love, as we shall discover further on.

There is more. Punishment is not an accident, or the whim of some vengeful imagination. It is chosen, studied, prepared with the most meticulous of precautions and attention. The punishment of justice is a product of rational justice.

It becomes clearer now why justice, in performing its duty of punishment, never does so gladly, unless we confuse gladness with the corrupt jubilation of sadistic and vengeful souls. And the sadness which accompanies the punitive function does not emanate, properly speaking, from a moral scruple, from pity or from some affected and snivelling sensitivity. The crisis is of a metaphysical nature. Radical punishment lifts the veil from the incompetence of judicial reason, from human reason, in short. Amazing! Because of this strange power, reason, man believes himself superior to the animals and invested with his supreme dignity. But the crisis of radical punishment brutally shakes the myth and confirms instead the perpetual crisis of reason. In other words, the reasons of radical punishment are without sufficient reason. So long as penitentiary specialists persist in "justifying" punishment on the basis of justice, they will be forced to concede the impossibility of reaching any conclusion.

Thus far, we have chosen primarily to emphasize *one* way in which punishment gives birth: as justice's faithful companion and mistress, punishment is creative in its administration of evil as an antidote to evil. But it is not only as an "anti-evil" cause, principle or foundation that punishment exercises its strange productive influence. Punishment *is*, that is, punishment is a given, something which exists. Punishment performed or punishment performing is an evil produced, a lasting evil. A cause, but also an effect. A principle, but a source as well, a point in time, in duration, and at the same time a line, an occupying and occupied space. Thus it is part of the already existing heritage when the new creation appears. But because it is a heritage, it creates in the same way that any patrimony brings growth: through a contribution of "presence" — a support, a provision, a resource, a reference point to which we can attach our lives' ideals, our projects, our rules of conduct. For a heritage is not merely a gift and an offering; it is a seed, a source of vitality, growth, hope. For a heritage cannot be reduced to that which is given; it provides meaning to the force which gives and establishes.

What seemed relatively unlikely at the outset is now clear: radical punishment is an evil which can never be dissociated from the new regime which it generates. Even transformed into correction, the punishment of justice is not and has not the means of creating a world free of evil and violence, for presentation to the rising generation, the generation which has never known the existing world. And it is unnecessary to resort to the Rousseauist snare of natural goodness to realize that the heritage of radical punishment is foreign to the concepts of purity and innocence and that it remains essentially a model of mimetic violence, endlessly repeated. On this latter point, child psychology proves astonishingly close to our anthropological hypothesis. Let us look closer.

Our aim is to demonstrate that the child, despite his own internal logic of genetic progression, begins very early to learn through imitation. To do so, we shall limit ourselves to the problem of moral development, or, more specifically, to the concept of justice. Piaget's unique work will serve as our primary reference.[13]

The ethological roots of imitation in the child are apparently at the same time the roots of moral development. "There are indisputably psychobiological roots to the idea of sanction. Blows lead to blows, kindness to kindness, etc. The instinctive reactions of defence and sympathy thus determine a sort of elementary reciprocity which constitutes the field of development essential to retribution." The child is neither good nor bad by "nature". His first dependence is mimetic in nature. Consider the few known cases of children abandoned at birth and left completely without human influence. The only part of their human heritage they retain is their human form, while all their behaviour is perfectly adapted to, consistent with and determined by the environment which has served as their model. But the "average" child, who is introduced to the world by an adult human being — what is he given as a model to imitate? Orders and rules. "So long as there are no rules, vengeance, even disinterested vengeance, will be determined solely by individual sympathies and thus will remain arbitrary: the child will not experience the feeling of punishing an evildoer and protecting an innocent, but simply of conquering an enemy and defending a friend. However, as soon as there are rules..., there are judgments of guilt, innocence and the moral "structure" of retributive justice. These rules are the product of adult instruction and are considered "sacred" by the child because he loves and respects his parents and adults in general. Through them, the "desinterested vengeance" of the child is polarized and "becomes an expiatory sanction", the first type of retributive justice. Thus, with adult intervention, "even before the appearance of language", the child is introduced to sanctions. In and through his extreme dependence on the adult, he is constantly supervised and sanctioned by scolding or encouragement, by taboos, orders, punishments. Because he loves and respects his parents, the child considers adult reactions natural, legitimate and necessary. Indeed, they constitute the "psychological point of departure of the idea of the expiatory sanction". "The concept of expiatory sanction thus results entirely from the conjunction of two influences: the individual influence, which is the need for vengeance, including derivative and disinterested vengeance, and the social influence, which is adult authority imposing respect for orders and respect for vengeance in the case of violations."

In sum, the first morality of the child can be defined as a morality of adult constraint or a morality of heteronomy, Piaget continues; the idea of the expiatory sanction in the child appears to be bound up with the unilateral respect which he demonstrates for adult authority; and the concept of retributive justice, his first allegiance to justice. This unilateral imposition is so strong that the child must learn to resist it in order to develop. In fact, it is despite adult orders, against and in opposition to them in a sense that the child slowly, and according to his own pattern, develops a morality of solidarity, co-operation and autonomy, in which the concept of distributive justice dominates and the thesis of expiation is modified into a thesis of reparation and reciprocity. Although he does not expand upon this profound intuition, Piaget notes the great wisdom of the child, who seeks, as if by instinct, to liberate himself from the yoke of vengeance as he develops. "The child places forgiveness above vengeance, not through weakness, but because with vengeance 'it's never over' (10-year-old boy)." Somewhat later, Piaget touches on our problematics again in attempting to answer the question: "how can the child be turned away from evil?" Through the practice of evil or through the practice of good? Durkheim opts for the first path, in defending the thesis of punishment within the school. Piaget criticizes him for this stand and explains his oppositon to it at length, demonstrating the preferability of "self-government", that is, in his opinion, the practice of good.

How can we avoid seeing the striking parallel which exists between Piaget's discovery and our own hypothesis? The first lesson learned by the mimetic child is the lesson of expiatory justice. Our society, for all its noble and generous intentions, has made no effort to improve this first teaching. In order to ensure that the child, from infancy, is perfectly at ease and established in the territory of what is due, it has offered him a charter of the rights of the child. Definitively, penal justice seeks to be definitive. It also poses the vital question: how are we to be turned away from evil? Its answer, as we have pointed out so often, is always the same: punish evil and correct evil. In other words, do evil to eliminate evil. "In the execution of the most ordinary punishment, in the most faithful observance of legal forms, reign the active forces of vengeance."[14]

Beyond a doubt, penitentiary education will not find its principal justification in the judicial function, whether punitive or curative. Over and above all our arguments, the fundamental reason lies perhaps in the essentially irreconcilable marriage of convenience between justice and the world. A wise old rabbinical saying expresses it best: "If you search the world, you will not find absolute justice. If you search absolute justice, you will not find the world."

NOTES

1. See Edward Shea, "Teaching Prisoners", *Education Canada*, Summer 1980. Based on a study by A.R. Roberts, *Readings in Prison Education* (1973), the author states: "There is a general dearth of reports on empirical studies of correctional education. For example, between 1940 and 1968 only six doctoral dissertations focus on the subject" (p. 40). This is even more true with respect to the determination of reasons other than the utilitarian to justify the role of education in prison.

2. Three texts have been of particular value: *Mensonge romantique et vérité romanesque*, Paris, Grasset, coll. "Pluriel", 1979 (1961); *La violence et le sacré*, Paris, Grasset, coll. "Pluriel", 1980 (1972); *Des choses cachées depuis la fondation du monde*, Paris, Grasset, 1978.

3. J. Lacan, *Écrits*, Paris, Seuil, 1966, p. 502. He adds: "Hence we can say that it is in the chain of the signifier that meaning *insists*, but that none of the elements of the chain *consists* of the signification of which it is capable at the actual moment". *Ibid*.

4. Paul Claudel, *Réflexions sur la poésie*, Paris, Gallimard, "Idées", 1967, pp. 55-57.

5. It would be impossible to measure by page references what this study owes to René Girard's hypothesis. It is not that our conclusion would be different without it; rather, our study itself would not exist.

6. Heidegger, *Kant et le problème de la métaphysique* (Kant and the Problem of Metaphysics), Paris, Gallimard, 1953, p. 266.

7. "La violence et le sacré, Discussion avec René Girard", *Esprit*, November 1973, p. 531.

8. V. Jankélévitch, *Traité des Vertus*, Paris, Bordas, 1959, p. 423. This "oxygen" is charity, the author continues: "the will of justice is charity", p. 436.

9. Michel foucault, *Nouvel observateur*, May 30 — June 5, 1977.

10. Bossuet, *Sermon sur la justice*.

11. Thomas Aquinas, *Summa theologica*, Ia IIae, q 60, art. 31.

12. St-Exupéry, *Citadelle*, Paris, coll. "La Pléiade", 1959, p. 709. "And they all departed enriched, so they thought, with their pieces of temple, but dispossessed of that which was divine in them and now merely rubbish."

13. J. Piaget, *Le jugement moral chez l'enfant* (The Moral Judgment of the Child), Paris, PUF, 1973 (1st edition 1932). The following quotations are all from this work.

14. M. Foucault, *Surveiller et punir*.

13. THE IDEA OF FAIRNESS AS THE BASIS FOR THE EDUCATIONAL REFORM OF THE PRISON

Peter Scharf

Conceptions of Punishment Used in the Definition of Inmate Rights

The years since the Attica uprising have seen numerous legal and political efforts to define the legal and political rights of incarcerated felons. While there has been ample discussion on which specific rights should be granted prisoners, there has been little debate on the more abstract question of whether from a philosophical point of view, prisoners need be granted any rights at all. This paper seeks to offer a philosophic justification for the minimal legal rights of prisoners. We will offer a conception of punishment derived from social contract theory which differs from utilitarian and retributive theories of punishment. We will suggest that the rights of offenders should not necessarily be based on considerations of either rehabilitation or general utility. Rather, we hope to argue, prisoner rights should be based on a notion of the social contract which specifies clearly which liberties may agreeably be lost when a person commits a serious felony. We will further argue that critical to the maintenance of inmate rights is the existence of justice mechanisms which allows inmates to claim rights in everyday prison practice. We will offer that a working democratic framework seen in T.M. Osborne's "Mutual Welfare League" as one model capable of assuring *de facto* as well as *de jure* inmate rights. This problem of inmate rights seems

Paper presented to the World Congress in Education: Values and the School; Symposium on Prison Education, Université du Québec à Trois-Rivières, July, 1981.

essential to any fundamental reform of either prisons or the idea of imprisonment. Reform efforts have lacked any fundamental direction, in that they have failed to present a reasoned philosophic defense of inmate rights, rather relying upon the cliches on "inmate power" or the romantic rhetoric of liberal humanistic sentiment. In our view, a far more reasoned view is required. We must carefully define the moral limits of punishment and ensure that they are respected in the everyday reality of the prison.

We will further argue that programs such as have been described elsewhere by Scharf, Hickey and Scharf, Duguid and Ackley advocating education as a strategy of prison reform might be better defended in terms of a conception of fundamental social right than they are by justifying them in treatment, social control or other psychological theory. It might be argued that education may be conceived of as a social good, much like money, right to life, health or other such social intangeables. Viewed from this perspective, society distributes educational goods unevenly and perhaps unfairly. The reformer's task, given this line of reasoning, is not simply to create an educational prison program for some psychological aim directed at the inmates. Rather, the goal of prison reform should be posed in terms of establishing the optimum balance of educational goods, focusing upon the rights of one of the least advantaged groups in society: the prisoner population.

It should be noted that efforts in prisoner reform have always raised the issue of social justice; however, this issue was usually discussed in terms of the prisoner himself becoming more morally mature or just. Here we will depart from conventional developmental theory asserting that moral educators involved in prisoner education have confused means with ends. Rather than creating an educational program as a means towards prisoner change, it might be suggested that a proper end of prison may be the creation of a broad humanistic education for the prison inmate. In reviewing theories of inmate rights, we will argue that a prisoner can reasonably expect such a quality education to be his due in a democratic and just society in that conviction of a serious felony cannot reasonably diminish a person's right to expect relative equality in social goods, including educational services.

The Moral Limits of Punishment

Since the first prisons were constructed, there has existed an ongoing debate as to what should constitute the prison inmate's moral and legal rights. That some limits must be placed upon punishment seems obvious. Were we to castrate all parking violators or even confidence men, we would all be outraged. Yet, philosophers widely disagree both at to what these limits might be as well as the moral principles underlying such limits. This discussion of the limit is, of course, related to the more general aspect of the rationale for punishment itself.

Prior to the Enlightment, society offered merely religious or revenge justifications for punishment. The criminal was paying a debt to the victim, meted out by outraged individuals. Such notions of vengeance carried little sense of limit or proportion. More recently, the utilitarian theory of punisment of Hobbes (1953), Bentham (1970), and later Mill (1859), and the theory of desert posited by Immanuel Kant (1957), and Pincoff (1972), suggest discrete justification for imprisonment with clear morally definable limits.

Utilitarian theory offers that imprisonment is justified in order to maximize the sum of individual welfares (i.e., "greatest good for the number"). The Utilitarian doctrine of specific deterrence suggests that people who are tempted to misbehave, to trample the rights of others, to sacrifice public welfare for private gain, can be deterred from such conduct by fear of punishment. Similarly, it is argued that potential criminals, viewing the criminal's plight, will be similarly deterred (general deterrence). Utilitarian theory suggests that the mandate to imprison derives from the obligation to maximize the sum of individual welfares, rather than simply to protect the existing state. John Mill (1859), a liberal utilitarian, argues that punishment should be limited by the minimal deterrent necessary to deter wrongdoers from jeopardizing others. This view tends to argue for both the humanization and liberalization of prison sentences. Other utilitarians, such as Bentham (1970) himself, have argued that the pain exacted from the criminal is justified by the welfare gains attained by others. Thus, the inflicting of pain throughtout imprisonment represents a social good when judged by other overall sum of welfares in society.

One problem with the utilitarian doctrine is that the justification for inmate rights rests on the notion that a prison which allows maximum prisoner rights will, in fact, reform the inmates involved as well as remain as a deterrent to other future crimes. Thus, the greatest good might be enhanced if a fair and just prison would return its prisoners to society thoroughly reformed as well as would still serve as a deterrent to future crime by the prisoner as well as others. Critical to this justification of inmate rights are the empirical facts as to whether or not a prison which guarantees inmates basic social and legal rights will rehabilitate offenders as well as maintain a deterrent function. The evidence from such recent studies such as that conducted by Martinson (1974) questions whether liberalization of the prison has any rehabilitative benefits to inmates. This study also questions whether a prison which guarantees full legal rights would deter future crimes as well as would a more restrictive facility. Given the utilitarian notion of inmate rights, there is little reason to reform the prison other than to reform the offender; rights given this view are a means to an end: the achievement of the greatest good for the greatest number. In the absence of gains in terms of rehabilitation, inmate legal rights are neither necessary nor even desirable.

While long dominant among penologists, the utilitarian theory of punishment has been challenged repeatedly by what is referred to as retributive theory of just desert. This position is not to be confronted with simple "eye-for-an-eye" retribution. Such theorists as Fogel (1973), a penologist, Pincoff (1972), a philosopher, and Von Hirsch (1976), a lawyer, have recently argued following Kant (1952), that punishment must not be justified as a means to an end. Utilitarian theory, they argue, justifies the punishment of one individual as being necessary to protect the state or other person's welfare. Imprisonment, they assert, is justified only when a "moral wrong" justifies imprisonment. The criminal, through his act, is either morally deserving of punishment, or there should be no imprisonment at all. To argue that we should imprison a man because we wish to "rehabilitate" him or to "protect others" cannot be just.

The retributive desert theorists generally are not primarily concerned with either deterrence or rehabilitation. They seek, rather, to give the criminal a deserved punishment regardless of the consequences to the criminal or society. This notion assumes that wrong acts "deserve" blame as good acts deserve praise. A crime demands that we punish the criminal, even if this act were to have no perceptible effect on future crime by the offender himself or on other potential offenders. The limits of punishment similarly set by the wrongness of the act. Any price may be exacted providing the offense is sufficiently heinous. Given this formula, the rights of prisoners are rarely considered. The limits of punishment is determined more by the moral nature of the crime rather than the consequences of either the crime or its punishment.

Recent work by Hart (1968), Morris (1974), and Rawls (1971), have sought to philosophically disentangle some of the contradictions in both utilitarian and desert theory of punishment to offer both a coherent theory of punishment as well as some sensible notion of the moral rights of the offender. For example, Rawls' *Theory of Justice* (ibid.) offers a contractual notion of social justice distinct from a utilitarian or desert arguments. He postulates a hypothetical stage of nature in which abstract persons meet prior to the incorporation of a future society. Rawls asks, "What ethical principles could any person agree to were he *not* to know what position he would occupy in the future society?" For example, he must agree to principles of income distribution, not knowing if he were to be rich or poor, ditch-digger or medical specialist. This

> ... ensures that no one is advantaged or disadvantaged in the choice of principles by the outcome of natural change of the contingency of social circumstances. Since all are similarly situated and no one is able to design principles to favor his particular condition, the principles of justice are the result of a fair agreement or bargain (1971).

Rawls suggests that only two ethical principles which may be intutively agreed to from this "veil of ignorance" are:

> First, each person is to have a basic right to the most extensive basic liberty compatible for a similar liberty to others.
> Second, social and economic liberties are to be arranged so that they are both reasonably expected to be everyone's advantage and (are) attached to positions and offices open to all (1971).

Rawls' position differs from the utilitarian formulation in that, using utilitarian calculations, one may subordinate another person's welfare to another's gain. For example, we can kill a murderer to save future lives from deterred murders. Similarly, President Truman could justify the dropping of the Atom bomb on Hiroshima to save the American "G.I.'s" and Japanese who would have died were the allies to have invaded the Japanese mainland. Also one can justify the imprisoning of a political agitator to save the social cost of a riot were he to remain free in a hostile community. Rawls offers the example that Utilitarian logic could be used to justify slavery in that the social costs of freeing the slaves (i.e., Civil War) might outweigh the gains of freeing them.

The fairness of 'punishment' becomes a question of the degree to which the loss of liberty through imprisonment is consistent with the losses a person could ideally agree to were he not to know if he were to become a criminal. This differs with the utilitarian justification of imprisonment, as the utilitarian logic leads us to allow one man to suffer for the greater good of *other* members of society. This is unfair as it conflicts with a core Rawls axiom that all people in society should be treated as moral ends in themselves:

> ... treating men as ends in themselves implies at the very least treating them in accordance with the principles to which they would consent in an original position of equality. For in this situation men have equal representation as moral persons who regard themselves as end and the principles they accept will be rationally designed to protect the claims of their persons (1971).

Rawls' notion of ideal agreement leads us to accept what Morris calls a "moral limit on punishment" (1974). We must limit punishment to what might be agreed to from the original position; that is, we must only punish to the extent that the loss of liberty would be aggreeable were one not to know whether or not he were to become a criminal; and the loss of liberty must be justified as the minimal loss consistent with the maintenance of the same liberty among others.

Kohlberg and Elfenbein (1981) argue that such a definition excludes certain penalties — for example, the use of capital punishment to deter murder. They offer:

> would persons in the original position contract into a system of capital punishment? For one thing, we can be absolutely certain that whatever appeal the ideal of retributive punishment may have in the abstract, vanishes altogether once we put ourselves into the original position. For no rational person who thought that he himself might be the object of retribution would contract into a penal system founded thereon, particularly when the retribution is to be exacted in the form of death. Even if such a system would promote the validation of the social order in the mind of the average citizen, this objective is simply not worth risking one's life for. Persons in the original position would, however, be inclined to agree to some forms of punishment that fulfilled a deterrence function. That is, they would be willing to run the risk of turning out to be a criminal and suffering some forms of punishment if such an arrangement would materially reduce their chances of being victimized by crime if they turned out

to be noncriminal. But recognizing that they might be the criminal, they would opt for the minimum punishment that would effectively deter the crime. The optimal punishment would be that which is just severe enough to offset the gains which might be realized from the commission of the offense... No murderer can gain enough by murdering to offset the cost of losing his own life. The "rational" murderer, therefore, who engages in a sort of cost-benefit analysis before killing, can theoretically be deterred by a penalty that falls short not only of death but of life imprisonment as well. What about the irrational murderer? Even though the punishment whose cost just exceeds the benefit to be gained will not deter him, persons in the original position would never agree to impose a more severe penalty upon such a killer. In the first place, a harsher punishment would not commend itself on deterrence ground, since by definition the irrational murderer is not deterrable. Moreover, the death penalty would never be an attractive arrangement to persons who themselves had to run the risk of being the criminal. Even if there were reasons to expect an additional deterrence payoff to capital punishment, persons in the original position would still reject the death penalty because rationality would dictate that they forgo (sic) the additional protection which they would enjoy as the potential victim, rather than take the chance of being executed if they turned out to be the murderer (1981).

Prisoner Rights Reconsidered from Rawls' Theory of Justice

The problem of prisoner rights is conceptually related to our articulation of a coherent theory of punishment. Yet even beyond such a theory one is forced to ask a rather specific and difficult question: which rights might agreeably be retained by the convicted felon? Revealing is the fact that in Ernest Van de Haag's otherwise almost encyclopedic book, *Punishing Criminals* (1975), there is almost no discussion as to this problem of prisoner rights.

Perhaps related to the philosphic difficulty of this problem is that the courts have taken what has been referred to as a "hands-off" position on the subject of the rights of offenders. In one court decision, the inmate was legally "a slave for a while." Similarly, in a nineteenth-century decision, he had forfeited not only "his liberty, but all his personal rights, except those which the law in its humanity grants to him." In more recent federal court decisions, the judicial "hands-off" policy toward the prison has been somewhat modified. In a number of key cases (cf. "Sostre vs. Rockefeller, Johnson vs. Avery," etc.) there have been successful suits to ensure at least minimal procedural justice for the inmate. The clearest areas are the most obvious. Prison officials are legally able to protect the health and safety of their prisoners. An Arkansas federal court decision held that, under the Cruel and Unusual Punishment doctrine, the officials of the notorious Commins Farm must protect its inmates from rape and assault by other inmates. Similarly, most states have outlawed the use of corporal punishment. With many restrictions, the courts have upheld the right of inmates to receive religious materials and, in some cases, have allowed observance of religious dietary practices and ensured other first ammendment liberties such as the right to receive political materials. On other issues as the offender's right to rehabilitation, sexual expression, access to the courts, freedom of assembly, etc., there have been potentially explosive but ambiguous replies from the courts. In many cases, judges have been simply unwilling to mandate changes which the corrections system has argued would throw its institutions into "anarchy and chaos."

Underlying this legal debate on prison rights has been the obscured philosophical issue. Why should the offender be able to claim any rights at all? Why should an offender morally claim the right to participate in disciplinary decisions, to be allowed to engage in political debate or be free to assemble with other inmates? Which rights claimed by citizens at large can the offender claim to be his? Is there any reasonable standard which the prison must honor in the context of a democratic and fair society.

Needless to say, Utilitarian Desert, and Contractual theories all yield different responses to these questions. As we earlier noted, Utilitarian arguments tend to demand the preservation of prisoner rights *providing* that it serves to increase the "greatest good for the greatest number." The rights of offenders are a means towards other social ends. If maximization of social goods is achieved by a benign prison, this aids rehabilitation. If, on the other hand, we find that general utility is served by harsh exemplory punishments, then the prison becomes severe and cruel. Considering recent research which indicates that the rehabilitativeness of any prison is at least questionable, then both the liberalization and humanization of the prison becomes extremely tenuous.

The desert position, in contrast, in its ideal form proscribes different levels of severity independent of the effect of such severity on either offender of society. A cruel sex offender using the principle of desert might receive harsher and longer punishment than would a check forger. This assumes gradients of severity or cruelty of imprisonment which fit the moral wrongness of specific crimes. Assuming that crimes were considered sufficiently morally heinous, the desert prison might be quite brutal, meeting out pain in response to the grievous wrong of the offender.

In contrast to the utilitarianism and desert theorists, the contractual perspective as articulated by Rawls, allows for the loss of social rights only under clearly specified conditions. Rawls argues that the liberty of a person within the social contract can only be reduced, compared with other members, when it is the good of the least advantaged as well as most advantaged, considered, of course, from the veil of ignorance (i.e., assuming that we do not know who is the most or least advantaged). Losses are *only* justified when the prisoner himself might agree that they were for his good as well as *any* other member of society. Thus, a loss in freedom of speech, assembly, due process, *habeas corpus*, etc., is only justified when the prisoner could agree (from the veil of ignorance) to this loss. Such an agreement might only be attained under specific conditions. For example, when the maintenance of freedom of assembly presented danger to either the prison or to the larger community, it might be reasonable for the prison, as well as any member of society to agree to its *temporary* curtailment. Similarly, the right to jury by peers (i.e., other inmates) might only be revoked when there was clear evidence that the process of fairness implied in the jury system was being subverted. Stated in other terms, this conception of inmate rights assumes that rights granted other citizens at large belong to the inmate *unless* society can show them incompatible with common welfare so that any reasonable inmate might agree to their temporary suspension. The only social right which should automatically be abrogated is the right to freedom of movement. Other legal rights consistent with agreeable social welfare of the prison remain with the prisoner.

Needless to say, many dilemmas still remain. For example, should the prison restrict freedom to sexual access, right to wages, or the right to form a corporation? From Rawls' perspective, such losses, while allowable, using either utilitarian or desert arguments, do not follow from the original position. Take the rather simple case of the right to earn wages (Thirteenth Amendment). When can a prison, for example, deny the inmate the right to sell his labor? In contrast to the utilitarian position where such rights might be revoked to provide examples to deter future criminals, or the retributive position where such rights might be revoked as necessary retribution, using Rawl's, there would be rather restrictive conditions where Thirteenth Amendment liberty might be revoked : such a liberty, as others, might be revoked, or curtailed *only* when it was to the advantage of *both* the prisoner as well as other members of both the prison and larger society. The only condition we think of which would satisfy this condition, would be cases where the prison society would be on the brink of near social chaos, and that a "free" labor system was contributing to this chaos. Even the most pessimistic observers of prison life would agree that such conditions are rather rare. While constraint in the name of order might be claimed by prison authorities, the burden of proof (that chaos was imminent) would remain with society.

This argument implies that the one loss which prisoners in democratic society might suffer is the loss of liberty. All other rights, political, economic, educational, should be maintained as they exist with other citizens. This, needless to say, is a somewhat radical argument for prisoner rights. It represents an ideal to be attained in a truly democratic society, an extension of the contractualist argument that rights which are now granted to citizens at large, be extended to prison inmates. The prison given this notion of an ideal conception of justice is given an affirmative obligation to uphold the rights of offenders. Unless it can establish that a loss in rights will, in fact, aid the least advantaged (i.e., the prisoner) as well as the most advantaged, all rights granted other citizens *must* be granted the prisoner as well.

Some element of what is proposed here has already been implemented into Swedish penal law. Inmates in Sweden are guaranteed under Swedish law bargaining, work, unionization and even 'vacation rights.' The right to sexual access is now being discussed. The intent of these reforms is to approximate for the prisoner the political rights of other Swedish citizens. Similarly, the American Friends Service Committee's *Struggle for Justice* (1972) has proposed for American prisoners a similar "Bill of Rights." This, of course, represents a future ideal, rather than a concrete proposal for contemporary prisons.

Guaranteeing Inmate Rights in Prison Practices

Even if society were to acknowledge legal rights as suggested by the Swedish or Quaker proposals, there remains the bewildering dilemma of how these rights granted by law are to be guaranteed in practice. Rights even if protected by the courts must be operation-alized in day to day prison practice. Unless a structure is developed to handle day to day conflicts, equitably and fairly, a legal change in the inmates' status would be practically meaningless. As Weber has noted, there is the critical distinction between *possessing* and *claiming* these rights. As Goldfarb and Singer (1973) observe, "the courts are hesitant to review prisoner grievances for fear of being inundated with claims." In practice, few inmates have the consciousness or the means to redress grievances through legal channels. Gelhorn (1968) for example argues:

> Nowhere is the need for external examination of grievances greater than in America's prisons, jails, and other places of detention... Inmates, many of them ill-adjusted socially and resistant to discipline, live perforce in an authoritarian setting; they are poorly equiped by nature or training to participate in rational planning for themselves or their companies. Those whom a court has condemned to loss of freedom cannot expect, then, to find behind prison walls a fully fashioned democracy, keenly sensitive to individual wishes. Nonetheless, the man under detention continues to be a man. He is not free, but neither is he without rights. The question to be considered is how the prisoner's residual rights can best be protected without destroying a penal institution's discipline...

A number of ideas have been tendered to address this problem of non-judicial remedies within prisons. Chief Justice Warren Berger favors a system of judicial state inspectors. Others have suggested allocating funds to increase access to law libraries, legal counselors, social workers and conflict mediatorys. Most popular among these non-judicial means of ensuring prison justice is the idea of the correctional Ombudsman, implemented in Minnesota (as well as in Scandinavian prisons). The Ombudsman, in this model, acts to complement the mechanisms available to a prison disciplinary system. Most typically, he has the power to reverse disciplinary actions, advocate changes within prison conditions (i.e., new books in the library, fewer macaroni and cheese dinners), and, as well, to give inmates legal advice.

Experiments in democratic self government provide another means to implement inmate legal rights. This is one avenue to reform we consider both promising and largely unexplored. T.M. Osborne's "Mutual Welfare League" provides a working historical model of both inmate legislative and judicial participation as well as a model of workable prison justice. Following a constitutional convention, the inmates elected two men from each workshop to act as their representatives. This "congress" of delegates became Sing Sing's working governmental body. In times of crisis, a general Community Meeting would be called to either support or contest the actions of the delegates. The delegates elected an executive board of nine inmates who coordinated routine decision-making. The executive board, in turn, elected a Sergeant at Arms who might be described as Sing Sing's "police chief." Policy decisions were routinely delegated to the executive committee. When for example the men in the foundry shop needed special shoes or when a guard needed money to visit a sick relative, the request would be adjudicated by the executive committee. Conflicts between inmates and staff were mediated as well. When for example the workers in the shoe shop appeared to be malingering, an order to return to work was delivered by the executive committee upon receiving a complaint (judged legitimate) by the Captain of the Shoemaker. A league court was responsible for nearly all disciplinary infractions committed in the prison. At Sing Sing, five inmate-judges served for five months each. The hearings were open to all members of the League. Appeals might be made to the warden. At the appeals hearing, the inmate-judges would be forced to explain the justice of their decision. Often, more than one-hundred inmates would attend an appeals hearing. Tannenbaum (1933) suggests that such appeals served to articulate the judicial principles implicit in prison discipline as to affirm the inmate community and the warden's commitment to the League's punitive judicial system:

> When appealed, the cases served many useful purposes. Appeal gave the culprit a sense that he had had a fair trial. It compelled the judges to defend their decision in public before the Warden and before the community on grounds that would (seem fair) to both; the interests of the Warden and the prison community thus united against the law-breaker. It gave the Warden an opportunity to know what was going on and an opportunity to lay down fundamental rules of policy which would govern not only the action of the prisoners but of the law-enforcing machinery. And it compelled the Warden to behave in a manner which the prison community would recognize as just and fair.

Such experiments such as Osborne and later efforts by such reformers as Thomas Martin (1976) and on a more minor scale by the author (1980) to encourage inmate participation in self-governance may be justified by the ideal of inmate rights rather than by a utilitarian based concept of rehabilitation. Viewed in this way the fundamental task of the prison becomes the guarantee of social justice. Reform should be based not on the tenuous expectation of rehabilitation but rather to guarantee rights which legitimately follow from a just social contract.

Conclusions

This paper has attempted to define a philosophically reasonable conception of inmate rights. We have suggested that a Rawlsian conception of social justice provides a perhaps more philosophically reasoned basis for defining inmate rights than does either utilitarian or desert theory. We also suggest that critical to operationalizing this position is a strategy to guarantee inmate rights in reality as well as in law. We have further suggested that experiments in prisoner democracy (often justified in terms of citizenship education) may be more reasonably and sensibly defended in terms of the goal of ensuring social justice for the convicted felon. Our own work using developmental theory to create just community programs in schools, and prisons, for example, might be best justified in terms of ensuring social rights than in terms of lowering inmate recidivism rates or other similar objectives. In a similar vein, educational programs, such as are described by Duguid might be better justified in terms of principles of social right and social justice, than in terms of utilitarian crime control criteria. Rawls, for example, speaks of his principle of social distribution as including such goods as educational and health related intangeable rewards. Thus, the just society must strive to ensure a fair distribution of educational devices if it is to act consistently with Rawls' conception of social justice. Viewed in this sense a program such as conceived of by Duguid may be more appropriately considered a fundamental social right than an experiment in prison reform. From this perspective, all men (or women) have a *prima facie* right to expect to have access to a quality education, especially one that concerns itself with fundamental issues of social living such as is offered in the core Matsqui University Program. By creating such a program, it is possible (in addition to providing social useful stimulation and humanization) to provide what any man should be reasonably able to expect from a just society — the experience of a structured intellectual community in the search for truth. It should be noted that from the perspective we have offered this expectation should be honored independent of the crime committed by the offender, in that there is no reason that the loss of this right should logically follow from the act of his conviction of a crime.

From this perspective, educational reform should be conceived of in terms of a theory of justice rather than as an aspect of a psychological theory of prisoner reform. Given this premise, such interventions as have been described by Duguid, Hickey and Scharf, Ackley and others follow not from societies' instrumental desire to "reform" the prisoner, but rather as a social commitment to insure educational fairness in a just society.

REFERENCES

AMERICAN FRIENDS SERVICE COMMITTEE
1972: *Struggle for Justice*, Cambridge, Mass.

BENTHAM, J.
1970: *An Introduction to the Principles of Morals and Legislation*, Hart, London, Athlone Press, 1970.

FOGEL, D.
1973: *We Are the Living Proof*, Cincinnati, Ohio, Anderson.

GELHORN, H.
1968: *Systems of Arbitration*, Unpublished paper.

GOLDFARB, R., SINGER, L.
1973: *After Conviction*, New York, Simon and Shuster.

HART, H.
1968: *Punishment and Responsibility*, New York, Oxford University Press.

HOBBES, T.
1953: *Leviathan*, New York, Dutton.

KANT, I.
1952: *Critique of Practical Reasoning*, Chicago, Encyclopaedia Britannica.

KOHLBERG, L.
1981: *The Philosophy of the Psychology of Moral Development*, San Francisco, Harper and Row.

MARTIN, T.
1976: *The Dilemma of Prison Reform*, New York, Holt, Rinehart and Winston.

MARTINSON, R.
1974: What Works: Questions and Answers about Prison Reform, *Public Interest*, vol. 35.

MILL, J.S.
1859: *On Liberty*, London, Longman.

MORRIS, N.
1974: *The Future of Inprisonment*, Chicago, University of Chicago Press.

PINCOFF, R.
1972: *Desert and Punishment*, Unpublished paper.

RAWLS, J.
1971: *A Theory of Justice*, Cambridge, Mass., Harvard University Press.

SCHARF, P. Hickey, J.
1980: *Toward a Just Correctional System*, San Francisco, Jossey Bass.

TANNENBAUM, F.
1933: *Osborne of Sing-Sing*, Capitol Hill, University of North Carolina Press.

VAN DE HAAG, E.
1975: *Punishing Criminals*, New York, Basic Books.

VON HIRSCH, A.
1976: *Doing Justice: A Choice of Punishment*, New York, Hill and Wang.

14. THE MAJOR PSYCHOLOGICAL PROCESSES IN MORAL BEHAVIOR

James R. Rest

In recent years the rationale of many value-education programs and intervention programs in prisons have drawn from research in developmental psychology. The work of Kohlberg on the cognitive development of moral judgment has been particularly influential. Currently, about a hundred studies have investigated the association of moral judgment development with measures of behavior, (including criminal and delinquent behavior) and in general, there seems to be a consistent, significant link between the two (Blasi, 1980; Rest, 1979a). However the link is not very strong, and many things besides moral judgment seem to be influential in determining behavior. Currently, many intriguing educational programs have been developed and evaluated. But it is still too early to know how successful these programs will be, particularly when operated as on-going, routine programs by personnel who don't have a doctoral dissertation riding on the outcome. Some critics have challenged the rationale of these programs as buying into a too-narrow conception of morality, a conception of morality that is too cognitivist, too intellectual and too cerebral; the critics point to other research in morality which emphasizes non-cognitive and affective aspects as the crucial factors in morality. The question arises then, are the moral education programs which appeal to moral judgment research really based on a viable foundation? Must one first become a "true believer" in the Kohlberg vision of things before these programs

Paper presented to the World Congress in Education: Values and the School; Symposium on Prison Education, Université du Québec à Trois-Rivières, July, 1981.

make sense? If one emphasizes moral judgment as the critical element in morality, must one deny the existence and importance of other factors?

In the present paper I shall examine the various aspects of morality that have been emphasized in psychological research, and I shall propose a more general model of the ensemble of psychological processes involved in the production of moral behavior. The general drift of this discussion is that moral judgment is a crucial part of morality, but so are other factors. I do not advocate an uncritical, anything-goes eclecticism, but rather will attempt to portray what the major factors are in morality, and how they interact and interrelate in the production of moral behavior. Hopefully, a more encompassing and integrated view of morality as an ensemble of psychological processes will provide a firmer basis for programs in moral education.

Indicators of Morality in Psychological Research

Psychologists have used a variety of criteria as indicators of a person's morality: (1) behavior that helps another human being, (2) behavior in conformity with social norms, (3) the internalization of social norms, (4) the arousal of empathy and/or guilt, (5) reasoning about justice, and (6) putting another's interests ahead of one's own. Each of these notions captures something important about morality, but as a complete definition of morality, each has limitations.

Behavior that helps other human beings is certainly part of morality. Indeed, whenever a person's behavior affects the welfare of another person, a question of morality is involved. But morality cannot be defined as *any* activity that helps people. Otherwise we would have to regard intestinal bacteria that aid digestion as behaving "morally," or the ozone layer in the upper atmosphere that filters out harmful rays of the sun as behaving "morally." If we define morality in terms of helpful consequences, we would have to regard as moral the actions of a wife who tries to poison her husband by putting harsh chemicals in his food, but instead of killing him, cures his gout. *Moral* behavior implies activity regulated by certain internal processes, not any and every activity that helps human beings.

Behaving in conformity with social norms also touches on an important aspect of morality. Morality is a social enterprise, involving the establishment of cooperative social structures (promises, institutions, laws, roles, and contracts) that individuals must support to accomplish shared goals (e.g., mutual protection, economic coordination, and education of the young). Individuals who violate group norms are refusing to accept their part in making that system work, and as well might be showing contempt for the shared goals of the group.

Sometimes, however, particular norms of a society are actually inconsistent with cherished social goals; and sometimes certain social arrangements may place a disproportionate burden on some members of the society. There can be various types of non-conformists: those who protest norms that are unjust or inconsistent with ideal social goals and who are willing to incur punishment to dramatize their cause. Nonconformists such as Socrates, Sir Thomas More, Gandhi, and Martin Luther King obviously differ from nonconformists such as Al Capone, Lee Harvey Oswald, and Jack the Ripper. Conformity to group norms, therefore, is an inadequate criterion of morality. Furthermore, many matters of conformity are not primarily *moral* matters, such as eating etiquette, dress styles, and many customs of business, politics, and social intercourse. In addition, the smooth functioning of a society need not imply a high level of morality. The societies of bees and ants are well-coordinated but we do not regard their behavior as *moral*, because such coordination is not governed by individual choice and a desire to cooperate for shared goals, but by instinct. Likewise, a society tyrannized by a few people enslaving the masses may have a high degree of conformity to social norms, but we would regard that coordination of activity as based on coercion, not morality.

Some writers have described moral development as an "inter-nalization" process whereby behavior comes to be governed by internal standards in the absence of external reinforcement. This notion is consistent with the comment above, namely, that behavior produced by coercion cannot be regarded as morality. The internali-zation notion is appealing in that it emphasizes that morality involves an internal governance system. Indeed, one aspect of moral development is a person's becoming increasingly independent of the pressures and temptations of the immediate situation and more governed by long-term plans and more encompassing goals. Yet the notion of "internalization" by itself does not capture the active *social* constructive side of morality, involving the balancing of one's interests with other's interests and the coordination of long-term

plans and goals with other persons in unified schemes of cooperation. "Internalized behavior" usually is described as a pattern of
behavior originally established by external pressure, that later
persists in the absence of external pressure. But such behavior
would include phobias and mindless habits, and this misses the
social-constructive character of morality. Becoming increasingly
"internalized" *per se* (free of external constraints) could mark the
onset of autism or schizophrenia.

The arousal of empathy is an important motivator of moral action.
Acting in accord with empathy is not necessarily moral, however; for
instance, the new medical intern who can not administer an injection
into the arm of a crying child because he empathizes too much; the
teacher who gives certain children advantages because he empathizes with some children more than others; the mother who over-
protects her child because she is too emotionally identified with the
child for its own good. Similarly, the arousal of guilt indicates the
presence of inner standards, and that emotion also is an important
motivator. However, the capacity for guilt cannot be the defining
characteristic of morality, for then guilt-ridden neurotics would
have to be regarded as the height of moral perfection. Theories that
define morality in terms of behavior driven by the emotion of
empathy and guilt are deficient in two respects: first, as cited above,
these emotions are not always dependable guides; second, the
emotions of empathy and guilt are generally considered "good"
emotions in contrast to the "bad" emotions of envy and sadism. The
value placed on the emotions of empathy and guilt is grounded on
some more fundamental criteria of goodness; it is not correct that
any behavior that follows from a strong human emotion is good.
Otherwise we would promote envy and sadism as much as empathy
and guilt.

Reasoning about justice must surely be part of the moral process
because so many moral problems involve finding some balance
between competing claims and interests. Yet moral reasoning *per se*
is not all there is to morality; good reasoning does not necessarily
translate into good deeds. Furthermore, sophisticated reasoning can
sometimes mask or defend self-serving behavior.

Putting another's interests ahead of one's own is the operational
definition of much recent research on "prosocial" behavior. In the
typical study of prosocial behavior, the subject is given the choice of
acting to help another at cost to oneself or to help oneself at cost to
another. If the prosocial act costs something to the decision-maker,

we have more assurance that helping another is not really selfishly motivated. But considering only situations in which self-interest is opposed to another's interests eliminates cooperative situations (in which the self both gains and gives). Consequently cooperation is not included as "prosocial." In cooperative arrangements one does not martyr self-interest (the self's interests are as important as anyone else's, although not more so). Some pro-social writers seem to suggest that self-interest is intrinsically less important than someone else's interest (by labeling the *pro-social* alternative as the one in which the self loses and the other gains). But in many situations, self-sacrifice is not morally justified (e.g., the demonstrator who sets fire to himself to publicize a grievance when other means could have been effective; the wife who sacrifices her integrity and individual development to cater to the whims and conveniences of her husband). Moreover, if the prospects for a more moral world rest solely on the martyrdom of self-interest (instead of cooperation), then can we be very optimistic about the future?

Psychologists who have used one or another of these characteristics of morality have not claimed to be offering a comprehensive definition of morality, but have proposed operational definitions so as to be able to identify subjects as more or less moral for the purposes of their studies. Much of this research has contributed to our understanding. Nevertheless, the limitations of these conceptions need to be noted because each by itself leads to an underestimation of what is involved in morality. We need to attempt a more integrated picture of morality and to envision how the part-processes are organized.

The conception of morality proposed in this paper borrows from some moral philosophers (for instance, Frankena, 1970), although it must be admitted that moral philosophers are not in agreement on the matter. Alston (1971: 276) states: "It is notorious that moral philosophers agree no more about what is distinctive of the moral than about anything else"; see also Wallace and Walker, 1970. Nevertheless, along with Frankena and others, morality (considered abstractly as a domain of human functioning) can be regarded as a guide to social interaction in which the effects of one's actions on another is considered not just in terms of the actor's interests, but also from the other's point of view; given that people live together and that their activities affect each other, it is the function of morality to provide an action guide (and a rationale) for how each person's behavior should affect each other's welfare (how rights, duties, and responsibilities are to be determined). The implications of this conception of morality will be elaborated in the course of the paper, but at the onset it may be useful to note that not all human values or ideals are regarded as *moral* values (for instance, morality is distinguishable from aesthetic and religious values, and from ideals of personal perfection); also to note that morality at least in principle deals with *sharable* values since moralities are proposals for a system of mutual coordination of activities and cooperation among people.

Major Components of Morality

Reviews of morality commonly subdivide the area into thoughts, behavior, and emotions. Cognitive developmentalists are said to study moral thought, behaviorists study behavior, and psychoanalytic psychologists study emotions. This kind of presentation suggests that three basic psychological elements exist, each governed by different processes (equilibrating cognitive structures, conditioning and modeling, and identification and the operations of the superego). Such reviews usually end by lamenting the uncertain relationships among the three elements and calling on future research to elucidate how cognition and affect are connected, how thought relates to action, and so on.

Dividing morality into these three sub-areas is inadequate in several respects. First, the three sub-areas of morality do not represent empirical clusters; various "moral" behaviors (e.g., resistance to temptation, altruistic behavior) are no more highly correlated among themselves than are the correlations between thought and behavior (cf. Blasi, 1980; Burton, 1976; Rushton, 1976, 1980). Second, dividing reality into thoughts, behavior, and emotions does not provide theoretically clear units of analysis. What is an emotion disembodied from cognitive referents? What is a behavior without intention, or thoughts without any feeling component? Third, cognitive developmentalists are not the only psychologists interested in cognition. Social-learning theorists (e.g., Bandura and Mischel) and many social psychologists (e.g., attribution theorists) also study cognition, although not in the Piagetian tradition. There are many kinds of cognition now, and therefore, cognition is no longer the private property of cognitive developmentalists. Fourth, a considerable amount of research undertaken in the past ten years indicates many kinds of cognitive-affective interactions, and there is not just *one* interface between cognition and affect, cognition and behavior.

To represent the diverse kinds of cognitive processes involved in morality, and in an attempt to present a more integrated picture of morality, I propose a fourpart framework. Let us imagine that the production of moral behavior in a particular situation involves (1) interpreting the situation in terms of how people's welfare is affected by possible actions of the subject; (2) figuring out what the ideally moral course of action would be; (3) deciding what one actually intends to do; and (4) executing and implementing what one intends to do.

Component I

Component I, interpreting the situation, involves the perception that something one might do, or is doing, can affect the welfare of someone else (or may affect others' welfare indirectly by violating a general practice or commonly held social standard). Many factors complicate such interpretation and people often have difficulty realizing how or that their actions affect others. Sometimes the other people who are affected are distant, not personally identifiable, and are affected indirectly through a complicated chain of events (for instance, I may be unaware that my use of a certain brand of coffee supports the exploitation of peasant workers in South America). Political decisions almost always involve uncertainty in how one's action will affect various people because the effects are mediated through complex social structures and involve unpredictable chains of events (e.g., who knows with certainty what abolishing the draft will accomplish, or what tighter credit will do). The prediction of the effects of one's action entails knowledge about how the world works, and often our knowledge is not very good (e.g., the surgeon who isn't sure whether to perform an operation, the diplomat who wonders how certain policies will work out). Sometimes we are not very accurate in knowing what other people really want or what their real needs are. Sometimes we are not aware of alternative courses of action that would do more good than the options we are considering.

Psychological research indicates that many people have difficulty in interpreting even relatively simple situations, that striking individual differences exist among people in their sensitivity to the needs and welfare of others, and that the capacity to make these inferences generally develops with age. Consider first some striking findings from the research on bystander reactions to emergencies.

For instance, a New York woman, Kitty Genovese, was repeatedly attacked and stabbed by an assailant — why didn't her fellow apartment dwellers do anything to stop the attacks? Interviews with the apartment dwellers indicated that they were uncertain about what was happening to Genovese — some thought the commotion might be a lover's quarrel and did not want to interfere. Systematic studies find that the ambiguity of situations (and hence, the ability to carry out Component I processes) is significantly related to bystander helping behavior in emergency situations. (Staub, 1978: 79-97, 105-106). Interpreting such situations often entails identifying the pattern and meaning of behavior of several people in interaction with each other, inferring what their respective wants and needs are, imagining what one might do to help in the situation and how the participants would likely react to such an act. To the degree that the subject has difficulty in interpreting the situation in any of these regards, moral behavior is less likely to occur.

Research by Schwartz (1977) indicates individual differences in "the spontaneous tendency to attend to possible consequences of one's behavior for the welfare of others" (p. 243)., and finds significant relations of this variable with measures of helping behavior. Some people seem to recognize how their actions affect others only when the most blatant signs of human suffering are present, whereas other people are supersensitive, seeming to see momentous moral implications in every utterance, gesture, and sneeze, and a moral problem under every bush.

Social cognition research (e.g., Shantz, 1975) documents the developmental character of the ability to make inferences about the thoughts, feelings, and perceptions of others. Insofar as a person was unable to make these inferences, the ability to understand how one's actions would affect others would be limited. The development of these abilities is generally seen as a process of becoming less egocentric (although recent research indicates that "egocentrism" is not a unitary process and that many factors affect role taking abilities). A considerable amount of research has investigated the linkage between social cognitive development and "moral" behavior (Kurdek, 1978; Rushton, 1980; Shantz, 1975; Staub, 1978, 1979). Many studies show a significant relationship, although results are mixed. A variety of methodological issues and differences in assessment procedures may explain the inconsistent results. It should be noted, in addition, that social cognition measures are not designed to measure what I have described as Component I, but rather are designed to assess more elementary parts of that. Social-cognition measures primarily assess whether a subject can infer the perceptions, feelings, or thoughts of one other person in a fairly simple, static encounter; typically, social cognition is not assessed of several people interacting in complex ways, with multiple motives, presented in a flood of information in which relevant cues are embedded and scattered. As a notable exception, research by Collins and associates has attended to social inference-making in more complex situations (1973, 1974, 1978), using television programs to portray the situations. They find that young subjects have trouble understanding the motives of the characters and misunderstand their patterns of interaction; young children miss relevant cues, fail to integrate information from various parts of the presentation, and consequently draw false inferences, make erroneous moral evaluations, and advocate inappropriate behavior. Studies of more complex forms of social cognition as in Collin's research are more likely to show linkages between social cognition and moral development since these assessments of social cognition are closer to what is involved in Component I processes.

So far, the discussion of Component I has emphasized the cognitive aspects of perceiving and interpreting a situation. Also involved is the arousal of affect. Affective arousal does not seem to wait for an unambiguous interpretation of events, and even misperceptions of situations can trigger strong emotional arousal (for example, "I'm extremely agitated because I thought for a moment you were hurting him, even though I knew it couldn't be true"). Even when we don't fully understand social situations, we experience alarm, empathy, anger, envy, exhilaration, etc. Zajonc (1980), for instance contends that affective reactions precede complex cognitive operations and can be elicited independently of extensive cognitive encoding. Our own affective arousal then is part of what needs to be interpreted when faced with a social situation. Sometimes the affective arousal serves to highlight salient cues and motivate our "better" selves, as for instance when we strongly empathize with a victim and go to his aid. But also sometimes the affects aroused in a situation can hamper our better judgment, as for instance when juveniles feel anger from always being pushed around or taken advantage of, when a person feels envy at seeing how much everybody else seems to have and how the world is passing him by, or when crime is one of the few exciting adventures in a person's life.

Hoffman (1975, 1976, 1979) has emphasized the role of empathy in morality, and like Zajonc and others views the arousal of empathy as a primary response which need not be mediated by complex cognitive operations. The rudiments of empathy (distress triggered by distress in another) can be aroused in very young infants and requires very little cognitive development for its activation (Hoffman, 1976: 131). Hoffman's account is particularly interesting in tracing out how this primary affective response comes to interact with cognitive development. At first,

> The child's response is rather a conditional, passive, involuntary one based on the pull of surface cues associated with elements of his own past. If there is action, its dominant motivation is hedonistic — to eliminate discomfort in the self (Hoffman, 1976: 132).

As cognitive development proceeds, the child begins to see that it is another person in distress, not the self; further, the child becomes more accurate in inferring what precisely the other needs or wants; and eventually the child comes to infer distress from very subtle cues, and becomes accurate and effective in relieving the other's distress.

In Hoffman's account of the interaction of affect and cognition, the role of cognition is as a mediator of emotion: cognition serves as the "eyes" for empathy, integrating information from various cues so as to detect the distress in another person (who may be trying to disguise the hurt, or may not be immediately present at all). Accordingly, development is portrayed as a matter of more complex inference that someone is in need, and of greater accuracy in diagnosing how the need can be satisfied. This is surely one of the important roles of cognition, and one of the important affective-cognitive interfaces in morality. Yet we would not want to regard this as the only important role of cognition in morality. Furthermore, as a general paradigm for morality, empathetically responding to another person's wants or needs is not sufficiently inclusive of the various conditions and complexities of moral situations. One deficit, as mentioned before, is that empathy is not a reliable guide to moral action (e.g., teachers may play favorites with children they more easily empathize with; lack of empathy does not release us from moral obligations; being "tough" in some circumstances is much better for another person). Therefore another level of cognitive processing is necessary to arbitrate the claims of empathy with other considerations. Going directly from empathy (or any other aroused emotion) to action may not be moral. A second deficit is that many of our moral problems involve more than simply responding or not to one other person's welfare, but involve responding to the multiple needs of several parties (e.g., tax program, affirmative action, abortion). The crux of these problems is to figure out how and to what degree those needs will be served. Thirdly, the single-person-in-need situation, as a general paradigm for moral psychology, is inadequate, too, in its isolation from a social or historical context. Although some moral problems may involve two strangers in isolation, many moral problems must be considered with reference to social institutions designed to meet human needs and to on-going human relationships. The history of promises and expectations is often a crucial consideration in moral problems. Any paradigm of morality that neglects the social-historical context of human interaction is likely to underestimate institutional and programmatic ways of meeting human needs, and one's duties and rights within a set of on-going social arrangements.

In summary, being aware of other people's needs and how one's action affects them is the outcome of Component I processes. The emotions that are aroused in perceiving the situation are also part of what is carried forward to further processing. When empathy is aroused for each participant, the individual is more likely to act morally. When anger, envy, or avarice is aroused, the other components may have to override these emotions to act morally.

Some intervention and education programs have been designed to affect Component I processes in the hope of improving the subject's morality. For instance, Hoffman (1970) advocates that parents use "inductive" disciplining of their children, pointing out to the children the consequences to others of action and thus stimulating empathy. Mosher and Sprinthall's program (1971; *Counseling Psychologist*, 1977, issue 4) for "Deliberate Psychological Education" emphasizes empathy training and "role taking experiences" to foster general personality development, including moral development. Indeed, the rationale for widespread psychotherapy and group counseling in prisons seems largely based on the assumption that criminality is an emotional disease, and so the goal of rehabilitation is to rearrange the arousal of bad, antisocial emotions with good, prosocial ones (for instance, see Ayers, 1979).

Component II

Component II involves figuring out what the ideally moral course of action would be in a given situation. In Component II, the person tries to integrate the various considerations (e.g., person A's needs, person B's needs, my needs, expectations founded on previous promises or roles or instituted practices) insofar as they count for or against the alternative courses of action available. In other words, Component II involves determining what course of action would best fulfill an ideal. Since this paper deals with morality, we will attend to the formulation of a course of action in fulfillment of *moral* ideals, however a subject may simultaneously (or as a substitute) formulate a course of action that optimizes other non-moral ideals as well (for instance, religious ideals). Later, in discussion of Component III we will consider how a person decides between conflicting ideals or goals (e.g., to decide for the moral ideal as opposed to an aesthetic ideal), but in discussion of Component II we consider how a subject determines what the moral ideal is.

Consider Kohlberg's well-known moral dilemma about Heinz:

> In Europe, a woman was near death from a special kind of cancer. There was one drug that the doctors thought might save her. It was a form of radium that a druggist in the same town had recently discovered. The drug was expensive to make, but the druggist was charging ten times what the drug cost him to make. He paid $200 for radium and charged $2,000 for a small dose of the drug. The sick woman's husband, Heinz, went to everyone he knew to borrow the money, but he could only get together about $1,000 which is half of what it cost. He told the druggist that his wife was dying, and asked him to sell it cheaper or let him pay later. But the druggist said, "No, I discovered the drug and I'm going to make money from it." So Heinz got desperate and broke into the man's store to steal the drug for his wife. Should Heinz have done that? Was it wrong or right? Why?

Note that in such verbally presented dilemmas, much of the processing of Component I is already verbally encoded. The needs and motives of the chief actors are identified, as are the ways that the actions of the participants affect each other; the situation is already represented as a moral dilemma in that Heinz's action to help his wife is also clearly hurting (stealing from) the druggist; therefore the consequences to others by an action are already identified. Given these considerations, the subject is asked to make a judgment about the proper course of action and to explain the rationale. This is the business of Component II.

Two major research traditions offer descriptions of mechanisms involved in Component II: one from social psychology postulates that *social norms* govern how a moral course of action is to be defined. Social norms are of the form, "In a situation with X circumstances, a person is expected to do *Y*." A variety of social norms have been postulated: social responsibility (Berkowitz and Daniels, 1963), equity (e.g., Adams, 1963; Walster, Berscheid, and Walster, 1973), reciprocity (e.g., Gouldner, 1960), the norm of giving (e.g., Leeds, 1963). For instance, the norm of social responsibility prescribes that if you perceive a need in another person and the other person is dependent on you, then you should help the other person. This norm might be applied to the Heinz dilemma as follows: Heinz should steal the drug because his wife needs the drug and cannot get it herself.

Norms are rules or widely held expectations taught by socializing agents and reinforced by one's culture either subtly, by sensing what people expect, or not so subtly, through concrete reward and punishment. Social norms prescribe forms of behavior that are useful and necessary for the regulation, coordination, and prosperity of the social group. According to the social norm explanation, when a person is confronted with a moral problem, first, he or she interprets the situation, and in doing so, notices a particular configuration of circumstances relevant to a particular social norm (e.g., in the above example, the circumstance that someone dependent on Heinz is in need).

> Exposure to the need of others often leads to the activation of social expectations (norms) which define the appropriate responses in a given situation. Activation means a directing of attention to expectations sufficient to bring them into the stream information processing. Activation does *not* necessarily bring the expectation into focal attention where the individual becomes self-consciously aware that he is considering them (Schwartz, 1977: 225).

"Activation", then, is sort of pattern recognition that classifies the situation as falling under a certain norm; in turn, the norm prescribes the moral course of action.

The second major research tradition dealing with the process of formulating a moral course of action is cognitive developmental research, notably that influenced by Piaget and Kohlberg. Instead of postulating several types of social norms activated by a configuration of features in the situation, cognitive developmentalists postulate *stages* of moral judgment, which are highly abstract, deep-seated interpretive frameworks for understanding social relationships. "Stages" are representations of subjects' understanding of how people cooperate. According to cognitive developmentalists, people not only learn many social rules and how to apply them, they also come to understand the logic of returning favors, of establishing enduring and loyal relationships, of establishing social organization with complex role structures, and of organizing society-wide networks of cooperation — in other words, development is not only the learning of more and more rules but also the progressive understanding of the function and purpose of social institutions and relationships. Each higher stage is a greater realization of the possibilities and conditions of cooperation — the "stages" are generalized "schemes of cooperation" which are stored in long term memory and which guide the subject's construal of specific social situations (see Rest, 1979a for elaboration of this interpretation of "stage").

For illustration, consider the Heinz dilemma again and how Kohlberg's Stage 4 might construct the situation. Stage 4, "Law and Order Orientation," views all human interaction as taking place within an organized social system, governed by formal law with rights and duties assigned to each role position. The people who occupy those role positions have rights and duties to each other as prescribed by the laws and institutions of the social system. Thus the social system provides society-wide coordination of human activity, stabilizes expectations about what people can expect from one another, provides protection from irresponsible individuals within and from the enemy without. Each person should do his job and stay within the law expecting that other people will do the same. Thus Heinz might believe that the druggist is a scoundrel and feel desperation about helping his wife; however, Heinz's moral duty is to stay within the law. What is involved is more than a transaction between Heinz and the druggist; maintenance of law and order of the entire social network is at stake. Far more human suffering and waste would occur if the system of law were undermined and people began taking the law into their own hands. If a legal way can be found to force the druggist to give up the drug, Heinz is certainly justified in using that recourse, but it can never be right to violate another person's legal rights (out of respect for the social system, not respect for the particular druggist).

Note that in such a formulation, the specific moral dilemma is assimilated into a way of looking at human relationships in general. The derivation of a moral course of action in a specific situation follows from a generalized structure that defines obligations and rights. In a sense, each moral judgment stage provides a "grammar" or a "deep structure" for integrating the various considerations in a case. Therefore a moral judgment "stage" differs from a "social norm" in that the former is a generalized view about how to define morality in general human relationships, whereas a "social norm" applies to a particular type of situation and does not involve a generalized view about society or human relationships, nor does it give a rationale for allocating moral rights and responsibilities; social norms entail a recognition of a pattern, and a prescription.

The application of Stage 4 concepts to the Heinz dilemma is actually less tidy than portrayed above. Stage 4 concepts could be applied in a different way to the Heinz dilemma. Some subjects focus on Heinz's duties as a husband (who presumably took a formal oath at the time of the marriage vows), and argue that Heinz has a duty as a husband in protecting his wife, possibly even to the point of stealing the drug. Thus the features of the Heinz dilemma can be organized in several ways in accordance with a Stage 4 perspective, and thus the general perspective of a stage does not always generate unique solutions to a dilemma. The subject must construct the linkages between a stage perspective and the features of a dilemma. This is not to say that a person's stage orientation should in principle have nothing to do with how he solves moral dilemmas, as some writers have contended. Rather, stage structure provides the rationale for formulating a moral course of action and in some multifaceted dilemmas, some stage structures can be used to formulate more than one rationale.

Although some writers regard Piaget's or Kohlberg's stage theories as furnishing a total theory of moral development (and some writers even seem to regard them as theories of general personality development), I regard their theories mainly as contributions to Component II processes. Reasoning about justice is no more the whole of morality than is empathy.

In recent years, many moral education programs have been targeted at influencing Component II processes. For instance the programs for public schools described by Hersh, Paolitto, and Reimer (1979), Kohlberg, (1973) are oriented towards improving scores on the Kohlberg test primarily through peer discussion of controversial moral dilemmas. Similar programs in a prison setting are described by Jennings (1979) and by Kohlberg, Kaufman, Scharf, and Hickey (1975). Programs also aimed at Component II but using the vehicle of university courses in the humanities and social sciences are described by Ayers, Duguid, and Montague (1980).

Component III

Component III involves deciding what one actually intends to do. In Component II, the morally ideal course of action is defined, but that does not entail that the person will actually choose to do it. Typically, a person is aware of a number of possible outcomes of different acts in a situation, each presenting different values and activating different motives. For instance, a student taking an examination might be asked by a classmate to allow a look at his paper. This situation might evoke a motive to resist temptation and not allow cheating; it might evoke a motive of affiliation, expecting that helping the classmate in this situation would solidify their friendship; it might evoke a motive of need achievement, if the student wanted to show his superiority over the classmate and others; it might evoke the motive of self-protection if the classmate was menacing. Therefore parallel to formulating a *moral* course of action, a person may be formulating courses of action oriented towards other values. Oftentimes, other values are so important to a person that they preempt or compromise moral values. For instance, John Dean writes in his book *Blind Ambition* that his activities as Special Counsel to President Nixon were motivated by his ambitions to succeed in the Nixon Administration, and that questions of morality and justice were preempted by more pressing concerns. Research by Damon (1977) is another case in point. Damon asked young children how ten candy bars ought to be distributed as rewards for making bracelets. In interviews, the children described various schemes for a fair distribution of rewards, explaining why they thought a particular distribution ought to be followed. However, when these same children actually were given the ten candy bars to distribute, they deviated from their espoused fairness schemes, and instead gave themselves a disproportionate number of candy bars. The children's espoused moral ideals thus were compromised by their self-interest in the actual behavior.

Three somewhat different questions are relevant to Component III: (a) How can we represent the decision making process? That is, what are the components and how are they organized and how do they interact? (b) How do we explain that various goals are valued differently by different people? What is the origin of values? What determines what is valued? (c) What temporary or situational factors influence or modify the decision making process?

Models of decision making. Behavioral Decision Theory (reviews

by Rapoport and Wallstan, 1972; Slovic, Fishchhoff, and Lichtenstein, 1977) offer some possible candidates for models. For instance,
Pomazal and Jaccord (1976) applied Fishbein's model (1967) to
moral decision making. They depict the human decision maker as
identifying the various consequences of each course of action,
calculating the value to the self of each consequence, calculating the
subjective probability of each consequence occurring, and calculating how significant other people would favor each action alternative; then all these calculations are algebraically combined to an
overall value for each course of action. Such models of decision
making have the advantage of including many variables which seem
to influence decisions and they have accounted for a sizable amount
of the variance in some studies (e.g., Pomazal and Jaccard, 1976).
However when the number of consequences are many and when
there is difficulty in estimating the probabilities of occurrence, it is
doubtful that many people actually carry out all these complex
calculations and algebraically combine them according to some
systematic algorithm — most human heads are boggled by too much
calculation (Slovic, et al., 1977). Another complication in applying
Behavioral Decision Theory to moral decision-making is that some
subjects, in some situations, may not calculate the gains and losses of
different courses of action, but may respond to "the call of duty"
without calculation. In some circumstances, people decide to fulfill
a moral obligation without weighing the costs and benefits — they
do it "just because it's right." Therefore, moral decision-making
may sometimes have a different dynamic than other forms of decision-making which assume a "maximum gain" orientation. Indeed,
one of the interesting aspects of moral decision-making may be to
determine whether or when moral obligation overrides cost-benefit
calculations. A third complication in modeling moral decision-
making is that sometimes subjects engage in defensive evaluations to
deny or neutralize feelings of moral obligation. As the costs of moral
action are recognized, a person may neutralize the feelings of
obligation by denying the need to act, by denying personal responsibility to act, by re-appraising the situation so as to make other
alternatives more appropriate, or by devaluating persons in need
(e.g., Bandura, Underwood, and Fromson, 1975; Lerner, 1971;
Schwartz, 1977; Staub, 1978: 151ff; Walster and Walster, 1975).
In summary, at present we have some notions about what elements have to be considered in models of moral decision making
(in the sense described as Component III), but it has been studied

very little and its development character is virtually unknown.

Origins of moral values. Answers to the second question (what determines what is valued?) are as elusive as the first. This problem is of course not unique to the explanation of *moral* values, and this chapter is not the place to delve into the topic. A brief consideration, however will relate this aspect of morality to other aspects, and will describe further affect-cognitive interactions. Several classical approaches to the determination of values are theories that appeal, respectively, to human biology, to human understanding, and to social influence.

Psychologists have long recognized the power of basic biological drives such as hunger, thirst, pain avoidance, temperature regulation, sex and need for oxygen. Indeed, when such biological drives were posited as the only motives for behavior, *Moral* values seemed to pose a problem: why should any human care about the needs of *other* humans? Some writers have claimed that the problem was only apparent. If the subtleties of complex reinforcement schedules and extinction curves were carefully examined, one would always find that apparent "moral" behavior was governed by the same reinforcement mechanisms as other behavior (e.g. Goldiamond, 1968). Some writers have attempted to solve the paradox by postulating biologically based altruistic instincts. Wilson (1975), for instance, cites cases of animals helping fellow species at cost to the self, and argues by analogy for a genetic basis for altruism in human beings. Hoffman (1976), though not arguing for altruistic genes, nevertheless believes altruistic motivation in humans is as basic and inevitable as egoistic, self-serving motives; and even if altruistic motivation isn't established at birth, by early childhood its rudiments are established in the form of empathic distress (experiencing negative affect at the sign of distress in others). "We are built in such a way that distress will often be contingent not on our own, but on someone else's painful experience" (Hoffman, 1976: 132). It is human nature to relieve that distress. According to Hoffman, the basic motive system for altruism is established very early in development, and with cognitive development, the motive comes to be aroused by more subtle cues and the expression of the motive is channeled in more effective and complicated ways. Presumably individual differences in moral values might be explained in terms of the different conditionability of humans (e.g., Eysenck, 1976) and different cognitive "pick up" systems.

In contrast, cognitive developmentalists have proposed that basic motive systems change, just as cognitions change. According to this view, development involves more than changes in the cues that trigger the motive and in the channels through which affect is expressed — instead, development involves fundamental changes in the types of outcomes and goals that are valued. Although Piaget's 1932 book on moral judgment is usually regarded as concerned only with cognition, it also presents a view about motivation. Piaget's position is essentially that social understanding leads to moral motivation — that is, as a person comes to understand the possibilities and conditions for human cooperation, the person comes to appreciate his stake in supporting certain social arrangements; his ego boundaries are extended to include others in a social system of "mutual respect" whereby each individual values the other. At first, the child is coerced to obey externally dictated moral rules, but with development the person is motivated by mutual respect for others, who likewise realize that by cooperating they can do much together in creating a social world of great value. At the beginning of development, the child is not cognizant of the possibilities that later become the major motivator of morality. Therefore, according to this view, moral motivation is not just rechanneled or retargeted with cognitive development but is fundamentally transformed.

The notion that "social understanding leads to moral motivation" is not unique to Piaget or cognitive developmentalists, but is part of the ideological tradition of "liberal enlightenment." This tradition has assumed that education can cure prejudice and provincialism, that one of the outcomes of schooling is "broadening one's perspectives," that exposure to great thinkers fosters social responsibility, that tax-supported public education must be provided for the electorate in a democracy to ensure "enlightened" participation in the democratic process. Indeed, the ideal of democracy presupposes that understanding motivates decision-making (cf. Scheffler, 1976, Rest, 1979b).

Moral education programs based on cognitive developmental rationale have usually assumed that as people gain understanding about how the social order works and their stake in it, they become motivated to participate in it and support it. More recently these programs have added another condition for effective motivation: that a person must not only become cognitively aware of the possibility of a moral order but must also actually experience the mutual support and reciprocity and solidarity of a moral community. Discussions of a "just community" in a prison setting (Duguid,

1980; Jennings, 1979; Kohlberg, Kauffman, Scharf, and Hickey, 1975) indicate that at least people who are discouraged, cynical, self protective and brutalized need to have more than just the cognitive awareness of the possibility of harmonious living; they need to see a just community concretely in operation they need to experience that their commitment and contributions to the community are reciprocated and that support from others is really there, and to be confirmed and reconfirmed that cooperation is a workable (and even preferable) way to live. Cognitive understanding is thus linked with self validating experience to build the motivation that mobilizes one work for a moral order.

A third view of the origin of moral values is the "socialization" view, which attributes moral motivation to the impact of social influence. The socialization view also has a long and venerable tradition — including Emile Durkheim (1965), who emphasized the power and authority of the group in regulating individual activity, and also including many child developmental researchers in the areas of personality and social development who stress the mechanisms of reinforcement, modeling and didactic teaching. Developing moral values is the accretion of influence by parents, peers, schools, media and other socialization agents. The influence on behavior of social pressure via reinforcement, modeling, and didactic teaching is so extensively demonstrated that it need not be documented here (see Staub, 1978, 1979). However, the question remains whether social influence offers an explanation of the *origins* of moral motivation, or only of temporary modifications.

Education programs based on the socialization view emphasize the systematic use of reinforcers and conditioning procedures. Behavior Modification has been widely used in public schools and prisons, and typically effects on the students' and prisoners' behavior can be demonstrated. Transfer of those effects to other settings has been the problem.

Temporary and situational influences on moral values. There is no doubt that social pressure can exert at least temporary influence on choices. Rewards administered by others contingent on specific behavior, exposure to other people performing the behavior, instructions or demands to perform particular behavior — these are all potent influences.

Recent research indicates another influence: mood. Isen (1970) found that subjects who were induced to feel happy by being provided a success experience (being told they did "extremely well" on a perceptual-motor task) tended to donate more money for charity than subjects with a failure experience (being told they did "extremely poorly") or than controls. Similar results have been found in studies of children donating more to charity after success in a bowling game, of college students volunteering to participate in a study after being given a cookie, of people who helped pick up spilled papers after finding a dime in a pay phone, of children "who had reminisced about happy experiences", giving more to charity (see review in Staub, 1978: 278-302).

The general finding is that people who are in a good mood (from remembering pleasant memories, from a recent success-experience, from having been given something) usually are more positive, generous, and willing to cooperate. These researchers talk about "the warm glow of success" and the "positive effects of looking on the bright side." Isen, Clark, Shalber and Karp (1978: 2) speculate on the cognitive-affective processes that may produce this relationship between good mood and decision-making:

> When a person is confronted with a situation in which he or she can help, presumably, cognitions concerning both the advantages and disadvantages of helping are available in memory from past experience in similar situations. These advantages and disadvantages, however, may not all be equally accessible or retrievable to the person at the moment, and thus, they may not all come to mind. What we are suggesting is that mood plays a role in what comes to mind.

Component IV

Components I, II, and III have accomplished the interpretation of a social situation, the formulation of a moral plan of action, and the decision to carry out that plan rather than other alternatives. And yet, as popular wisdom advises, good intentions are a long way from good deeds. Component IV, executing and implementing a plan of action, involves figuring out the sequence of concrete actions, working around impediments and unexpected difficulties, overcoming fatigue and frustration, resisting distractions and other allures, and keeping sight of the eventual goal. Perseverence, resolutions, competence, and "character" are virtues of Component IV. Psychologists sometimes refer to these processes as involving "ego strength" or "self-regulation skills." Somewhat earlier, Paul the Apostle noticed that intentions to perform a course of action sometimes fall short: "The good that I would, I do not; but the evil which I would not, that I do" (Romans 7:19). "Weakness of the flesh" is Biblical terminology for failures in Component IV processes. However, firm resolve, perseverence, iron will, strong character, ego strength, and so on are qualities that can be used for ill or good. One needs ego strength to rob a bank, prepare for a marathon, rehearse for a piano concert, or carry out genocide.

Mischel and Mischel (1976: 98) discuss research on "ego strength" and delay of gratification:

> Correctional studies indicate that the person who chooses larger delayed rewards or goals for which he must either wait or work... is more likely to be oriented toward the future... and to plan carefully for distant goals..., have high scores on ego-control measures, high achievement motivation; to be more trusting and socially responsible; and to show less uncontrolled impulsivity and delinquency.

Grim, Kohlberg, and White (1968) reported significant correlations between measures of attention (resistance to distraction on monotonous tests — an "ego strength" index) and resistance to temptation on a cheating task. In another study, Krebs (1967) reported that Stage 4 "Law and Order" subjects on Kohlberg's measure who were high on a measure of "ego strength" showed less cheating than Stage 4 subjects who were low on ego strength — presumably those subjects with high ego strength had "the strength of their convictions," whereas the Stage 4 subjects with low ego strength had such convictions but didn't act on them.

Various other lines of research also suggest that a certain inner strength, an ability to mobilize oneself to actoin, is a factor in the production of moral behavior. Barrett and Yarrow (1977) found that social assertiveness was an important component in children's prosocial behavior. London (1970) interviewed people who were involved in saving persecuted Jews in Nazi Germany, and remarked on their adventurousness. Hornstein (1976) describes a motivational force that maintains goal-directed behavior and increases in intensity as the desired goal is approached — a "Zeigarnick effect" in moral behavior. Mischel (1974), and Masters and Santrock (1976) describe techniques for enhancing persistence in effortful tasks — these however are small scale laboratory manipulations, and educational programs have not as yet been developed.

Conclusions

The conception of morality in this paper implies that failure to behave morally (i.e., behavior that is morally commendable) can result from deficiencies in any component. If a person is insensitive to the needs of others, or if a situation is too ambiguous to interpret or if too strong antisocial affect is aroused, the person may fail to act morally (deficient in Component I). Or a person may be deficient in formulating a moral course of action or may have simplistic and inadequate moral reasoning (Component II). Or moral values can be compromised or pre-empted by other values, or a person may just not feel motivated to risk oneself for a moral order (Component III). Or it may be that a person has decided upon a moral course of action, but loses sight of the goal, is distracted, can't implement a decision, or just wears out (Component IV). Moral development entails gaining proficiency in all these component processes. Moral education should be concerned with all these processes.

REFERENCES

ADAMS, J.S.
1963: Toward an understanding of inequity, *Journal of Abnormal and Social Psychology*, 67: 422-436.

ALSTON, W.P.
1971: Comments on Kohlberg's "From is to ought." In T. Mischel (Ed.), *Cognitive development and epistemology*, New York; Academic Press: 269-284.

AYERS, J.D.
1979: Education in prisons: a developmental and cultural perspective. Paper presented atSymposium on Education as a cultural alternative for prisoners and delinquents, Canadian Society for the Study of Education, June 5-8.

AYERS, D., DUGUID, S., and C. MONTAGUE
1980: Effects of University of Victoria program: A post release study. Report to the Ministry of the Solicitor General of Canada.

BANDURA, A., UNDERWOOD, B., and M.E. FROMSON
1975: Disinhibition of aggression through diffusion of responsibility and dehumanization of victims, *Journal of Research in Personality*, 9:253-269.

BARRETT, D.E. and M.R. YARROW
1977: Prosocial behavior, social inferential ability, and assertiveness in children, *Child Development*, 48: 475-481.

BERKOWITZ, L. and L.R. DANIELS
1963: Responsibility and dependency, *Journal of Abnormal and Social Psychology*, 66: 429-436.

BLASI, A.
1980: Bridging moral cognition and moral action: a critical review of the literature, *Psychological Bulletin*, 88: 1-45.

BURTON, R.
1976: Honesty and dishonesty. In T. Lickona (Ed.), *Moral development and behavior*, New York, Holt, Rinehart and Winston, 173-197.

COLLINS, W.A.
1973: Effect of temporal separation between motivation, aggression, and consequences: a developmental study, *Developmental Psyc.*, 8: 215-221.

COLLINS, W.A., BERNDT, T.J., and V.L. HESS
1974: Observational learning of motives and consequences for television aggression: a developmental study, *Child Development*, 45: 799-802.

COLLINS, W.A., WELLMAN, H.M. KENISTON, A. and S.D. WESTBY
1978: Age related aspects of comprehension and inference from a televised dramatic narrative, *Child Development*, 49: 389-399.

COUNSELING PSYCHOLOGIST (THE)
1977: *The Counseling Psychologist*. (Special Issue on Developmental Counseling Psychology), 6 (4).

DAMON, W.
1977: *The social world of the child*, San Francisco, Jossey-Bass.

DUGUID, S.
1980: From prisoner to citizen: theory and practice of moral education in the prison. Unpublished manuscript, University of Victoria.

DURKHEIM, E.
1961: *Moral education*, New York; the Free Press.

EYSENCK, H.J.
1976: The biology of morality. In T. Lickona (Ed.), *Moral development and behavior*, New York; Holt, Rinehart and Winston: 108-123.

FISHBEIN, M.
1967: Attitude and prediction of behavior. In M. Fishbein (Ed.), *Readings in attitude theory and measurement*, New York, Wiley.

FRANKENA, W.K.
1970: The concept of morality. In G. Wallace and A. Walker (Eds.), *The definition of morality*, London, Methuen: 146-173.

GOULDNER, A.W.
1960: The norm of reciprocity. *American Sociological Review*, 25: 165-167.

GRIM, P.F., KOHLBERG, L. and S.H. WHITE
1968: Some relationships between conscience and attentional processes. *Journal of Personality and Social Psychology*, 8: 239-252.

HERSCH, R., PAOLITTO, D. and J. REIMER
1979: *Promoting moral growth from Piaget to Kohlberg*, New York, Longman Inc.

HOFFMAN, M.
1970: Moral development. In P. Mussen (Ed.), *Carmichael's manual of child psychology*, Volume II, New York, Wiley: 261-359.
1975: Developmental synthesis of affect and cognition and its implications for altruistic motivation, *Developmental Psychology*, 11: 607-622.
1976: Empathy, role-taking, guilt, and development of altruistic motives. In T. Lickona (Ed.), *Moral development and behavior: theory, research and social issues*, New York; Holt, Rinehart and Winston.
1979: Development of moral thought, feeling and behavior, *American Psychologist*, 34 (10): 958-966.

HORNSTEIN, H.A.
1976: *Cruelty and kindness: A new look at aggression and altruism*, Englewood Cliffs, Prentice-Hall.

ISEN, A.M.
1970: Success, failure, attention and reaction to others: the warm glow of success, *Journal of Personality and Social Psychology*, 15: 294-301.

ISEN, A.M., SHALKER, T.E., CLARK, M., and L. KARP
1978: Affect, accessibility of material in memory, and behavior: a cognitive loop? *Journal of Personality and Social Psychology*, 36: 1-13.

JENNINGS, W.S.
1979: The juvenile delinquent as a moral philosopher: the effects of rehabilitation programs on the moral reasoning and behavior of male youthful offenders. Unpublished doctoral dissertation, Harvard University.

KOHLBERG, L.
1973: *Collected papers on moral development and moral education*, Cambridge, Mass., Laboratory of Human Development, Harvard University.

KOHLBERG, L. KAUFFMAN, K., SCHARF, P., and J. HICKEY
1975: The just community approach to corrections: a theory, *Journal of Moral Education*, 4: 243-260.

KREBS, R.L.
1967: Some relations between moral judgment, attention, and resistance to temptation. Unpublished doctoral dissertation, University of Chicago.

KURDEK, L.A.
1978: Perspective taking as the cognitive basis of children's moral development: a review of the literature. *Merrill-Palmer Quarterly*, 9: 299-240.

LERNER, M.J.
1971: Observer's evaluation of a victim: Justice, guilt and veridical perception, *Journal of Personality and Social Psychology*, 20: 127-135.

LONDON, P.
1970: The rescuers: Motivational hypotheses about Christians who saved Jews form the Nazis. In J. MACAULAY and L. Berkowitz (Eds.), *Altruism and helping behavior*, New York, Academic Press.

MASTERS, J.C. and J.W. SANTROCK
1976: Studies in the self-regualtion of behavior: effects of contingent cognitive and affective events, *Developmental Psychology*, 12 (4): 334-348.

MISCHEL, W.
1974: Processes in delay of gratification. In L. Berkowitz (Ed.), *Advances in social Psychology*, Vol. 7. New York, Academic Press.

MISCHEL, W. and H. MISCHEL
1976: A cognitive social-learning approach to morality and self-regulation. In T. Lickona (Ed.), *Moral development and behavior*, New York, Holt, Rinehart and Winston: 84-107.

MOSHER, R. and N. SPRINTHALL
1971: Deliberate psychological education, *The Counseling Psychologist*, 2 (4): 3-82.

PIAGET, J.
1965: *The moral judgment of the child* (M. Gabain, trans.), New York, The Free Press (Originally published, 1932).

POMAZAL, R.J. and J.J. JACCARD
1976: An informational approach to alrustic behavior, *Journal of Personality and Social Psychology*, 33: 317-327.

RAPOPORT, A., and T.S. WALLSTEN
1972: Individual decision behavior, *Annual Review of Psychology*, 23: 131-175.

REST, J.R.
1979a: *Development in judging moral issues*, Minneapolis, University of Minnesota Press.
1979b: *The impact of higher education on moral judgment development*, Minneapolis, University of Minnesota, Minnesota Moral Research Projects.

RUSHTON, J.P.
1976: Socialization and the altruistic behavior of children. *Psychological Bulletin*, 83: 898-913.
1980: *Altruism, Socialization and Society*, Englewood Cliffs, Prentice-Hall.

SCHEFFLER, W.
1976: The moral content of American public education. In D. Purpel and K. Ryan (Eds.), *Moral education... it comes with the territory*, Berkeley, California, McCutchan.

SCHWARTZ, S.H.
1977: Normative influences on altruism. In L. Berkowitz (Ed.), *Advances in experimental social psychology*, Vol. 10, New York, Academic Press.
SHANTZ, C.
1975: The development of social cognition. In E. M. Hetherington (Ed.), *Review of Child Development Research*, Vol. 5, Chicago, University of Chicago Press.
SLOVIC, P., FISCHOFF, B., and S. LICHTENSTEIN
1977: Behavioral decision theory, *Annual Review of Psychology*, 28: 1-39.
STAUB, E.
1978: *Positive social behavior and morality: social and personal influences*, Volume I, New York, Academic Press.
1979: *Positive social behavior and morality: socialization and development, Volume II*, New York, Academic Press.
WALLACE, G. and A.D.M. WALKER (Eds.),
1970: *The definition of morality*, London, Methuen.
WALSTER, E., BERSCHEID, E., and G.W. WALSTER
1973: New directions in equity research, *Journal of Personality and Social Psychology*, 25: 151-176.
WALSTER, E. and G.W. WALSTER
1975: Equity and social justice, *Journal of Social Issues*, 31: 21-43.
WILSON, E.O.
1975: *Sociobiology: The new Synthesis*, Cambridge, Mass., Belkap Press of Harvard University Press.
ZAJONC, R.B.
1980: Feeling and thinking: preferences need no inferences, *American Psychologist*, 35: 151-175.

15. MORAL DEVELOPMENT, JUSTICE AND DEMOCRACY IN THE PRISON

Stephen Duguid

There are several ways to reconcile theory and practice in an analysis of a social reality. One may engage in the perverse, twisting observation and data to fit an inherited theory or allowing the theory to blind the observer or to refract observation to more amenable forms. Conversely, one may become a revisionist and bend the theory to fit apparent observation, hoping that in the process the essential integrity of the theory remains intact. Finally, assuming the absence of a logical 'fit' with an existing theory, one can allow theory to grow out of practice. Generally, elements of all these approaches seem to be present in most attempts to place social reality in a larger context. In this paper I propose to analyze the relation between theory and practice in a prison education program, focusing on the crucial role of theory and the difficulty of maintaining its integrity and developmental thrust in the restrictive context of a prison.

In dealing with the social reality of a prison and a group of prisoners within it, I have been attempting for several years to discover, adapt, or create a theoretical framework that will describe and analyze the static reality of the prison and the developmental process occurring within the education program. Prisons as institutions have an odd relationship with theory. There are a multiplicity of theoretical approaches available to prison administrators, from behaviour modification to religion to the work ethic. All have been and are being promoted and funded by the prison system and social scientists, yet in the reality of the prison they are peculiarly absent or perverted. With a few exceptions, most prisons operate in

This paper appeared in the Canadian Journal of Criminology, *23: 2, 1981.*

a theoretical vacuum, stressing order, punishment and protection. When theoretical approaches are tried they tend to be short-lived or applied in such a manner as to doom them to either an early collapse or bureaucratized atrophy.

Prisons remain warehouses in spite of their increasingly modern appearance and experimentation with new forms. These new forms, in Canada the 'living unit concept' being the most prevalent, promise much but in the end deliver only form, not content. The dangers inherent in this failure to consider the larger, theoretical meaning or purpose of incarceration was recently commented upon by Dr. Peter Scharf following a visit to a new maximum security penitentiary in British Columbia which proudly displayed its commitment to the living unit concept. After discussing the prison with its staff, he predicted its potential for chaos because it had the practice of living units but no theory, i.e., no sense of purpose or plan for using this form for anything other than warehousing.

Dr. Scharf was visiting British Columbia at the invitation of the University of Victoria program at Matsqui Institution. For the past seven years the University of Victoria has been offering university courses to prisoners at Matsqui in the context of an off-campus facility within the prison. During that time a separate building has been acquired, course offerings expanded to include a full four year program and seven prisoner/students were awarded BA degrees with many others attending university upon release. The program attracts about 20% of the prison population (average of fifty students per term) and has been described as the most successful program of its kind in North America (Griffin, 1978).

Theoretical Assumptions

Like most programs in prisons, the University of Victoria program started with a theory, based loosely on Lawrence Kohlberg's work on moral development and on various theories of attitude change accompanying cognitive growth. Unlike most prison programs, it has tried to retain a strong sense of theory. Having attained a sometimes remarkable degree of empirical success in seven years and having demonstrated some theoretical success as well (Parlett, 1975; Ayers, 1979, 1980). Dr. Scharf was invited to discuss with the students and staff the general question of "where do we go from here"? In raising this question, however, both students and staff discovered that it was crucial to first discover where in fact we had been or, put another way, to explore the relationship between theory and practice during the last seven years before considering either elaborating on the theory or adopting a new one.

Our theoretical assumptions were firmly grounded in the cognitive-developmental tradition, flowing from Piaget's work in cognitive development through Kohlberg's linking of those stages to levels of moral reasoning ability. The emphasis, consistent with Kohlberg, was never on morality per se nor even on moral content, but on moral reasoning, the development through the cognitive growth implicit in higher education, of higher levels of empathy (role-taking) and improved decision-making capabilities. Nothing in our experience to date has persuaded us to alter this basic direction.

We assumed throughout that our students had certain deficits and that we were not there to 'change' but rather to develop, to facilitate a natural process of growth that had been stunted or distracted by environmental and social factors, what Ayers has called "habilitation" (1979). Our model co-opted aspects of several theories of criminality. We incorporated the 'criminal as victim' approach in the sense of recognizing the socio-economic factors involved in the creation of cognitive and moral reasoning deficits. We also viewed the criminal as a 'decision-maker' within the context of his level of development and thus as ultimately rational.

The theory, as elaborated by Piaget/Kohlberg, is based on a genetic approach to human development. Rejecting the crucial role of learned attitudes stressed by Freud and advanced by the social learning theorists, the developmentalists argue that levels of moral thought (reasoning) are inherent in each of us. In an ideal state, we move consecutively through the stages of moral reasoning, each correlated to a Piagetian stage of cognitive development.

Chart 1: Stages of Moral Development (Scharf, 1978)

Basis of Moral Levels Judgments   *Stages of Development*

I. Moral values reside in external, quasi-physical happening, in bad acts, or in quasi-physical needs rather than in persons and standards.

Stage 1. Obedience and punishment orientation. Egocentric deference to superior power or prestige or to a trouble-avoiding set.

Stage 2. Naively egoistic orientation. Right action is that which instrumentally satisfies the self's needs and occasionally others' needs. Awareness of relativism of value to each actor's needs and perspective. Naive egalitarianism and orientation to exchange and reciprocity.

II. Moral values reside in performing good or right roles, in maintaining the conventional order and the expectancies of others.

Stage 3. "Good-boy" orientation to approval and to pleasing and helping others. Conformity to stereotypical images of majority or natural role behavior, and judgment by intentions.

Stage 4. Authority and social order maintenance orientation. Orientation to "doing duty" and to showing respect for authority and maintaining the given social order for its own sake. Regard for earned expectations of others.

III. Moral values reside in conformity by the self to shared or sharable standards, rights or duties.

Stage 5. Contractual, legalistic orientation. Recognition of an arbitrary element or starting point in rules or expectations for the sake of agreement. Duty defined in terms of contract, general avoidance of violation of the will or rights of others, and majority will and welfare.

Stage 6. Conscience or principle orientation, not only to actually ordained social rules but to principles of choice involving appeal to logical universality and consistency. Conscience as directing agent.

The cognitive stage is a necessary but not sufficient condition for the parallel moral stage, just as the moral reasoning stage is a necessary but not sufficient condition for parallel moral behaviour. Thus a crude determinism is avoided but an attempt made to establish causal links between intellectual growth (cognitive), growth in moral reasoning, and evidence of moral behaviour. Many dispute the validity of this linkage, but Kohlberg maintains that there is "...clear evidence that persons reasoning in a more morally mature way act in a more mature way" (Kohlberg, 1974; Mischel, 1976; Kurtines, 1974; Levine, 1979).

There are many assumptions here. First, there is the notion of progress, i.e., growth. It is this factor which excludes the word 'change' from the vocabulary of the developmental approach as being too connotative of replacement and rehabilitation (Ayers, 1979). Second, there is the rigidity of the sequence. At least up to Stage 4, the process must be consecutive, that is, stages may not be skipped. An individual can reason at his own stage and can understand the next higher stage as well as those below, but reasoning two or more stages above is imcomprehensible to him. Third, there is the philosophic sense of the absolute, the superiority and finality of Stage 6 and the use of 'justice' as the arbiter in the evaluation of each stage.

It must be stressed at this point that the emphasis throughout is not on behavior, but on reasoning or the rationale for behaviour. Thus Stage 2 and Stage 5 individuals are notorious in the literature of the field for engaging in similar behaviours, yet the behaviour of the Stage 5 individual is judged qualitatively superior because of the more advanced reasoning which led to the behaviour (Fishkin, 1973; Kohlberg, 1973). The argument is that each of us has a possible range of explanations and reasoning tools for acting in the world, a definite repertoire available to us. That repertoire is determined not by lessons our parents taught us, by knowledge of rewards and punishments, nor by moral knowledge itself. Rather, it is determined first of all by our level of cognitive development, how we see the world, and secondly by our level of moral development, how we interpret what we see.

Assuming that our research and that of others is correct, we start in the prison with men who are primarily at Stage 1 or Stage 2 in terms of moral reasoning (Kohlberg, 1972; 1974). Assuming also a retarded level of cognitive development relative to age, we start at the base by developing the cognitive abilities of the men through education. (The average age of prisoner/students in the U-Vic program is 31 and the average completed grade is 8 (Ayers, 1980). As stated earlier, however, this is only a necessary, not a sufficient condition for growth in moral reasoning. To facilitate the latter, the concept of moral education is introduced. This does not mean a *moralizing* education, the old 'bag of virtues' approach, but rather an approach which in its most basic form is issue oriented (Baier, 1971; Muus, 1976; Kohlberg, 1972). Within the education process, particularly in the humanities and social sciences, issues are debated within a moral context, i.e., within the context of justice. Since for many of us all good teaching is issue oriented, this need present no special problems. For the strict moral relativist, however, it produces some conflict since it can be argued that even justice is not a universal criterion for the judgment of acts (Simpson, 1974).

There are thus three steps in the program. The education process leads inevitably to cognitive development and even to moral knowledge. That, in turn, opens the door to the possibility for growth in moral reasoning. Advancement in moral reasoning makes possible dramatic alterations in behaviour. Obviously a very shaky paradigm which could result in stagnation at any level. Finally, to complicate matters even more, Kohlberg insists that justice (moral reasoning) can only be taught in just schools. The implications of this are indeed profound for the prison and a direct challenge to a prison education program based on moral development.

Before discussing that problem which in many ways is the central issue of this paper, another factor must be considered. Assuming all of the above is in fact valid, that these stages are real and that growth is possible through education; how does this affect the problem of criminality? That is, is there a connection between low cognitive and moral development and criminality and will raising those levels of development eliminate criminal activity?

To argue that most criminals are at Stage 1 or Stage 2 of cognitive/ moral development and that raising their levels of development would mitigate against further criminal activity does not mean that all Stage 1 and 2 adults are criminals. Were this the case we would in fact have isolated a type of criminal 'personality' in line with the recent work of Yochelson and Samenow (1978). No such claim is made here. What is said is that research in the United States and other countries indicates that criminal offenders are remarkably lower in moral judgment development than are non-offenders of the same social background (Kohlberg, 1974; Scharf, 1979). Thus sociological or economic factors could remain dominant causative factors for crime as a generalized phenomenon, but retarded cognitive/moral development may explain the individual choice to act on these factors in a criminal manner. While the issues of the criminal personality and the origins of crime itself are too complex to be properly discussed here, some relevant points must be made.

First, not all prisoners are at Stage 1 or Stage 2. Many men in prison are at Stage 3, Stage 4, or even Stage 5. They obviously do not fit the pattern, having engaged in criminal activity for different reasons. Thus generalizing about prisoners is dangerous from the beginning once the focus is shifted from the act to the basis for the act or the reasoning behind it.

Secondly, while Stage 1 and 2 adults undoubtedly exist in society and avoid criminality, they are the exceptions. Most adults in North America mature at levels 3 and 4, stages of basic conformity to the existing rules and values of society. Something has gone wrong in the developmental process for an adult or even an older adolescent to be reasoning at the pre-adolescent Stage 1 or 2 level. Given the definition of these stages, the likelihood of such egoistic thinking leading to a criminal act is much greater, though by no means inevitable. Suffice it to say that it is dangerous for the social order to have too many of these individuals within it.

Returning to an earlier statement, I argued that criminals were at base decision-makers, that is, they are not driven to crime nor is their decision based on an overwhelming predilection for crime (Taylor, 1973; Letkemann, 1973). Rather, the decision to commit a crime can more productively be seen in situational terms. In a society with a consumerist ideology and persistent disparities in the means of consumption, coupled with persistent and deep feelings of alienation, there are valid criminogenic situations. Not everyone, however, who finds himself in such situations will behave criminally. This is, of course, the central issue for all concerned with understanding deviance. Merton's anomie theory and his notion of "illicit innovation" springing from incomplete internalization of norms and means provides the basis for understanding the parameters of individual choice in these situations (Merton, 1971; Cloward 1961). Within the context of the situation, the state of anomie, and the possibility of supportive sub-cultural ties, there remains room for a decision and it is at this point that perceptual and cognitive processes come into play; how the individual perceives the situation and the various judgments he makes about it (Spivak, 1976). These could include the seriousness of the offence, the perceived ease or difficulty of committing the offence, the consequences of apprehension, and the moral issue of the individual's relationship to the act (Clarke, 1977). A 'willingness to offend', therefore, can be seen as a decision reached in a particular set of circumstances rather than as a generalized behavioral disposition. The circumstances can be the individual's physical state at the time (economic, personal) as well as his level of cognitive/moral development which will determine the reasoning process he uses to correlate all these circumstances with the situation. Thus rather than "conversion" (Schmalleger, 1979), development or 'habilitation' may be the key to a different decision-making process.

Just Schools and Moral Development

The fact that most incarcerated criminals operate at a Stage 1 or 2 level of cognitive/moral reasoning may in part be a result of the vicissitudes of their lives but it is also a result of their sometimes extended residence in the criminal justice system, especially this prison in all its forms. What we see in the adult as a fully developed 'criminal personality' is really a personality formed in large part by the justice system, and cognitive/moral deficits are a major part of that personality. As Scharf says:

> ... time spent in prison does little if anything to increase the offender's awareness of the purpose of law or of the nature of constitutional democracy. Because the criminal leaves prison with the same social conscience with which he entered, he faces a continuing probability of remaining morally alienated from society and its institutions (1976).

In a recent follow up study of 72 men released through the University of Victoria program from 1976 to 1979, it was found that 62 (86%) had extensive juvenile and/or adult criminal records. It can be argued that the justice system arrests not only the criminal but the cognitive/moral development of the criminal as well, thus perpetuating the cycle.

This raises a whole series of questions, all revolving around Kohlberg's statement that the teaching of justice requires just schools. Scharf clearly perceives that criminals must attain a new perspective of the purpose of law, they must gain some empathetic 'verstehen' of the nature of a democratic society, and they must develop a social conscience if the cycle of criminality is to be broken.

These are all 'social' developments in the sense that they occur in conjunction with others, not in isolation. Moreover, unlike the Freudian tradition, the developmental approach sees the evolution of a sense of justice as being autonomous, not something passed on from parent to child. While the parent or teacher plays an important role as the necessary model for more advanced reasoning, justice is only internalized through interaction with peers in the context of mutual respect and solidarity (Craig, 1976; Maccoby, 1968; Tapp, 1971). Finally, without these kinds of developments, Scharf rightly concludes the growth of an even more fierce sense of moral alienation following incarceration.

The prison as an institution and a community creates a clear Stage 1 or 2 environment. It is authoritarian by nature and encourages the formation of social relations among individuals for the purpose of self-protection (Stage 2) or outright deferral to unquestioned authority or force (Stage 1) (Roebuck, 1963; Bowker, 1977). Prison staff, like police officers and military personnel, can be seen to function at a Stage 2 level while on the job, responding in part to the rules of the institution and in part to the situation. In terms of moral development, within the prison staff and prisoners are two sides of the same coin. The prison, obviously, is perceived by the prisoners as being unjust and authoritarian and is thus negated as a factor in cognitive/moral development. Worse still, since individuals can either temporarily or permanently regress in the Piaget/Kohlberg model, prisoners who enter the prison above Stage 2, may in fact be forced to move backwards on the developmental continuum (Kohlberg, 1974). Garabedian's findings that this regression (what he calls prisonization) may be temporary (1963) is mitigated by Bettelheim's account of regression among concentration camp inmates (1979). It is in these situations that we can best refer to prisons as schools for crime.

In response to this situation the University of Victoria program in effect created an island within the prison, an area in which all Kohlbergian stages above Stage 2 were operational or possible. After several years of experimentation a form of just community was created within the educational program. This could be done because the cumulative effect of taking university courses in the humanities and social sciences was cognitive development which in turn made possible movement in terms of moral reasoning which in turn made possible a more civil and just set of social relations. Just as important, the staff of the university, not being part of the prison hierarchy, felt no pressure to conform to the Stage 2 environment and were thus able to model and encourage thought and practice at higher levels.

There are, of course, tremendous limitations to justice in a prison. The first limitation lies with the prisoners themselves. Far from crying out for democracy or a just community, a significant number of prisoners find the prison quite compatible with their world view. As Norman Holt says, "Inmate leaders have traditionally had a strong vested interest in maintaining a quiet, orderly and respectable prison routine for only under these conditions can they maintain their status and positions of privilege" (1977). Given that they are both at Stage 2, this is quite logical. For those prisoners above Stage 2, there is an impulse toward change or reform, but it is controlled and intimidated by the authoritarian nature of the institution and the hostility of their peers. The experiment in democracy within the U-Vic program, therefore, did not come about by 'popular demand', but rather was initiated and manipulated by the staff.

The community established within the program was democratic or just in both a formal and an informal sense. Relations between staff and prisoner/students were emphatically non-authoritarian. The authoritative quality of the staff's administrative and academic role was always implicit, never explicit. All students know that the teacher has the power to fail, but if that power is not flaunted in daily social relations it need not be a constant limiting factor in the quality of those relations. There were few points of contact with prison staff during the day, all administrative matters with the prison being handled by the Superintendent of Education and most disciplinary matters taken care of by the students themselves.

The more formal democratic structures evolved as the community matured, i.e., as the students demanded practices more in line with their more advanced perceptions and reasoning. These structures took the form of student involvement in staff selection, student administration of the library and a student council with an understood right to involve itself in virtually all aspects of the program.

As in all communities, this one is never static. Leaders retire or are released and there is a constant influx of new members from the prison community. Not only are these men not "socialized" into this alternative community, they are generally not ready to partake of the practices of that community. Thus, as in real life, at any one time the university program will have members functioning at all stages of cognitive/moral development and this results in the same disruptions and frustrations as in any other community (Duguid, 1980).

Unlike other communities, however, this one remains an island in a hostile sea. This prison atmosphere remains pervasive, each student spending more time as a prisoner than as a student. Many students insist that the prison must remain the norm and resist the alternative community, actively or passively undermining its further development. Finally, the prison itself cannot be kept out of the program. It intrudes within the consciousness of each student as he struggles with its authoritarian demands and impositions and it all too frequently intrudes into the operation of the program with arbitrary rules and prohibitions.

There are several conclusions possible at this point concerning the relationship of theory and practice in this program. I have argued that the cognitive/moral development approach does have relevance to the issue of criminality, both in a causative and a curative sense. To that degree it is a useful theory. Program staff have observed in the last seven years that cognitive development in the prisoners/students does indeed take place in the university program. In testing, interviews, observations and follow-up studies we have concluded that development of moral reasoning also occurs, frequently at quite dramatic rates (Parlett, 1975; Ayers, 1979; Duguid, 1979; Ayers, 1980). The speed and extent of this development is probably indicative of earlier retardation of this development or even regression and the fact that we are dealing with adults who can draw on a considerable life experience to supplement their development of cognitive skills and moral reasoning. We can further conclude that this developmental process results in certain kinds of changed behaviour. Clashes with institutional rules are certainly less frequent with the students than with other prisoners. Behaviour within the university program, and even personal appearance, undergoes marked change. There is a strong sense of group identification among the prisoner/students, a great deal of verbalized 'identification' with the program. Finally, among many of the students there are stated and acted upon ambitions to continue their academic endeavours upon release with the intention of using their education to begin a new career. In the most recent follow-up study of 75 program alumni, virtually all were employed and in the three year term of the study only eleven (15%) had been reincarcerated. It would seem, then, that the theory works (Ayers, 1980).

There is, of course, a difficulty in assessing the process of development and the specific results of this program, namely the issue of self-selection. Were these prisoners already an 'elite' group prior to entry into the university program, many of the developments described in this paper would be less than significant. The prisons in which the U-Vic program operates are not strictly 'graded' prisons, each containing virtually the entire range of offence types, ages, educational and social backgrounds and men fitting all the various prisoner typologies designed by Schrag (1961), Cohen and Taylor (1972), Sykes and Messinger (1960), and so forth. The university program follows a virtually open admissions policy, encouraging prior completion of the GED but admitting all students under the 'mature student' category. The program consistently attracts 20% of the prison population and from the data collected in the recent follow-up study indicates that the prisoner/students are typical in all relevant categories to a matched group of non-student prisoners. While 'motivation to join' is a factor that contributes to the success of the program it may not be decisive since in practice the university is just one work location among many in the prison and one of the most demanding in terms of effort.

While motivation and tenacity to continue are factors which affect the university program, their impact is probably not as great as might be supposed. The development described above would be significant even if the students were a prison elite and since all indications are that they are not, the program itself remains more likely the causal agent. There is a further difficulty, however, the prison itself.

The Prison and the Just Community

In the observed and statistical results of the U-Vic program we may be witnessing more compliance than internalization, even conscious or unconscious manipulation of tests and behaviour in order to present the best possible case for release or simply to please the staff. For internalization the theory demands the praxis of justice, the putting into daily practice of the moral reasoning engendered by the program (Tapp, 1971). Political development is in fact a crucial part of the development of moral reasoning. Kohlberg turns to Plato on this point: "Civic or political education means the stimulation of development of more advanced patterns of reasoning about political and social decisions and their implemen-

tation in action. These patterns are patterns of moral reasoning"
(Kohlberg, 1975). The transition from compliance to internalization must come with action in the world, and by definition that
action is political.

The political world of these men, however, is dualistic. The
existence of two communities with opposite values between which
each individual must move each day produces an obvious tension,
both within the individual and within the two communities. It can
be argued that the tension is creative, that it heightens the positive
aspects of the just community when compared to the authoritarian
community. Or it can be destructive tension which perverts and
eventually destroys the challenger. It is on this point that the theory
runs into the greatest conflict with practice. The two communities
are perceived by most prisoners to be unequal. The just community
is a refuge in a storm that never abates. The prison has the power and
while a few individuals see the impotence of that power and in fact
transcend the conflict, most do not. The common perception is that
the alternative community is utopian which, while very nice, is
impractical and will eventually conform or be crushed. Tied to this
Hobbesian view is the other logical perception that the society
outside the prison more clearly resembles the prison than the just
community of the university program.

How is this conflict between theory and practice to be resolved? It
can be ignored and the two communities continue to co-exist, the
program remaining satisfied with limited goals. The theory can be
revised by rejecting the emphasis on "just schools", i.e., on the
praxis of justice in daily life as the key to internalized moral development. Since this part of the theory is by no means empirically
proven, this is an attractive possibility. The creative aspects of the
tension can be emphasized and manipulated and any notion of 'real'
democracy postponed until the student leaves the prison. Finally,
the praxis can be changed and the community expanded into the
prison.

The reader might infer by the juxtaposition of these options that
the last was the preferred solution. The first two are, of course,
closely connected. If the conflict is ignored and the program
continues to co-exist with the prison, the theory is automatically
revised, assuming a strong sense of theory is retained. There are
substantial theoretical and practical bases for such an option. In a
recent address, M.C. Wittrock makes a strong case for the purely
cognitive approach to development, arguing that "People learn not

only by acting and experiencing the consequences of their actions but also by observing others, by imitating models, by watching television, by seeing a demonstration, by discussing issues, even by listening to a lecture; sometimes without practice, without reinforcement, and without overt action (1978)." The 'social learning approach' of Bandura (1979) and others certainly proposes behaviour change without corresponding moral reasoning development and in a recent external review of the U-Vic program, R. Ross criticized the moral development aspect as unnecessary and incapable of empirical validation (1980). Thus the just school need not, according to these views, be a crucial or even essential part of cognitive/moral development. While I have serious reservations concerning the effectiveness of this approach in linking learning with behaviour, it would certainly ease the problems of education in the prison. In fact, the problems implicit in trying to establish and maintain a just community in a prison may make this the only practical alternative.

Bringing justice to the prison — creating a just community in which the practices implied in moral education may be put into action — presents some very specific problems and some very promising prospects. First the problems and a few solutions and then the prospects.

I am assuming that a just community must be a democratic community, that is, it must be founded on democratic forms based on a system of representation and a set of rules commonly agreed upon by all factions in the community. It must contain within it the mechanisms for adjusting conflicts of interest in a way that avoids the tyranny of the majority and limits the tendency toward elite or authoritarian rule (Kohlberg, 1974).

This type of community presents obvious problems for the prison administration but even more complex problems for the prisoners. Dostoevsky in his prison diaries observed that he did not meet a single prisoner in the Siberian work camps who thought he deserved to be incarcerated (Arendt, 1963) and contemporary observers report much the same (Davis, 1976). For whatever reason and through whatever mechanisms, prisoners are seldom repentent or wracked with guilt for their acts and in fact feel a deep sense of injustice at being in prison at all (Seashore, 1976; Sykes, 1957). Thus besides the operation of the prison being perceived as unjust, the prison by its very nature is perceived as unjust. Prisoners can develop role-taking capability and, as Ayers reports in his interviews with Matsqui prisoner/students, state that "I now understand that policemen have a role to play in society", but to move from that to an acceptance that the role includes putting them into prison is too dramatic and personal a leap (1979).

How, then, can a community universally seen as unjust and which enforces membership at the point of a gun, become a just community? From the prisoners' perspective this is an almost insoluble dilemma. To work for a just community in the prison serves to at least indirectly legitimize the prison, their sentence, and to some extent their guilt (Kasinsky, 1977). Nevertheless, in the interest of expediency, material self-interest and a recognition that some form of change/development is in their best interest, some prisoner/ students in the Matsqui program have either transcended or temporarily side-stepped this problem and are actively investigating the possibility of such a community.

There are several factors at work within the Matsqui program which make this movement possible. Few individuals can or wish to live with the consciousness of oppression always present (self-defined 'political prisoners' are the exception). In a prison, therefore, alternative realities are constructed within the larger environment, realities which are perceived as being 'other' than the prison. Thus our students repeatedly refer to "leaving the prison" when they enter the university area and the meaning attached to those words can be quite literal. For a few hours each day the prison assumes a different position in the daily life of the prisoner, never forgotten to be sure, but more abstract.

This created reality within the prison can occur in a variety of settings but is certainly made more pronounced by certain key aspects of the university program. First, there is the geographical distance from the physical centre of the institution, the academic centre being in a separate building in the corner of the prison. One must physically leave the living, eating and recreation areas of the prison to get to the university. Second, there is the fact that the university program is contracted to another institution, the University of Victoria, and all staff are university staff. Once in the university area, there are no uniformed prison staff and only one prison administrator who keeps a low profile in the operation of the program. Finally, there are a whole range of decorative and cultural aspects of the academic centre which mark it off from the rest of the prison as well as a totally different relationship between prisoner/ student and staff. Taken together, this makes possible a unique set

of social relations among the students themselves, further rein-
forcing the sense of a different reality.

These two factors, the need for alternative realities and the form
of the university program, have resulted in a type of just community
within the prison. As discussed in more detail elsewhere (Duguid,
1979), this community has evolved from an early paternalist form, to
one based on a sense of *krugovaya poruka* (group solidarity in the
Soviet manner), to the present attempt at a more principled community based on justice and democratic participation. As referred to
earlier, in all its forms it has remained an island within the prison, a
fact which accounts for much of its strength and to the questions
posed in this paper.

The search for a just structure for social relations is a crucial part
of any moral education. As a cursory knowledge of history demonstrates, such a search has no end but rather is a process that has
served to define much of human history. To settle for a static model,
a steady-state community, rather than to risk the extension of justice
and its democratic forms into the rest of the prison denies the
educative role of that process and endangers the continued existence
of the present community. There are risks involved on the other side
as well. Creating a just community among an "elite" group of
prisoners sensitized and made sympathetic to such project by an
extensive education program, with a staff fully supportive of the
project and with a minimum of custodial interference is not that
difficult. It is quite another matter to extend that community into
prison work areas where no such sympathetic clientele or supportive
staff exists and into living unit areas where hostility and security are
the paramount considerations. The source community may be
labeled a troublemaker by the administration and forcibly
disbanded; the prisoners may become discouraged by the difficulties and abandon both efforts: or the possible impossibility of the
project may serve to heighten the essential unreality of the university
community. Nevertheless, for reasons outlined above, the process
must continue and the community must expand if the practice is to
be reconciled with the theory, to keep alive the sense of process, and
to preserve the integrity and existence of the original community.

Summary

Several issues have been dealt with in this paper — one has not. The necessity of a strong theoretical base in prison education has been shown as well as the need to correlate that base with practice. The development of one such program at Matsqui Institution has been analyzed along with the logical political and social extension of that program, the creation of a just community. Finally, it has been argued that to survive such a just community must be extended into the prison at large and that this process is a central ingredient in the individual growth associated with moral education. What is not discussed here is the question of how this just community is to be expanded into the prison. There are historical precedents which are relevant and there is the history of the University of Victoria program itself, but in the end there can be no blueprint (Scharf, 1979; Kohlberg, 1972). Manipulation, plans, and the 'hidden hand' were essential features in the creation of the university community at Matsqui, but such tactics have inherent dangers and limitations.

The most exciting aspect of this kind of project is that once even an 'island' community is created, the members of that community begin to take it upon themselves to expand it. The cognitive and moral reasoning growth engendered by the learning process and the praxis of democracy lead inevitably to a drive to eliminate or minimize the dissonance between theory and practice in all aspects of life. The 'how' will be discovered in the praxis of struggle by those most directly involved in and affected by the process, the staff and the prisoners. The result could be citizens, not necessarily contented citizens, but individuals who will express their discontents and frustrations in legal and socially agreed upon forms.

Thus we end with a strange alliance of Kohlberg and Maoist philosophy; "If the people lead a democratic life, their habits will naturally be transformed. Only through the practice of democracy can you learn democracy (Belden, 1970)." In the prison as in Maoist theory, it is practice with a theory and practice with onmipresent guidance, but practice nevertheless which makes possible the internalization of values.

REFERENCES

ARENDT, H.
1963: *Eichmann In Jerusalem*, New York, Viking.

AYERS, J.D.
1978: Perspective in Education in Prisons, paper presented to Ontario Institute for Studies in Education *Review* of Penitentiary Education and Training, Toronto.

1979: Education in Prisons: A Developmental and Cultural Perspective, paper presented at Canadian Learned Societies Conference, Saskatoon, Sask.

AYERS, J.D., DUGUID, S.R., MONTAGUE, C., WOLOWYDNIK, S.
1980: Effects of University of Victoria Program: A Post Release Study. Prepared under contract with the Ministry of the Solicitor General of Canada.

BAIER, K.
1971: Ethical Pluralism and Moral Education, in Beck, C., et al., *Moral Education*, Toronto, University of Toronto.

BANDURA, A.
1979: The Social Learning Perspective in Toch, H., (Ed.) *The Psychology of Crime and Criminal Justice*, New York, Holt, Rinehart and Winston.

BELDEN, J.
1970: *China Shakes the World*, New York, Monthly Review.

BETTELHEIM, B.
1979: *Surviving and Other Essays*, New York, Alfred A. Knopf.

BOWKER, L.
1977: *Prisoner Subcultures*, Toronto, Lexington Books.

CLARKE, R.
1977: Psychology and Crime, *Bulletin of the British Psychological Society*, 30.

CLOWARD, R. and OHLIN, L.
1961: *Delinquency and Opportunity*, London, Routledge and K. Paul.

COHEN, S. and TAYLOR, L.
1972: *Psychological Survival*, Hammondsworth, Penguin.

CRAIG, R.
1976: Education for Justice: Some Comments on Piaget, *Contemporary Education*, 47: 2.

DAVIS, M.
1976: The Prison Dilemma in McGrath, W. (Ed.) *Crime and Its Treatment in Canada*, Toronto, MacMillan.

DUGUID, S.

1979: History and Moral Development in Correctional Education, *Canadian Journal of Education*, 4: 4.

1979: The University in Prison: Moral Development and the Alternative Community, paper presented at Canadian Learned Societies conference, Saskatoon, Sask.

1980: Post Secondary Education in a Prison: Theory and Praxis, *Canadian Journal of Higher Education*, 10: 1.

FISHKIN, J.

1973: Moral Reasoning and Political Ideology, *Journal of Personality and Social Psychology*, 27: 1.

GARABEDIAN, P.

1963: Social Roles and the Process of Socialization in the Prison Community, *Social Problems*, 11.

GRIFFIN, D.

1978: Report to Reviewers; OISE Review of Penitentiary Education and Training.

HOLT, N.

1977: Prison Management in the Next Decade, *Prison Journal*, 57: 2.

JONES, C.

1976: The Contribution of History and Literature to Moral Development, *Journal of Moral Education*, 5: 2.

KASINSKY, R.

1977: A Critique on Sharing Power in the Total Institution, *Prison Journal*, 57: 2.

KOHLBERG, L.

1970: Education for Justice: A Modern Statement of the Platonic View, in Sizer (Ed.), *Moral Education*, Cambridge, Harvard University.

1973: Continuities and Discontinuities in Childhood and Adult Development Revisited, in Kohlberg, L., *Collected papers on Moral Development and Moral Education*, Moral Education Research Foundation, Harvard University.

1975: The Cognitive-Developmental Approach to Moral Education, *Phi Delta Kappan*, June.

KOHLBERG, L., SCHARF, P. and HICKEY, J.

1972: The Justice Structure of the Prison: A Theory and an Intervention, *Prison Journal*, 51: 2.

KOHLBERG, L., KAUFMAN, K., SCHARF, P. and HICKEY, J.

1974: *The Just Community Approach to Corrections: A Manual, Part I*, Moral Education Research Foundation, Harvard University.

KURTINES, W. and GREIF, E.
1974: The Development of Moral Thought: Review and Evaluation of Kohlberg's Approach, *Psychological Bulletin*, 81: 8.

LETKEMANN, P.
1973: *Crime As Work*, Englewood Cliffs, Prentice Hall.

LEVINE, M.
1979: The Form-Content Distinction in Moral Development Research, *Human Development*, 22: 4.

MACCOBY, E.
1968: The Development of Moral Values and Behavior in Childhood, in Clausen, J., *Socialization and Society*, Boston, Little Brown.

MERTON, R.
1971: Social Problems and Social Theory, in Merton, R. and Nisbet, R., *Contemporary Social Problems*, New York, Harcourt, Brace, Jovanovich.

MISCHEL, W. and MISCHEL, H.
1976: A Cognitive Social-Learning Approach to Morality and Self-Regulation, in Lickona, T., *Moral Development and Behavior*, New York, Holt, Rinehart and Winston.

MUUS, R.
1976: Kohlberg's Cognitive-Developmental Approach to Adolescent Morality, *Adolescence*, 11: 41.

PARLETT, T., AYERS, D., and SULLIVAN, D.
1975: Development of Morality in Prisoners, *Yearbook of the Canadian Society for the Study of Education*.

ROEBUCK, J.
1963: A Critique of Thieves, Convicts and the Inmate Culture, *Social Problems*, 11: 2

ROSS, R.
1980: Socio-Cognitive Development in the Offender: An External Review of the U-Vic Program at Matsqui Penitentiary, report to Solicitor General of Canada.

SCHARF, P., and HICKEY, J.
1976: The Prison and the Inmate's Conception of Legal Justice: An Experiment in Democratic Education, *Criminal Justice and Behavior*, 3: 2.
1977: Thomas Mott Osborne and the Limits of Democracic Prison Reform, *Prison Journal*, 57: 2.

SCHARF, P.
1978: Indoctrination, Values Clarification and Developmental Moral Education as Educational Responses to Conflict and Change in Contemporary Society, in Scharf, P., *Readings in Moral Education*, Minneapolis, Winston.

1979: Law and the Child's Evolving Legal Conscience, in Sprague, R., *Advances in Law and Child Development*, New York, John Wiley.

SCHMALLEGER, F.
1979: World of the Career Criminal, *Human Nature*, March.

SCHRAG, C.
1961: A Preliminary Criminal Typology, *Pacific Sociological Review*, 4.

SEASHORE, B., and HABERFORD, S.
1976: *Prisoner Education: Project Newgate and Other College Programs*, New York, Praeger.

SIMPSON, E.
1974: Moral Development Research: A Case Study of Scientific Cultural Bias, *Human Development*, 17.

SPIVAK, G. et al.
1976: *The Problem Solving Approach to Adjustment*, San Francisco, Jossey-Bass.

SYKES, G., and MATZA, D.
1957: Techniques of Neutralization: A Theory of Delinquency, *American Sociological Review*, 22.

SYKES, G., and MESSINGER, S.
1960: The Inmate Social system, in *Theoretical Studies in the Social Organization of the Prison*, Social Science Research Council Pamphlet.

TAPP, J., and KOHLBERG, L.
1971: Developing Senses of Law and Legal Justice, *Journal of Social Issues*, 27: 2.

TAYLOR, I., WALTON, P., and YOUNG, J.
1973: *The New Criminology*, New York, Harper.

WITTROCK, M.
1978: The Cognitive Movement in Instruction, *Educational Psychologist*, 13.

YOCHELSON, S., and SAMENOW, S.
1978: *The Criminal Personality*, New York, Jason Aronson.

16. EFFECTS OF JUST COMMUNITY PROGRAMS ON THE MORAL LEVEL AND INSTITUTIONAL PERCEPTIONS OF YOUTHFUL OFFENDERS

William Jennings

Introduction

In 1975, the author became the director of an open group home in Florida for ten delinquent boys below the age of 17. Prior to the author's acquiring the directorship, the home had operated on a behavior modification model. Before assuming the directorship, the author administered a Kohlberg moral judgment interview (Colby, et al., 1978) and an "ethnographic" moral atmosphere interview (Kohlberg, 1980) to each of the residents. After assuming the directorship, the author attempted to implement a "just community" model of operation, along the lines developed earlier at the Niantic, Connecticut Women's Prison (Kohlberg, et al., 1972; Kohlberg, et al., 1975; Scharf and Hickey, 1980). The author served as director for only four months but the unit continued to operate on the just community model after his departure. Nine months after the initial interviews, the author again administered the moral judgment and moral atmosphere interviews to eight of the residents.

At a somewhat later date, the author had the opportunity to conduct similar interviews in a secure behavior modification unit and a secure transactional analysis program both located in a state

Paper presented to the World Congress in Education: Values and the School; Symposium on Prison Education, Université du Québec à Trois-Rivières, July, 1981.

hospital in Massachusetts. Residents were reinterviewed one year later.

The first basic hypothesis of the study was that there would be more upward development in moral stage in the just community program than in either of the alternative programs. The second hypothesis was designed to provide some explanation as to why the just community program would produce more developmental change than the alternative programs. The hypothesis was that the just community program provides a significantly "higher" stage or "better" moral atmosphere than do either of the alternative programs studied.

The second hypothesis was based on the idea that institutions for youth like high schools and correctional facilities tend to develop a characteristic "moral atmosphere," an atmosphere which may stimulate moral growth or retard it (Kohlberg, 1970; Kohlberg, et al., 1972; Kohlberg, et al., 1975; Kohlberg, 1980; Reimer and Power, 1978). Three distinguishable but overlapping meanings have been given to the idea of moral atmosphere. The first meaning (developed in Kohlberg, et al., 1972; Kohlberg, et al., 1975) is that the institutionalized rules, norms or justice structure of a setting or program has a definite stage, from the point of view of the "average" member of the institution. An "average" member of a correctional facility for youth is in transition from Stage 2 (instrumental reciprocity or exchange) to Stage 3 (mutual interpersonal concern) (Kohlberg, 1978). Based on responses to a set of "prison dilemmas" administered to inmates of a traditional reformatory, Kohlberg, et al. (1972) concluded that the average inmate viewed the justice structure of the traditional reformatory as either Stage 1 (punishment and obedience) or Stage 2 (making deals for exchange).

Because of the usual interpretation of behavior modification's exchange of point rewards for good behavior, it was hypothesized (Kohlberg, et al., 1975) that the average inmate would perceive the program as Stage 2 (instrumental exchange of points for behavior) even if the inmate had the cognitive-moral competence to perceive a setting as Stage 3 or Stage 4. Kohlberg, et al. (1975) hypothesized that the norms and justice structure of programs based on an insight therapy model, e.g., transactional analysis, would be perceived by the average inmate at his modal stage, i.e., as a mixture of Stage 2 instrumental exchange and Stage 3 mutual understanding and support.

Hypothetically a just community program would be perceived by an average resident at that inmate's growing edge, as Stage 3 (mutual understanding and support with loyalty to the group) with suggestions of Stage 4 (concern of each for the welfare of all and impartial justice representing the general will).

The second related meaning of moral atmosphere looks at the peer group's shared or collective norms as revealed by group meetings and by hypothetical dilemmas about issues requiring group norms. Such collective norms can be assigned a stage score as well as a phase score representing its degree of institutionalization. A "just community" alternative high school program was found to eventually solidify a Stage 3/4 moral atmosphere (Reimer and Power, 1978; Power, 1979; Kohlberg, 1980).

A third meaning of "moral atmosphere" focuses not upon the environment as a stageable normative structure but upon the ways in which an environment may stimulate moral growth (Kohlberg, 1970; Kohlberg, 1976; Kohlberg, et al., 1975). This last meaning was the focus of the present study. Following moral development theory, the following were hypothesized to be central to moral growth:

1. A relatively high amount of moral discussion and dialogue.
2. A relatively high amount of resident power and responsibility for making decisions about policies, rules, etc.
3. A relatively high perception of rules and decisions as being fair.

Given the well known phenomenon of institutional inertia, it was not at all certain that a change of director in the Florida house would lead to an actual change in moral atmosphere, as distinct from a change of verbal ideology of the staff. To document that a change of staff behavior actually occurred in the direction of a developmental moral atmosphere, the author analyzed logbook moral growth. In the present study, ethnographic moral atmosphere interviews with residents were used to compare presence of the conditions of growth in the behavior modification, transaction analysis and just community programs. It was hypothesized that the just community program would be highest on these conditions, transaction analysis next, and behavior modification lowest.

Method

Design and Subjects

Open Behavior Modification Unit. Ten youths were administered the Kohlberg Moral Judgment Interview and seven the Moral Atmosphere Interview just prior to conversion to the Just Community Program.

Just Community Unit. Data collected from the Open Behavior Modification Unit (before the first author became director) constituted the pretest scores on moral judgment and moral atmosphere. Post-tests of Moral Judgment Interviews were administered nine months later to eight of the ten residents and Moral Atmosphere Interview to seven of them. The age range of the seven subjects was from age 12 to age 17 with a median age of 15. I.Q.'s ranged from 70 to 106 with a median of 82. Grade completed ranged from fifth grade to tenth grade with a median completion of seventh grade. Four were white, three black. Father's occupations ranged from minister and business executive to carpenter. Offenses ranged from pickpocketing to arson and robbery with assault. Most were from broken homes.

Secure Behavior Modification Unit. Eight youths were given moral judgment pretests and one year later were post-tested. Seven were administered the Moral Atmosphere Interview. In general, the background characteristics were similar to those in the Florida program.

Transactional Analysis Unit. Seven youths were administered Moral Judgment Pretests and Moral Atmosphere Interviews. Only four received Moral Judgment Post-Test Interviews six months later. The youth's background characteristics were similar to those of youth in the other programs.

Program Descriptions

Just Community Program. The program was open with the ten residents attending public school, participating in school sports, etc. Staff included a director, a social worker and five day staff, one of whom slept in each night. Staff salaries ($5,000 per year) and educational background were relatively low. The heart of the just community program was the weekly community meeting. In the first weeks it was primarily to make and change rules and develop a "constitution." Later, meetings were used to discuss issues of rule enforcement, as well as interpersonal issues and conflicts. Emergency meetings were held when needed, e.g., in the case of a fight between two residents. "Marathon" meetings were held every two months to review and modify the rules and constitution. A full description of the program is provided in Jennings, 1979.

Open Behavior-Modification Program. The Open Behavior-Modification Program was the program later converted to the Just Community Program. Located in an urban residential house, it was an unlocked, long-term, community program. Considering that all of the residents and some of the staff later became part of the Just Community Program, this program was important to this study insofar as it provided measurable perceptions (through Moral Atmosphere Interviews) for the same residents after exposure to the Behavior Modification Program and after exposure to the Just Community Program.

The program was "open" in that it was located in the community and its residents were fairly free to go where they pleased (i.e., in contrast to the Secure Behavior-Modification Program discussed below).

There were approximately ten residents (ages 12-17) in the program. They attended public schools or alternative programs within the schools.

Their role in the program was passive, in that staff made all the rules and procedures. Residents were expected to perform correct behaviors in response to specific instructions with a reward and punishment system. This reward and punishment system was administered by the staff, and especially the co-directors. The directors, called house parents, "lived in" and worked with at least four line staff, an administrator, a social worker, and a cook. Only staff were active in formulating rules and procedures and enforcing punishments. They considered the residents to be suffering from behavioral disorders which could be cured through control and modification of specific behaviors. The primary goal, then, was to condition the adolescents to produce new behaviors deemed appropriate by the adults.

Secure Behavior-Modification Program. Like the Open Behavior-Modification Program, the Secure Behavior-Modification Program was a long term treatment program. It differed in that both the residential and educational components of the program were located in the same building on the grounds of a state hospital. It also differed in that it was a "locked" setting. The adolescents could leave only if accompanied by staff. Additionally, the residents' individual rooms were locked during the night.

This program was important to this study in that it provided a) data from a second behavior-modification program to substantiate or to discount the results obtained from the Open Behavior Modification Program, b) pretest and post-test moral judgment scores to be compared with moral judgment scores of just community residents and transactional analysis residents, and c) Moral atmosphere perceptions of its residents to be compared to those of just community residents, transactional analysis residents and open behavior-modification residents.

At any one time, there were approximately 12 residents living and going to school within the locked setting. All had been involved in illegal activities and had been committed to the program by a judge. The staff viewed the residents as having serious behavioral problems. Residents had a passive role in the program; they were expected only to comply with staff wishes and directives. The only exception to this approach was the school program, administered by teachers with training in the "just community" approach. Here, teachers allowed the residents some voice in deciding minor school rules and procedures and curriculum. The teachers also allowed residents to discuss and resolve problems as a method of learning. However, the overall program director made the major rules relating to the school (e.g. a resident has to spend 24 hours locked in his room if he does not attend school).

The residents were under the supervision of a director, assistant director, and line staff. The director made all critical decisions and reviewed any decisions by other staff. He had the power to change anything at any time, and often exercised this power. Essentially, the assistant director and line staff carried out the director's policies. The line staff worked regular eight-hour shifts with about six staff on duty during the day and three at night.

Transactional Analysis Program. Like the two behavior-modification programs, the Transactional Analysis Program was a long-term program. It was located in a large two-story brick building on the grounds of a state hospital. It was a locked setting, so adolescents could only leave if accompanied by staff.

There were approximately 14 residents who lived and attended school within the locked setting. All delinquents were committed to this treatment center by various courts. The program staff diagnosed the residents as either being character-disordered or as having characterological dysfunction. The role of the residents was a combination of activity and passivity. On the passive side, the residents had to follow program procedures and rules set by the directors. They were required to attend events, follow rules, and use a certain treatment language. On the active side, the residents took some responsibility for their lives within the set program. They were encouraged to take the initiative to be honest about what they did and why they did it, and to confront other people who were being dishonest by "conning" themselves and others.

The staff's primary function was to confront the residents about their unrealistic behavior and to encourage the residents to deal more honestly with the relevant issues of their lives. Staff were also responsible for security. They had to maintain contact with the residents at all times.

A psychologist consulted with the directors, trained other staff, and counseled residents. Two teachers taught basic skills and worked closely with the line staff to coordinate residential and educational activities.

By using the principles and transactional analysis techniques developed by Eric Berne, the program's treatment focused on examination of verbal transactions among residents. These transactions were talked about in terms of Berne's ego state categories of parent, adult, and child. The overall goal of the program was derived from what the directors considered to be wrong with the residents, i.e., character disorders primarily manifested by residents' childish denial of their plight by saying things like: "It wasn't my fault," "It was a bum rap," or "If it weren't for my stupid caseworker." Such denial might have been viewed as a result of control by one's "child" ego state. According to the director, "The goal was to teach the residents to become fully responsible for their actions and to develop effective thinking processes to appropriately test reality." Or, in Berne's terms, the goal was to activate residents' "adult" ego states as moderating or controlling influences over "child" ego states.

Instruments

Kohlberg's Moral Judgment Interview Form A was used to collect moral judgment data (Colby, et al., 1978). It consists of three moral dilemmas each followed by several probe questions aimed at revealing a person's reasoning about his choices in the dilemma. The dilemmas were designed to place in conflict moral issues or values basic to adolescents and adults in every culture. The moral issues represented in Form A of the Moral Judgment Interview are as follows:

Story III : Life vs. Law

Story III': Punitive Justice vs. Recognition of Conscience

Story I   : Contract vs. Authority

The interview sessions lasted approximately 30 minutes. Where possible, the interview was tape recorded and transcribed.

Data on the program environments was gathered through the use of the Ethnographic Moral Atmosphere Interview (Kohlberg, 1980; Power, 1979). The interview is termed "ethnographic" because it asks the interviewee to act as an informant describing to the interviewer the culture or atmosphere of the institution. The interview was a free clinical interview. All forms contain at least the following four global questions followed by more specific probe questions:

1. How were general problems resolved, and how were rules and procedures made in your program?
2. What kinds of relationships existed between residents and between residents and staff?
3. Was the program fair, why or why not?
4. What effect did the program have on you?

An example of an interview with Joe, a resident of the Just Community Program is as follows:

— *I want to ask you how the place is now. What do you think about this place now?*

— I think it is a pretty nice place and it has helped me a lot. And I really like it here, it is a pretty nice place, you don't have to worry about how everything is set up.

— *How do you think it has helped you a lot?*

— It has learned me to discipline myself more, with trouble with my emotions and stuff, what I do. I can control my temper more than I used to and I am able to talk things out with people instead of just turning my back and walking away.

— *Why do you think you can talk things out with people better now?*

— Well, all the counseling and stuff that I have had, I can see it in a better light, I guess.

— *Tell me about the program now. What are some things about the program that you like?*

— I like the way it is set up because like the community as a whole is the one who makes all the rules, and everything. And that is the main thing that I like about it and the staff members are pretty nice — they help you whenever you need it.

— *How was the program before?*

— Before it was like the director just did what he wanted to do. He made all the rules and everything, and there were no questions asked.

— *Do you think this program is fair?*

— I think it is, now the staff and the community get together about everything. In this program we should know the rules because we made them. Staff treats you like you was regular people. But at first it was like shit. The staff just carried out the director's orders and we didn't know what it was until he told us about what it was.

— *Do you ever get punished or disciplined in this house?*

— I haven't been since the new director came about 3 or 4 months ago. [*Why do you think you haven't been disciplined?*] Because I am following the rules and everything.

— *Why are you following the rules?*

— Because I am one of the ones that made the rules and if I am one of the ones that make a rule, I should follow it.

— *If people in this house get disciplined, how is it decided who gets disciplined?*

— We have a discipline committee with three or four of the residents and one or two of the staff, and they get together and decide what kind of discipline it should be. It is a fair discipline most of the time...

— *What do you see as the purpose of discipline?*

— It makes you see the problems you are having and things you have done wrong. If you see something wrong, you can appeal it. If you see something wrong with your discipline, you can appeal it, but most of the time you see what you have done wrong — what everybody else thinks you have done wrong. And if you don't, you appeal it.

— *Who decided discipline under the old program?*

— The director. [*Do you think that was fair?*] No. [*Why not?*] He liked one or two of the guys better than the others and the ones he liked he let slide, and the ones he didn't like he would come down real hard on.

— *What were some of the disciplines under the old program?*

— Scrubbing the entire house and this is a big old house — enough for one person... Standing in the corner with your nose on the wall and not being able to move, sitting at a table. [*How long did people have to do that kind of thing?*] How many hours he wanted you to do it? Most of the time it was about 20 hours you had to do.

— *Did you get any discipline under the old system?*

— Yeah. I had to sit at a certain table for 40 hours and had to stay in the house for 69 days and have 9 o'clock bedtimes for about 100 nights.

— *What was that for?*

— For going out to a party and coming back the next morning without calling. [*How would that be dealt with if you did that now?*] Now you would have to tell the community your reason why you were late and why you didn't come in or something. And you tell them and they sit and talk about it and decide if it was a good reason or not. And if the reason is good enough, then it is okay… And if the reason is not good enough, you would probably have to get a discipline… And I didn't feel like calling, that was not too good of a reason. But we was way out of town at this party and I tried to call and I couldn't get ahold of him. And it was pretty late at night and I didn't want to wake anybody up, so I just stayed all night and got back when I could.

— *What is the difference, why would you before and not now?*

— In the other program the director was Harold. And he didn't like me too much and anytime I did the slightest thing, he would try to bust me as hard as he could. And he did everytime, so to keep myself out of trouble, I had to lie sometimes. Like once I went outside without permission and I got 20 days just for walking around the house…

— *Do you think any of the rules you have in the house are unfair?*

— Not really, I don't approve of some of them. [*How do you go about changing them if you don't approve of them?*] You bring it up at community meeting and then everybody votes if they are going to change them or not.

— *How about the staff in the house, how are they involved in rule-making?*

— They are just like we are. [*Do they have more power than you guys?*] In enforcing they do, but not in making them. Staff members have to have a little more. We tell them what is going on and they tell the director or something.

— *What is the staff's job in this place?*

— To make sure we are getting along all right in school and social life and stuff. Just seeing that we are doing good things. [*Do you feel like the staff do their jobs?*] Staff do their job. They don't get paid much, but they do their job.

— *Do you think the staff cares about you guys?*

— Yeah. I know they do. By the way they are treating me and everybody else.

— *Do you think most of the guys in the house follow the rules?*

— They follow the rules. We have a couple in the house that mess around, but nothing much. [*Why do you think everybody follows the rules?*] Because we made the rules, nobody made them for us. We made them ourselves.

— *How about the guys in the house — how do you think they feel towards each other?*

— I don't like all the guys in here. I like some better than the others. I think they all feel like that, too. [*What are the guys like? What do you like about them?*] I like them being guys, but some of them act a little immature sometimes. [*What does immature mean?*] Doing childish stuff… stuff you do when you are 8, 9 or 10 years old.

— *Suppose you had a new resident come in the house, what would be some of the things you would tell him about the house?*

— There is not very much I can tell him. It is a nice house, and as long as you abide by the rules, you will make it. That's all I can tell them. That's all I can tell them. That's just where it is.

— How about the way the program worked before? What would you tell a guy who came in the house?

— I would tell him to avoid the staff and try to get by with as much as he could because the director would hang him, if he could...

— What would you say is the best thing about this program?

— The thing I like best is the way the staff and the residents get together and advise everything and the way that they feel towards each other.

— What is the one bad thing, worst thing, about this program?

— That you can't have girls in.

Moral Judgment Scoring

Moral Judgment Interviews were blind scored (as to pretest and post-test, and as to program) by an experienced scorer (C. Power) by the standardized issue scoring method (Colby, et al., 1978). A second scorer scored some of the interviews. There was a correlation of .74 between the two scorers. Scoring involves assigning an interview a major stage score (averaging 66% of the issues scored); and a minor stage score when relevant. For instance, a score of 3 (2) indicates a primary usage of Stage 3 and a secondary usage of Stage 2. Interviews were also assigned a continuous moral maturity score, based on multiplying the percentage of each stage used by its ordinal number value as a stage. A 3 (2) score of 267 if 67% of responses were Stage 3 and 33% were Stage 2.

Scoring Moral Atmosphere Interviews

The Moral Atmosphere Interviews were categorized on the following four dimensions: 1) effects of the program on the residents; 2) the fairness of the program as perceived by the residents; 3) the existence of discussion in the fairness form as a way of solving problems; and 4) the amount of decision-making power the residents experienced.

A statement was considered a unit of response when the resident talked about one of the above dimensions. This may or may not have been in response to a probe eliciting a response about that dimension. Also, any unit of response could provide information for more than one category. For example, "Man, this is a fair program because we discuss all the problems together," would go in both the "discussion" and "fairness" categories.

Once the resident's responses were placed in the categories, all responses were clinically analyzed and given a score. Two scorers were used to establish interjudge reliability yielding agreement of 955. The responses were scored on a four-point scale, ranging from the extreme negative to the extreme positive. The first scoring level was denying the existence of the category content (-1). For example, if a resident said, "We don't discuss nothing around here," this response was scored -1, indicating that he believed discussion of issues was not part of the program. The next scoring level was 0, indicating an ambiguous or contradictory set of responses. For example, if a resident said, "I don't get to discuss nothing, but there is one staff I discuss things with once in a while," it was score 0, indicating ambiguous or contradictory statements about the dimension. The next was + 1, indicating the resident saw the dimension as a definite or positive part of the program. For example, "We discuss things around here," would be scored + 1. The final category was scored + 2, indicating a *higher quality* or *intense existence* of the dimension. For example, "We discuss everything around here. We talked about *why* we do things," would be scored + 2.

If several responses from different places in the resident's interview were scored under the same category, the score given the resident was from the statement receiving the highest score. For example, a resident may have said on page one of his interview, "We discuss things around here," (+ 1); and, on page 6, have said, "It's the best thing about this program, that we always discuss what we did and why," (+2). He would then be given a +2 score for the total interview.

Results

Moral Judgment Changes

The mean moral maturity scores on pre-test and post-test for each program are presented in the bottom row of Table 1.

From pre-test to post-test, the just community residents had an average gain of 35 moral maturity points. Inspection of the individual scores in Table 1 indicate that each of the eight subjects gained at least one-third of a stage, i.e. they acquired a new higher stage or dropped a lower stage as a minor stage.

This one-third stage change in the just community group is equivalent to the amount of change found in "good" moral discus-

TABLE 1
GLOBAL STAGE CHANGE SCORES
AND MORAL MATURITY MEANS FOR THREE PROGRAMS

Subjects	Just Community Pre	Post	Behavior-Modification Pre	Post	Transactional Analysis Pre	Post
1	2	2(3)	2(3)	2(3)	2(3)	2(3)
2	3(2)	3	2	2	3(2)	3(2)
3	2	3(2)	2(3)	3(2)	3(2)	3(2)
4	2	3(2)	2(3)	2(3)	3(2)	3(2)
5	2(3)	3(2)	2(3)	2(3)		
6	2	2(3)	2(3)	3(2)		
7	2	2(3)	2(3)	3(2)		
8	2(1)	2	3(2)	3(2)		
Mean Moral Maturity	211	246	236	251	260	257

sion or just community educational interactions with junior high and high school students in the schools (Blatt and Kohlberg, 1975; Lockwood, 1978; Power, 1979). It is larger than that found in moral discussion or just community interventions with older offenders (Hickey, 1972; Scharf, 1973).

In contrast to the change in the just community residents, the transactional analysis group remained unchanged (change = -3 moral maturity points) and the behavior modification residents changed slightly (mean change = 15 moral maturity points). As Table 1 indicates, only two of the eight behavior modification residents showed the one-third or more change found for all of the just community residents.

An overall test of the differences between the mean-change scores showed the three groups to differ significantly (F = 8.86, P <.005). A post-hoc test among group-means revealed the just community mean change to be greater than the behavior-modification mean change (P <.05), and also greater than the transactional analysis mean change (P<.05).

Because the scores on the pre-tests showed the just community group with the lowest pre-test scores (and pre-test was correlated with change (R = -.205), an analysis of co-variance was performed to determine if the change-score differences were due solely to the pre-tests.

An analysis of these scores showed there was still a statistically significant difference between the just community and transactional analysis groups (P < .05), but the difference between the just community and behavior modification groups was only marginally significant (P <.10) (the existence of a just community model for the school program within the behavior-modification program may in part explain the positive change).

Moral Atmosphere Differences

Self-Perceived Changes

The Just Community Program led to greater moral change by an "objective" measure, the Kohlberg Moral Judgment Interview. Did these changes correspond to subjective self-perceptions of residents about change in the programs? The Moral Atmosphere Interviews were coded as follows with regard to these dimensions:

– *1 Score*. These were statements which indicated that the program had no positive effect or had a negative effect.

— *What has been the best for you about being here?*
— *What's been the best?* Ah, nothing.
— *How has this program affected your life and way of thinking?*
— It aggravates me.

0 Score. These were ambiguous statements which made it unclear whether the resident saw the program as having a positive or negative effect.

— *Are you getting anything out of the program?*
— Yeah. [*What?*] Before I came here, I used to like fighting a lot and stuff. And I had a real bad temper and liked to hit people and stuff like that. But since I have been here I don't do that too much. I don't get in too many fights.
— *Why do you think you don't do it too much? What do you think helped you?*
— Well, nothing really helped me. It don't help me. But you know, because I don't get in too much trouble since I have been here, like coming in late from school, I might be a minute late. But I don't get in any real bad trouble like smoking and stuff.

+1 Score. These were statements which indicated the program had a positive effect on the resident's personal functioning, such as an improvement in self-understanding or in his ability to discuss problems.

— *What do you now like best about this program? Why?*

— Just overall making progress for myself. I'm finally making a lot of progress that I couln't have done on my own.

— *How has being in this program affected your life and way of thinking?*

— Before, if I was going to do something I wouldn't really think I would just go ahead and do it. Now, I think about some of the things. I still have a little "go ahead and do it" in me.

+2 Score. These were statements which indicated changes in personal function (+ 1) and also changes in moral functioning such as respecting other people's feelings or caring about other people.

— *Has this program helped you?*

— Yeah. I think a lot more. Like, before I'd just hit someone. Now I think first and try to talk to them. I respect people more.

The distribution of these categories of response about self-perceived change in each of the three programs is presented in Table 2.

The modal response (72%) of just community residents was +2, e.g., that the program had changed their actions toward other persons in morally relevant ways. The modal response (72%) of residents of the Transaction Analysis Program was +1, that it had improved self-understanding. It should be made clear that these were not two alternative responses since the categories formed a

TABLE 2
PERCENTAGE OF RESIDENTS IN EACH PROGRAM RESPONDING TO CATEGORIES OF SELF-PERCEIVED PROGRAM EFFECTS

Level	Just Community	Open Behavior Modification	Secure Behavior Modification	Transactional Analysis
+ 2 Moral effects	72%	—	14%	—
+ 1 Personal effects	28%	—	—	72%
0 Ambiguous effects	—	29%	14%	—
− 1 No effects or bad effects	—	57%	42%	14%
No comment	—	14%	28%	14%

rough cumulative Guttman scale. Thus a resident who perceived himself as changing morally (+2) usually also saw himself as having increased self-insight or ability to verbalize problems or conflicts (+1). Finally, the modal response of both Behavior Modification Programs was -1, no effects or bad effects.

Two examples of the modal (+2) responses from the Just Community Program are:

Resident 3:
Before I'd fight. Now I talk it out or bring it to the group. This place has taught me to respect the feelings of others.

Resident 4:
To handle my temper and respect people, sit down and talk. I'm friendlier, before I didn't give a shit about anybody.

An example of the modal (+1) response of the Transaction Analysis Program is:

Resident 5:
The transaction analysis helped me figure out where my attitude came from.

Two examples of the modal (-1) response of the Behavior Modification Programs are:

Resident 5:
It ain't doing nothing. The clerk system just made me madder.

Resident 4:
Nothing about the program, it made me want to get out of here. But I learned in school.

While the +2 responses of the Just Community residents and the +1 responses of the Transactional Analysis Program may be viewed merely as "testimonials" to the ideology of each program, such "testimonials" may be viewed as necessary, if not sufficient, indicators of desired change. Their absence in the Behavior Modification Program may be interpreted, at the minimum as indicating that these programs do not have ideology which the residents can accept and verbalize.

Presence of Moral Discussion

The distribution of resident responses in perceiving the presence of moral discussion in the four programs is presented in Table 3.

TABLE 3
PERCENTAGE OF RESIDENTS
RESPONDING TO THE CATEGORY OF DISCUSSION

Level	JC	OBM	SBM	TA
Discussion in the fairness form (+2)	71%	0%	0%	14%
Interpersonal conflict discussion (+1)	28%	0%	0%	14%
Ambiguous or discussed some things and not others (0)	%	14%	0%	0%
No discussion (−1)	0%	57%	85%	0%
Never mentioned moral discussions	0%	28%	14%	72%

The modal (71%) perception of the Just Community Program was +2, i.e., that there was moral discussion of conflicts in the form of considerations of fairness. The modal perceptions of the Transactional Analysis residents was a failure to mention such discussions. The modal perceptions of the Behavior Modification residents was -1, that there was an absence of such discussion.

Two examples of the modal +2 category for Just Community residents are:

Resident 6:

You discuss everything. In community meetings you explain why you did it and whether it was right.

Resident 2:

When we had bad times we talked about it, why we did it. We had arguments about it, a discussion of how food can ruin the carpet. It influences other people to think.

Two examples of the +1 perception (though not the modal category for transactional analysis) taken from residents of the Transactional Analysis Program are:

Resident 4:

Arguments are resolved by talking it out.

Resident 5:

Now kids have to talk about why they fight, what's going on in their heads.

Two examples of the modal (-1) perceptions in the Behavior Modification Programs are:

Resident 4:

When there's a disagreement they either get in fights or staff give them bad checks.

Resident 7:

If you discuss something, it will get used against you. Why should we discuss things, we'd just get more time.

Resident Decision-Making Power

The distribution of resident perceptions of resident decision-making power is presented in Table 4.

As Table 4 indicates, the modal perception of the just community residents was that they had power both to influence the program and their own personal lives (+2). The modal perception of the transactional analysis residents was ambiguous, in some ways they had power, in some not. The modal perception of residents in the two behavior modification programs was -1, that they had no power. Two examples of the modal+2 perception by just community residents are:

Resident 2:

We make the rules. Even the staff have a vote in it. You run your own life, it's your responsibility.

Resident 5:

The community as a whole makes all the rules. It helps you govern your own

TABLE 4
PERCENTAGE OF RESIDENTS IN EACH PROGRAM RESPONDING TO THE CATEGORY OF DECISION-MAKING POWER

	Just Community	Open Behavior-Modification	Secure Behavior-Modification	Transactional Analysis
Program and personal power (+ 2)	57%	0%	0%	0%
Program power (+ 1)	43%	0%	0%	28%
Ambiguous or power over some things and not other (0)	0%	14%	14%	43%
Having no power (–1)	0%	85%	71%	0%
Never mentioned power	0%	0%	14%	28%

life. We discuss issues at the community meeting and anybody we have to bring up for discipline we bring up here. We have a constitution.

It should be noted that not only do the just community residents perceive that democracy means self governement in their own personal lives, but that it leads to a "we-feeling" or a sense of ownership of the program.

Two examples of the − *1* perceptions of the transactional analysis residents are:

Resident 5:
Everybody is involved on decisions except restrictions. The staff decide those. Residents are in on most staff decisions.

Resident 6:
Certain rules you can change but some you can't do nothing about. On restrictions they say what you can and can't say.

Two examples of the modal -*1* perceptions of behavior modification residents are:

Resident 1 (Open Behavior Modification):
Rules were made unfairly. We never got a chance to discuss them.

Resident 2 (Closed Behavior Modification):
We say things but we never get a response. The director makes the rules.

Fairness of the Program

Most residents in all five programs responded to this dimension. Their diversity of responding is presented in Table 5 as the percentage of residents who perceived the program as extremely fair (+2), perceived it as generally fair (+1), perceived some program aspects as fair, and others unfair (0), and perceived their program as unfair (-1).

As Table 5 indicates, the modal perceptions of the just community residents was +2, that their program was very fair. The modal response of the transactional analysis residents was *0*, in some ways it was fair, in some not. The modal response of the closed behavior modification residents was also ambivalent, that is the open behavior unit was -*1*, that it was actively unfair.

Two examples of the modal resident perception of fairness (+2) in the Just Community Program are:

TABLE 5
PERCENTAGE OF RESIDENTS RESPONDING TO
THE CATEGORY OF PROGRAM FAIRNESS

	Just Commu-nity	Open Behavior Modification	Secure Behavior Modification	Transac-tional Analysis
Extremely fair (+2)	44%	—	—	—
Fair (+1)	28%	—	—	4%
Ambiguous about fairness (0)	—	28%	44%	52%
Unfair (–1)	—	72%	28%	—
No comment	14%	—	28%	—

Resident 2:
I think the system in this house is run about perfect. A very just structure.

Resident 6:
I think the program is very fair because you can discuss your side of the story, why you did it and that means something.

Two examples of the modal *0* response by transactional analysis residents are:

Resident 4:
Sometimes it's fair. The community makes rules about restrictions, some-times its unfair. I don't like a lot of the meetings, we do too much talking. You get stuff resolved but it makes me angry.

Resident 5:
What I like about the program is getting out. There ain't too much I like about it. But I think the way they deal with people on drugs is pretty good.

Two examples of the modal perception of the open behavior modification unit as -*1* actively unfair are:

Resident 1: (Open behavior modification unit).
The rules are unfair, especially table times.

Resident 5: (Secure behavior modification unit).
It's alright. Some of the rules are no good. We don't have any say about setting up the rules and I don't think that's fair.

Conclusions and Discussion

As hypothesized, the just community program for youthful

offenders led to significantly more upward moral stage change than did the behavior modification or transactional analaysis program. The amount of change found over nine months (an average of one-third stage) was equivalent to that found in "good" developmental moral education programs for non-delinquent high school students. While incarcerated delinquent adolescents are markedly retarded in moral judgment development compared to controls (Kohlberg, 1978), this retardation is not evidence of irreversible fixation in moral development due to earlier experiences. Further research is required to determine whether the change is in moral reasoning resulting from the just community program leads to any reduction of recidivism or antisocial behavior after leaving the program. Probably, because of both moral reasoning change and the moral atmosphere of the just community program, there was an improvement of moral attitudes and behavior within the program assessed by resident self-perception in the ethnographic interview and by staff reports of behavior in the logs (Jennings, 1979).

The moral atmosphere of the just community program was perceived by residents as high on the hypothesized conditions of moral growth including:

1. A high amount of moral discussion and dialogue.
2. A high amount of resident power and responsibility for making rules, policies and decisions.
3. A high amount of perceived fairness or concern about fairness in the institution.

As also hypothesized, the insight therapy program (transaction analysis) was intermediate between the just community and the behavior modification programs on these dimensions. There is nothing surprising about these findings. The ideologies of behavior modification and transaction analysis derive from psychological theories remote from the "common-sense" meaning making systems of residents. In contrast, the ideology of the just community program is close to the common understanding of adolescents who need no understanding of psychological theory to value the concern for democracy, fairness and reasoned discussion stressed by the just community ideology.

We currently live in a period of disillusionment with "treatment," with "rehabilitation" and with psychiatric diagnosis as solutions to the problem posed by youthful offenders. Even if we see no immediate strong prospects for rehabilitation of the offender, we need not settle for custodial warehousing as the only option left. Studies like the present indicate that residential custody of offenders is compatible with an atmosphere of fairness and the stimulation of social and moral growth, the right of every adolescent whether delinquent or not. A just community atmosphere of fairness and growth costs no more in-dollars or professional qualifications than does a more restrictive approach, as the Florida experiment indicates. The senior author was sufficiently convinced of this that he is now engaged in attempting to create a similar program in Massachusetts. This is a secure program for more "disturbed" and alienated groups of adolescents committed to both the Department of Mental Health and the Department of Youth Services.

REFERENCES

BLATT, M., and L. KOHLBERG
1975: The effects of classroom moral discussion upon children's level of moral judgment, *Journal of Moral Education*, 4: 129-161.

COLBY, A., KOHLBERG, L., GIBBS, J., CANDEE, D., SPEICHER-DUBIN, B., and C. POWER
1978: *Assessing Moral Judgment Stages: A Manual*, Cambridge, Mass., Moral Education Research Foundation.

HICKEY, J.
1972: The effects of guided moral discussions upon youthful offenders' level of moral judgment. Unpublished doctoral dissertation, Boston University.

JENNINGS, W.
1979: The Juvenile Delinquent as a Moral Philosopher: The Effects of rehabilitation programs on the Moral Reasoning and Behavior of Male Youthful Offenders. Unpublished doctoral dissertation, Harvard University.

KOHLBERG, L.
1970: The moral atmosphere of the school. In N. Overley, Ed., *The Unstudied Curriculum: Its Impact on Children*, Washington, D.C., Monograph of the Association for Supervision of Curriculum Development.
1976: Moral stages and moralization: The cognitive-developmental approach. In T. Lickona, Ed., *Moral Development and Behavior: Theory, Research and Social Issues*, New York, Holt, Rinehart and Winston.

1978: The cognitive-developmental approach to behavior disorders: a study of the development of moral reasoning in delinquents. In G. Serban, Ed., *Cognitive Defects in the Development of Mental Illness*, New York, Brunner Mazel.

1980: Exploring the Moral Atmosphere of Institutions: A Bridge Between Moral Judgment and Moral Action. In *The Meaning and Measurement of Moral Development*, Clark University Press.

KOHLBERG, L., HICKEY, J., and P. SCHARF
1972: The justice structure of the prison: A theory and intervention, *The Prison Journal*, 51 (2): 3-14.

KOHLBERG, L., KAUFFMAN, K., HICKEY, J., and P. SCHARF
1975: *Corrections Manual, Parts I and II*, Cambridge, Mass., Moral Education Research Foundation.

LOCKWOOD, A.L.
1978: The effects of values clarification and moral development curriculum on school age subjects: a critical review of recent research, *Review of Educational Research*, 48: 241-259.

POWER, C.
1979: The Development of the Moral Atmosphere of a Just Community High School Program. Unpublished doctoral dissertation, Harvard University.

REIMER, J., and C. POWER
1978: Moral Atmosphere: An educational bridge between moral judgment and action. In W. Damon, Ed., *Moral Development, New Directions for Child Development No. 2*, San Francisco, Jossey-Bass.

SCHARF, P., and J. HICKEY
1980: *Toward a Just Correctional System*, San Francisco, Jossey-Bass.

SCHARF, P.
1973: Moral Atmosphere and Intervention in the Prison. Unpublished doctoral dissertation, Harvard University.

17. COMPETENCIES OF THE CORRECTIONAL EDUCATOR

Douglas K. Griffin

The competencies required for corrections depend upon one's understanding of what the word "corrections" means. I believe that correctional educators will have a clear idea of the competencies they require when they stop accepting other people's nonsensical notions of what corrections is about. We have traditionally accepted notions developed elsewhere: that correction is punishment; that it is psychiatric therapy; that it is hard labour; that it is industrial production; or that it is hand-holding in the social-work model. We need no longer accept these notions of corrections, because they don't work, are extremely expensive, and deny any legitimate role for the educator.

By accepting others' definitions of corrections, we are forced to accept others' definitions of our place in corrections. The time has finally come for us to stand up and say aloud that corrections is re-education, and that our role is central in it.

The other approaches we have seen are not really *correctional*. They are simply applications of approaches used elsewhere. Like the snake-oil salesman, whose potion can cure every ill, the various practitioners have come along, each claiming that if he does what he does, it will correct criminals. The psychiatrist has said that we should cure the criminals' mental illness; the industrialist has said that we should put the criminal to hard labour; the social worker said that we should compensate for deprived social backgrounds. Educators must not fall into the same trap. We will not be any more

Paper presented to the Correctional Education Association, Nashville, Tennessee, July, 1980.

credible than the others if we simply talk about the three r's and vocational skills. What we do must relate particularly to the criminal.

Educators, of all these groups, have the opportunity to develop a truly correctional approach. In fact, I believe that the only reasonable meaning of the word corrections must be an educational one.

This is not to say that some criminals do not need therapy, or social care, or employment, or skills. What is generally called the "eclectic" approach to corrections is simply to say that crime has many causes — the cause might be psychiatric, social, or employment-related, and that the variety of approaches in today's prisons can remedy the various problems. This is a nice, comfortable, respectable, and popular idea, but I don't believe it.

Psychotic people are psychotic; socially-deprived people are deprived; the unskilled are unemployed, but none of that explains why any of these people are *criminals*; this nice, comfortable, respectable belief can account for everything except the one thing that concerns us: criminality. I believe that we need something more.

What we need is an understanding of why some of these mentally ill, socially-deprived, unemployed, unskilled or uneducated people are criminals, while the majority of them are not. What is missing from the nice approach is an elementary understanding of what makes a criminal different from any or all of these people. That is why a correctional educator must understand the difference between an un-educated non-criminal, and an un-educated criminal. The thing that is different about him will define the nature of the correctional educator's work.

What makes a criminal criminal? Apart from the simplistic answer that a criminal is one who is convicted for breaking the law, I believe, along with Yochelson and Samenow and a lot of other people, that crime is essentially a moral question, i.e., a question of social responsibility (not morality in the purely sexual meaning).

This means that the result of criminal action is harm and injury to other people. Harm and injury are wrong because they are immoral, and I don't believe that statement requires discussion. The task of the correctional educator is to intervene in such a way that the offender ceases or diminishes these actions. The process by which he does so, is correctional education, and the correctional educator must define himself or herself in these terms.

How is this done? Although crime is morally defined, its alleviation is not achieved by moral preaching. It requires at least three essential educational components in order to equip offenders to make morally-sound decisions. Speaking of the required competencies for correctional educators, then, I would say that correctional educators, in addition to being competent to bring their students to a given level of proficiency in a given subject area, must be competent in helping correct the kinds of cognitive deficiencies which contribute to the faulty decision-making processes of offenders, decision-making processes which lead to decisions for action which cause harm and injury to others. If we had these competencies, we would know that our role in education is even more relevant today than it has been in the past, because more and more, regular educators are coming to realize that skill proficiency is not enough; that North Americans are being faced with tougher and tougher decisions about the quality of life in a social order which appears to be crumbling before their eyes. Education for technical proficiency is not good enough, and neither is education for self-gratification. The role of the correctional educator in the 80's, while specifically relevant to our needs, is also relevant to the role of education in general — to equip people not only with the skills for employment, but also with the capacity to make morally-sound decisions. In the 80's and 90's, the educational mainstream should be looking to correctional education to show them the way.

What kinds of competencies are required for this different task? They are essentially of three kinds: they are competencies which enable students to overcome three kinds of cognitive deficits which contribute to faulty decision-making, and they are competencies which are based on an understanding of cognitive processes. Offenders must be helped to correct deficiencies in perception, in concept-formation, and in response repertoire. Let me explain.

Good decisions depend upon good perceptions — accurate perceptions. They depend upon the use of all the available relevant information. I don't purchase a car just because I like the colour, if I happen to know that the wheels will fall off it. Decisions that offenders make are often based on only a small part of the relevant information necessary. Through impulsiveness, or random attention to situational variables, offenders often jump to act without attending to important aspects of the situation. The attraction of stealing $100 today, can cost him a job worth far more. The appeal of a selfish and self-gratifying act of the moment can mean the loss of the companionship of a loved one, and a net loss to the individual.

Criminals' decisions are often faulty because their perceptions are faulty, and partial.

The second deficiency is that of concept-formation, i.e., the applying of meaning to the world. Correctional teachers know that their students make sense of the world in an abnormal manner. Correctional teachers who have the time or energy to engage in discussions with their students know that offenders interpret events and situations according to a unique set of meanings which are related to their goals and aspirations.

The socially responsible person sees opportunities for personal gain in a manner that does not harm others; the criminal sees opportunities for personal gain regardless of the degree of harm and injury caused to others. The socially-responsible person disallows many of the options entertained by the criminal, because his value system will not permit them. The criminal simply does not think of the options considered by the socially responsible person, because his value system does not include them. Value systems are composed of abstract concepts and meanings, and the teacher must help the inmate student to develop appropriate ones, to equip him to make responsible decisions.

The third competency is simply that of being able to equip the student with a sufficiently vast response repertoire, so that a range of appropriate responses is available for use. If a student's perception has been developed to the point where he now can attend to, and use sufficient perceptual input; if he has succeeded in developing useful and appropriate mental constructs, or meanings to apply to data, none of these will be useful to him, if his response repertoire is limited to bashing you over the head and running away. Responsible decision making also requires the ability to select an appropriate response from an available repertoire. If, when provoked, I can choose to be polite, to be conciliatory, to be evasive, to be rude, to be violent, to call the manager, to call a policeman, to telephone the press, to hire a lawyer, to punch the wall, or to shout an obscenity, I am in a better position than the poor fellow who only knows to bend a lead pipe over his opponent's head.

I believe that if we continue to develop our competencies in these three areas, the educational world will beat a path to our door. And that is how it should be.

The presenting problem, as they call it, however, looks different. While on the one hand I may believe that my ultimate objective is to be able to achieve the goals inherent in the kinds of competencies I have described above, when I actually walk into my prison class-room on Monday morning, the scene before my eyes makes all of the above seem remote and impractical. What I have in fact, is a class half empty because inmates have gone astray between their beds and the school. One inmate wants to know how he can get a replacement for a pocket calculator that "broke". Two inmates have their feet up on the desk and are hotly debating last night's poker game. I notice with chagrin that one inmate has his notebook open to the same page he has had in front of him all last week. I am told that there is a sports event that afternoon, and nobody will be at school. Two inmates already have passes to visit their classification officer and the chaplain. The floor is dirty. My primary job is simply to get some-thing — get anything — happening among this bunch of unwilling learners. Talk about perceptual abilities; talk about cognitive concept-formation; talk about skill repertoires — talk about getting me through until lunchtime!

My first experiences with prisoners in a classroom were devas-tating. I had ordered materials, based on the levels and courses of my students, and I had to wait two weeks for them to arrive. I thought it would be a nice opportunity to share in some off-the-cuff discussions of social class, perhaps, of the pyramidal structure of the educational system, which eliminates students as they move upwards. I thought that some common-garden psychology in popular language would go over well. Some basic economic theory, perhaps.

I lasted barely two days, with this approach. I was totally unprepared for the strength of the emotional onslaught of fifteen prisoners who were set on nothing else than to demonstrate their intellectual superiority over mine, and their total lack of need to imbibe anything I might have to say. I quickly learned what all new prison teachers learn, which is that inmates in a bunch are not the same thing as inmates individually. In fact, they are scarcely recognizable. I already thought of myself as something of a social radical, and I was surprised to find myself suddenly having to defend a social order I had devoted the past five years to tearing down (figuratively speaking). I found myself totally unprepared to deal with a concerted and forceful expression of social alienation; of opposition to me and my social class; of sophisticated self-justifi-cation and relationalizing that I was not prepared to counter. I retreated, and adopted the solution of most prison teachers faced with this problem: divide and conquer. I decided that I would deal with each of them individually, and that I would restrict my discussion to the matters closest to hand — division and multiplication of fractions, the use of metaphor and simile by William Wordsworth.

This was not a solution to the problem; rather, it was a means of avoiding the problem. Since I was alone in the prison (the only teacher there) I never developed the resources to do anything else. I detected later an even more insidious means of dealing with the antisocial attitudes of offenders: I found myself agreeing with their analyses of society and their perceptions of their own victimization, because that seemed to be a way of ingratiating myself them. This is a serious mistake, in my present opinion, because as an educator I am being paid to do more than simply support misinformed views of the world. It may not be dishonest in a personal sense, but it is dishonest in a professional sense.

The task of moving the teacher through all of the procedural problems and the administrative hindrances to a point where he or she has an effective means not only of presenting the subject of instruction but also of dealing with the underlying social attitudes and values of students, as well as dealing with the perceptual, cognitive deficiences which exist, is enormous. I know of no more difficult task than that of the correctional educator. In a few brief months he hopes to be able to have an impact on deficiencies and attitudes that are the product of a lifetime, and against which a host of complex and overlapping reactions and protections have been developed. He is dealing with individuals who have not been successful at school. He is dealing with the product of twenty years of influences that have led to a bad end. He accepts the principle that good influences can eventually overcome bad ones, but he faces the fact of the total influence of the prison on his students, and wonders if anything he does will counter that.

The teacher wants his students to pass their exams. He hopes that they might develop an autonomous appreciation of learning for its own sake. He hopes that they will use their intelligence to develop a new perspective on the world. He wants to get through each day without losing all his students, and without physical violence. The presenting problems are complex, immediate, and extremely challenging. But beyond these, the teacher knows that he also wants to have a more fundamental impact on his students, and I believe that in order for this to happen, the teacher must be aware of the nature of the underlying deficiencies which must be addressed to allow fundamental change to take place. That is why I discuss them in the context of competencies of the correctional educator. The correctional educator must be competent to deal with these, in the sense that he can identify when deficiencies are being displayed. Deficiencies of perception, of concept formation, and of skill repertoire can usually be perceived beneath the presenting problems, as they meet the eye. I am not denying the validity of the presenting problem, nor the teacher's need to deal with it. I am suggesting that "dealing" with it will be superficial unless the immediate problem can be related to a broader category of problem.

I believe also that there are important rewards for the teacher who is willing and prepared to deal with the underlying problems as well as with the immediate ones. There arises in the course of a normal teaching day (if any of them can be called "normal") many many opportunities for a teacher to deal with the social perceptions and concept-formation of his or her students. In my experience there are even too many of them to be able to deal with them all, and still get through the lessons. The willingness of the teacher to confront students when they demonstrate irresponsible concepts creates a great demand on the teacher. It also affords the opportunity for the learning experience to be stimulating and rewarding for the teacher, and motivating for the student. Inmates spend large portions of their time justifying their attitudes and actions, and proving to themselves that the social order which has imprisoned them, is unjust. Preoccupied with such concerns, they may lack interest in factoring whole numbers. The teacher who is willing to deal with such issues — issues of a social, political, and ethical nature, in the words of Dr. Douglas Ayers — will find he has activated a touchstone, and must be prepared to deal with the consequences. If he is not prepared to deal with them, as I was not in my first encounters with inmates, he would be better off to leave it alone. If he is prepared to deal with it, he has a real possibility of having a valuable impact on his students' lives, as well as making the learning experience rewarding and stimulating.

Most of us have not been forced to analyse our own values clearly enough to be able to deal with this kind of situation. Some teachers, in fact, hold basically anti-social attitudes themselves, and should be in another line of work. Our values, perceptions, and cognitive concepts are necessarily inter-related. None can be neglected without risk to the others. The competencies required of the correctional educator, then, include personal qualities as well. Adequate competencies cannot exist independently of them, for the teacher, and for the learner.

18. CORRECTIONS EDUCATION AND PRACTICAL REASONING: NEEDS, METHODS AND RESEARCH

Ian Wright

Since 1970, the Association for Values Education and Research (AVER), Faculty of Education, University of British Columbia, has been studying 1) how people reason about value issues, particularly those involving moral considerations, and 2) determining how people might become more rational in their thinking and acting. Its members have engaged in a variety of activities — conceptual and empirical research, curriculum development and evaluation, and education of teachers and other professionals through in-service workshops and pre-service and graduate courses in education. All of these activities are based on the assumption that a morally educated person will possess a complex set of abilities, understandings, attitudes and dispositions.

Coombs (1980) has conceptualized the attainments a person must have to be rational in moral reasoning. Briefly, these are:

1. Knowing that moral reasoning is guided by two principles:
   a) It cannot be right for me to do X unless it is right for any person in the same sort of circumstances to do X.
   b) If the consequences of everyone's doing X in a given circumstance would be unacceptable, then it is not right for anyone to do X in that circumstance.
2. Being sensitive to morally hazardous actions, that is actions which require assessment from the moral point of view.
3. Ability and disposition to seek out all the morally relevant facts about actions which are morally hazardous.

Paper presented to the World Congress in Education: Values and the School; Symposium on Prison Education, Université du Québec à Trois-Rivières, July, 1981.

4. Ability and inclination to imagine, when contemplating a morally hazardous action, the consequences that would ensue if everyone in your circumstance were to engage in the action.

5. Ability and inclination to put oneself imaginatively into the circumstance of another person and thus come to know and appreciate the consequences of a proposed morally hazardous action for the other person.

6. Ability and disposition to seek advice and counsel from others about moral decisions that one is making.

7. Ability and disposition to check the validity of moral arguments and to reject invalid arguments.

8. Disposition to require justifying arguments from others who propose morally hazardous actions.

9. Resolution to do what one has decided is right and refrain from doing what one has decided is wrong.

10. A sense of self-worth including the belief that achieving one's plans, pursuing one's interests, and so on, is important.

11. Knowledge of any way in which a person's perception of things harmful to himself differs radically from that of people in general.

In addition there are a number of attainments which are related to the above, and to practical reasoning in general. These include:

12. Skill in verbal and non-verbal communication.
13. Ability and disposition to assess the reliability of authorities.
14. Ability and disposition to assess the truth of empirical claims.
15. Ability and disposition to be clear in the language we use when deliberating about issues.

Many of these attainments are part of our everyday thinking. We do ask for evidence; we do ask, "How would you like that done to you?", and "What if everyone did that?"; we do ask for clarification of meaning; and we do expect people to act on their principles. We constantly use practical reasoning as this is the process by which we make decisions about what we should do or what we should value. Two sorts of reasons enter into the process of this type of reasoning: 1) motivational reasons concerning the person's wants, values, purposes or rules of conduct, and 2) empirical or factual reasons concerning actions which are likely to fulfill the wants, values, purposes or rules of conduct. For example:

1. Torturing people is wrong.
2. The government of X is torturing people.
Conclusion. Therefore the government of X is wrong.

In order to test the validity and defensibility of this argument, we have to ensure that the factual claim is true, the argument is valid, and the major principle or premise is justifiable. If the factual claim is untrue, then the conclusion does not follow — unless there are other grounds for claiming that the governement of X is wrong. If the factual claim is true, that the government of X is performing actions which are, by definition, torture, then the conclusion logically follows from the major principle and the argument is valid. In order to justify the major principle we have to appeal to tests (note I say *tests* not *proofs*) such as the role exchange test and the universal consequences test (see 1a) and 1b)) above, and be as certain as we can be that there are no exceptions to our principle i.e. there are no circumstances in which torture is justifiable. If there are then we have to modify our principle by appeal to another higher principle.

Practical reasoning is complex, yet it appears from the literature that prisoners are deficient in even the basic reasoning skills. Yochelson and Samenow (1976) identified a number of "automatic errors of thinking" which, they claimed, were exhibited by criminals and which impede rational judgment. Only a few of the "thinking errors" count as deficiences in the abilities and dispositions necessary for rational practical reasoning. However, their work does suggest the following hypotheses concerning possible deficiencies in prisoners' practical reasoning.

1. Prisoners will tend not to be disposed to imagine themselves in the situation of another person.
2. Prisoners will tend not to gather relevant information and weigh the pros and cons of a course of action before deciding upon it.
3. Prisoners will tend to be unwilling to suspend judgment on persons and courses of actions.
4. Prisoners will tend to be closed minded. They will not listen to evidence which contradicts what they already believe.

These hypotheses concern mainly the dispositions of prisoners. Yochelson and Samenow have little to say about what sort of thinking prisoners are capable or incapable of doing. However, studies based on Kohlberg's theory of moral development do provide some insight into prisoners' practical reasoning. These studies suggest that the majority of prisoners employ Stage 2 moral reasoning (Parlett *et al*, 1975, Kohlberg, 1972) which is characterized by the view that the right thing to do is that which best serves one's own interests. It is right to obey a law, help another person, or honor a contract if and only if it will benefit the self. Even the lives of others are seen as having only instrumental value (Kohlberg, 1976). Persons at Stage 2 will not understand that moral reasoning is based on the two generalization principles (1a) and 1b)); will not differentiate the moral point of view from the prudential point of view; will not be sensitive to morally hazardous actions; and will not be disposed to apply the role exchange test. This latter deficiency — the inability to see other persons' points of view — was found by Chandler (1973) to be a characteristic of delinquent boys. Although it is not certain that adult prisoners will have this same deficiency, there is a strong possibility that they will, either in terms of being able to see another person's point of view, or if they are able to role-take, being willing to consider another's viewpoint.

Another promising approach to understanding the thinking of juvenile delinquents and perhaps to adult prisoners, is to use the Harvey Conceptual Systems Model (1961). In Sub System 1 a person has not assimilated basic social norms. Thus he exhibits ego-centrism, negativism, and a disposition to seek immediate gratification. In System I he assimilates basic cultural norms and has a high positive dependence on authority. System II persons break away from social norms and their thinking is characterized by distrust of, and rebellion against, authority. In System III awareness of others' feelings and values develops. Only in System IV does a person adopt standards which are applicable to self and others.

Research using this model has found that delinquents are mainly in System I or II (Juers and Harvey, 1964), (Hunt and Hardt, 1965). Kipper (1971) using the Kahn Test of Symbol Arrangement, found that adult prisoners' thinking was characterized by concreteness and conceptual perseverance. There was little cognitive flexibility and they had difficulties in synthesizing diverse cognitive input.

If adult prisoners are in System I or II then it will be necessary to start at a fairly elementary level in developing practical reasoning skills.

Research concerning educational programs which attempt to develop reasoning skills is sparse. Projects using Kohlberg's moral development theory as a basis for raising the moral reasoning of prisoners have had some success (Scharf, Hickey and Moriarty, 1973; Scharf and Hickey, 1976). Parlett, Ayers and Sullivan (1975) found that a course in Humanities in which there were frequent opportunities for moral discussion was useful in raising the level of prisoners' moral reasoning. Scharf (1973) argued that the moral atmosphere of the prison inhibits the development of moral reasoning, and has combined counselling with a democratic governing process in a prison school. Duguid (1979) describes a program in which prisoners take university level arts courses in an "alternative community", which, because it is perceived as just, reinforces more advanced levels of moral thinking and behaviour. The most encouraging findings come from a study by Waksman, Silverman and Weber (1979). Using Feuerstein's Learning Potential Assessment Device, they found that even prisoners with low I.Q.'s and those who had failed in past academic efforts had the potential to learn new thinking strategies and skills.

On the basis of these studies there is reason to be optimistic that practical reasoning can be improved. However, it will require a concerted, long-term educational effort, and one which differs from previous interventions. Kohlbergian studies seem to assume that whatever thinking abilities and dispositions needed for rational practical reasoning will be picked up indirectly through dilemma discussions or taking part in democratic decision-making. This assumption is supported neither by evidence, nor by logic. University arts courses may well improve reasoning about the subject matter being studied, but the improvement in practical reasoning may only be marginal.

Yet many writers have called for a shift from the study of personality and / or socio-economic background variables to studies on, and programs in the thinking and reasoning of incarcerated offenders. Ayers (1979) and Wagner (1978) see prisoners as being deficient in reasoning skills and recommend educational programs to remedy this defect. Ayers (ibid.: 3) states:

> An alternative (to the medical model) and more tenable assumption is that most prisoners are deficient in certain analytical problem solving skills... If this alternative assumption is relevant then educational intervention models... are more appropriate for the majority of prisoners.

Wagner (ibid.: 26) claims that "An acquired proficiency in reasoning is clearly essential to successful criminal rehabilitation."

The research on prisoners' reasoning and the thesis that reasoning ought to be improved led the research group to decide that important information could be gained from trying out the AVER's existing teaching materials with a class of prisoners. These materials were developed for public school secondary students, but it was felt that field testing could facilitate modification to suit prisoner-students.

Over a six week period, seven students in the GED program at a medium security institution participated in twice weekly, two hour sessions of a course entitled "Critical Thinking." The course was taught by Dr. J. Coombs, Professor, Dr. I. Wright, Associate Professor, and Carol LaBar, a research associate. The purposes were:

1. To determine the appropriateness for adult prisoners of AVER's existing materials and methods for teaching practical reasoning.
2. To generate hypotheses concerning the most efficient techniques to use in teaching practical reasoning to adult prisoners.
3. To gain first hand experience of the context within which teaching and learning occurs in prisons.
4. To ascertain if adult prisoners felt that practical reasoning was useful in their studies and in their everyday lives.

The first two weeks were spent on activities such as distinguishing factual claims from value claims, assessing the truth or falsity of factual claims, judging evidence, observations and authorities distinguishing valid arguments from invalid ones, and recognizing informal fallacies. The remaining four weeks were devoted to learning the process of value reasoning and the application of value reasoning skills to the topic of war (AVER, 1979).

As no formal tests of achievement were given, observations are necessarily impressionistic. Activities designed to teach various skills appeared to be suitable. The readings from the *War* unit seemed to be appropriate but some questions related to the readings may have been too unsophisticated for adult audiences.

Students were apprehensive about the time spent on discussing the moral issues interest in wartime situations. Suspicion was present that we were attempting to ascertain student reasoning concerning violence and crimes of violence. Therefore it is important that issues be carefully chosen. The content is, after all, only a vehicle, and should be chosen on the bases of student interest and potential to raise moral questions.

During the course certain skills and concepts were taught and certain questions had right or wrong answers. However, much of the time was spent on debating value issues, and instructors attempted to adopt a Socratic approach involving questioning procedures designed to help people reflect upon their claims. Although this approach is not easy to operationalize, as by tone of voice or gesture the instructor's value stance can be inferred, there is reason to believe that the approach was successful. Discussion ensued and was at times animated. Initially students addressed their statements to and through the instructor, but, as classes progressed, there was far more student to student interaction. At various times students from other programs joined the class and participated in the discussion.

As in most classes, at whatever level, some people participated more than others. Although most students completed class assignments and appeared, in varying degrees, to be able to apply the skills and concepts taught, some were more prepared than others to engage in class activities. Presumably, the apprehension generated by the discussions of violence in wartime also mitigated against full participation.

Overall, we believe that prisoners' practical reasoning can be developed through suitable educational programs. AVER is in accord with Richard Peters (1972), who views education as initiation into worthwhile knowledge and understanding. This requires more than mere information, but rather, true belief and understanding of the evidence which warrants it. Moral education involves initiation into rational moral beliefs and the modes of reasoning used to justify them. As moral beliefs guide conduct, moral education involves, at least indirectly, initiation into rational modes of conduct.

AVER realizes that much research and conceptual work remains to be carried out, but our brief experience in this preliminary research has lent credence to the belief that our moral education approach would be suited to corrections education for a number of reasons. First, it is educational in that it equips people with cognitive skills and abilities which enable them to assess their own experience, and to make rational, defensible decisions about what should, or should not be done. Second, the focus on reasoning skills in the area of values, particularly in the domain of moral values, is precisely the area in which the majority of prisoners have demonstrated lack of reasoning ability. Third, as most adults have had considerable experience with moral questions and the complexity of resolving moral issues, they find them interesting. When they come to understand that moral reasoning fits into a rational framework requiring sophisticated abilities, they may also find the area intellectually stimulating.

The inclusion of values education in corrections educational programs would not only have the potential of producing positive effects on the future thought and action of people who have demonstrated disability in this area, but would make programs more educationally sound. As Cosman (1980) states:

Penitentiary education has simply not been conceived of in terms of the development of the powers of the intellect, in terms of enlightenment and the strengthening or reason, in terms of the development of man as an historical person, as a member of a society and a civilization.

Prison life, by its very nature, presents to both prisoners and staff, moral problems of the most difficult sort, problems which call for considerable competence in reasoning ability.

REFERENCES

AVER
1979: Teachers' guide and student reader, *War*. Value Reasoning Series, Toronto, OISE Publications.

AYERS, J.
1979: A model for prison education programs and guidelines for their operation, *Journal of Correctional Education*, 3 (1): 3-7.

CHANDLER, M.J.
1973: Egocentrism and antisocial behavior: The assessment and training of social perspective skills, *Developmental Psychology*, 9: 326-332.

COOMBS, J.
1980: Attainments of the morally educated person. In D. Cochrane and M. Manley-Casimir, Eds., *Practical Dimensons of Moral Development*, New Jersey, Praeger.

COSMAN, J.W.
1980: Penitentiary education in Canada, *Education Canada*, 20 (1): 42-47.

DUGUID, S.
1979a: *The university in prison: Moral education and the alternative community*, The University of Victoria, Mimeograph.
1979b: History and moral education in correctional education, *Canadian Journal of Education*, 4 (4): 81-92.

FEUERSTEIN, R., SHALOM, H., NARROL, H., HOFFMAN, M., KIRMAN, L., KATZ, O., SCHACHTON, E., and Y. RAND
1972: *Studies in cognitive modifiability: The dynamic assessment of retarded performers. Vol. 1, Clinical LPAD Battery*, Jerusalem, Hadassah-Wizo-Canada Research Institute.

HARVEY, O.J., HUNT, D.E., and H.M. SCHRODER
1961: *Conceptual Systems and Personality Organization*, New York, Wiley.

HUNT, D.E., and R.J. HARDT
1965: Developmental stage, delinquency and differential treatment, *Journal of Research in Crime and Delinquency*, 2: 20-31.

JUERS, E.H. and O.J. HARVEY
1964: *Conceptual Systems and Delinquency*, CONR Technical Report No. 6, Washington, D.C., United States Government Printing Office.

KIPPER, D.A.
1971: Identifying habitual criminals by means of the Kahn Test of Symbol Arrangement, *Journal of Consulting and Clinical Psychology*, 37: 151-154.

KOHLBERG, L.
1972: The justice structure of the prison: A theory and an intervention, *The Prison Journal*, 5 (2).
1976: Moral stages and moralization: The cognitive developmental approach. In T. Lickona, Ed., *Moral Development and Behavior*, New York, Holt, Rinehart and Winston.

PARLETT, T.A.A., AYERS, J.D., and D.M. SULLIVAN
1975: Development of morality in prisoners. In A.C. Kazepides, Ed., *The Teaching of Values in Canadian Education*, Edmonton, Yearbook of the Canadian Society for the Study of Education.

PETERS, R.S.
1972: *Ethics in Education*, London, Allen and Unwin.

SCHARF, P., and J. HICKEY
1976: The prison and the inmate's conception of legal justice: An experiment in democratic education, *Criminal Justice and Behavior*, 3 (2).

SCHARF, P.
1973: Moral Atmosphere and Intervention of the Prison. Ph. D. dissertation, Harvard University.

SCHARF, P., HICKEY, J., and T. MORIARTY
1973: Moral conflict and change in correctional settings, *Personnel and Guidance Journal*, 51 (9): 660-663.

WAGNER, P.
1978: Punishment and reason in rehabilitating the offender, *Prison Journal*, 58 (1): 37-46.

WAKSMAN, M., SILVERMAN, H., and K. WEBER
1975: Assessing the learning potential of penitentiary inmates: An application of Feuerstein's Learning Potential Assessment Device, Ottawa, Education and Training Division of the Correctional Service of Canada.

YOCHELSON, S., and S. SAMENOW
1976: *The Criminal Personality*, New York, James Aronson.